*

Understanding

the Language of Science

*

Understanding

the Language of Science

Steven Darian

University of Texas Press
Austin

First edition, 2003

Requests for permission to reproduce material from this work
should be sent to Permissions, University of Texas Press, Box
7819, Austin, TX 78713-7819.

⊗ The paper used in this book meets the minimum requirements
of ANSI/NISO Z39.48-1992 (R1997) (Permanence of Paper).

Library of Congress Cataloging-in-Publication Data

Darian, Steven G.
Understanding the language of science / Steven Darian.— 1st ed.
p.   cm.
Includes bibliographical references and index.
ISBN 0-292-71617-6 (cloth : alk. paper)—
ISBN 0-292-71618-4 (pbk : alk. paper)
1. Science—Language.   2. Science—Philosophy.   I. Title.
Q175.D2685 2003
501'4—dc21
2002154613

To Jack Evans

An Appreciation for the Gift of Friendship

Contents

Introduction

I had no desire to entice you with misleading premises, for there are, to be sure, many languages of science: the language of university science lectures and the explanatory inquiries of the elementary school classroom; the language of scientists debating issues in the laboratory; the language of papers presented at conferences and of articles in scholarly journals; plus the actual language of discovery. We also find pieces for the layman, from *Popular Mechanics* and *Scientific American* articles to accounts in print and broadcast journalism; and then, the language of textbooks, from primary and secondary school through university level, in textbooks introductory and advanced, on subjects from general biology to immunology.

This language of science, as we can see, is an *enormous* undertaking, with a nearly endless variety of audiences and participants, purposes, and degrees of complexity. A work encompassing this would be a lifetime's task, like tracing the declensions of the stars. Instead, I have chosen a more modest task, but one that, I would suggest, underlies the rest of them. I have taken, as my sample, university textbooks from a range of disciplines—geology and physics, biology and chemistry—with the thought that these illustrate, in a basic yet polished way, the language of science. For while these various languages seem to multiply as in an algebraist's dream, the tools, or *syntax*, of scientific inquiry are relatively few in number.

In contrast to textbooks, practitioners tend to reject the term "scientific method," arguing that there *is* no rigid sequence in the process of scientific discovery and validation. While this is true—as we will see in Chapter 1— we are still left with a limited number of tools, ways of thinking, or, as they are called in the humanities, rhetorical modes. These are the thought patterns I have focused on in our study. One problem, of course, is that textbooks do not peek beneath the covers, to show the conflicts and conundrums, the false starts and blind alleys that all scientists encounter in their search for truth. And we will try to catch some of these in our historical excursion.

Admittedly, as O. Régent remarks, the types of scientific discourse used in practice "contain none of the uniformity nor the simplicity of the expository discourse to be found in school or university textbooks" (in Riley 1985, 105). We even find differences in cultural attitudes. But the beauty of the texts is their closely argued, tight-fitting interaction between these various modes of thought: How do definitions and examples, cause-and-effect statements and classifying, hypotheses and experiments, figurative language and visuality relate to one another? How do they interact? What is the syntax of definitions? The vocabulary of hypotheses? These are some of the questions we will examine in our time together.

Our topic—the language of science—is important for a wide range of readers. I have tried to keep those readers in mind throughout the book—in my presuppositions and use of technical vocabulary. While at times the analysis goes deeper than some readers might need, the chapters also contain suggestions and activities for teaching the various thought modes. As such, I hope the material will be useful for all of you interested in the teaching of science and the teaching of thinking in general, as well as those involved in scientific and technical writing. This should include:

TEACHERS OF SCIENCE AT ALL LEVELS, elementary through graduate school. Underlying the teaching of science is the *language* of science. Crucial to *understanding* that language is mastery of the various thought modes that we've analyzed in the book. Normally, these thought modes are taught implicitly, if at all, in courses on science and other subjects. And it is unlikely that teachers, even science teachers, fully understand the structure of these thought modes—their lexical and syntactic patterning.

TEACHERS WITH LANGUAGE-MINORITY STUDENTS. Language-minority students include those whose first language is not English, as well as native English-speakers who have not developed the needed linguistic facility in some of the critical thought modes analyzed in our study. Again, these students are found at all levels—from elementary through graduate school. They may be ESL (English as a second language) students, those we traditionally classify as minorities, or any others who need developmental work. My own sense is that one of the major problems discouraging minority students from going into science is deficiency in the linguistic and sometimes cognitive mastery of the thought patterns discussed in this volume.

ALL THOSE CONCERNED WITH THE TEACHING OF CRITICAL THINKING. Clearly, the thinking skills—or rhetorical modes—found in our book are not the special province of science. It is important for *all* those involved in the teaching of thinking in general—and critical thinking in particular—to better understand the structure of those thought modes: defining, classifying, hypothesizing, and so forth.

SCHOLARS, IN ALL FIELDS, WHO ARE INTERESTED IN THE LANGUAGE OF SCIENCE. Inquiries into science and language—and especially into their interrelation—have expanded far beyond the discipline of the sciences, and have become a major concern for scholars in linguistics, English, rhetoric, anthropology, sociology, history, and philosophy. As a result, *Understanding the Language of Science* should appeal to scholarly readers from a wide range of disciplines.

PRACTITIONERS OF ALL SORTS, including people in scientific and technical writing, foreign scientists who want to publish their work in English (of whom there are a great number), and practicing scientists who are native speakers of English and who are interested in the language of their craft.

I have used the theoretical material of the book as the basis for a school text entitled *Skills Workshop: Reading in the Content Areas,* which— I hope—will also be useful for students at different levels and from different backgrounds.

Let's begin by exploring some of our thought patterns in their historical context. The history of science is, of course, a giant field in itself, and all we can do, within that universe of discourse, is to catch glimpses of our topics—such as classifying or defining—as they evolve across the centuries and eventually take their place as essential tools of scientific inquiry.

Understanding

the Language of Science

Chapter 1

The Development of Scientific Thinking

Facts . . . constitute only a part of what science has to teach us. . . . The truly influential and pervasive aspects of modern science are not its facts at all, but rather its method of inquiry and its criterion of truth.

STILLMAN DRAKE

(in Galilei 1957, 3)

❈

The distinguishing feature of science is its willingness to test the truth of theories by examination of facts; either facts discovered by experiment or those found by observation.

MARTIN GOLDSTEIN

(in Goldstein and Goldstein 1984)

❈

As long as man is in search of knowledge, he will make mistakes.

S. DARIAN

❈

As Edwin Hutchins says in an essay on Micronesian navigation, "the European colonization of the world must have led to the extinction of many species of ideas." While there is little doubt of this, we must pursue our traditions, realizing that the ideas we have connected will in some ways be partial, tentative, and fortuitous.

Science is one of the ways we have tried to understand the world around us and our place in this vast and lonely universe. And while the answers of science may not always comfort us as do those of other visions, they have helped us improve the human condition—in extending life, curing disease, greatly enhancing our physical needs, and, yes, helping us understand the world within us.

How does science differ from other kinds of inquiry? How does scientific thinking differ from other modes of thinking? Basically, in two ways. First, by the nature of its subject matter: The topics of scientific inquiry have been those that have *some* possibility of being verified—either through observation, experiment, or quantifying; in other words, by some objective and possibly replicable measure.

The second way is in the *language* of science. Let us confess, immediately, that the language of science is first and foremost—*language:* subject to the same facts and fantasies as ordinary language; and that the modes of scientific thinking are, to a great extent, an integral part of language in general. Such elements as quantifying and metaphor (as we will see in the following chapters) are almost as much a part of language as words themselves. The difference with scientific inquiry lies in its rigorous, close-fitting use of these thought modes. In this chapter, I would like to examine how these modes, or patterns, interact in the process of scientific discovery and explanation.

THE DIRECTION OF THOUGHT. In English—as in other Indo-European languages—writing is done from left to right and top to bottom. This fact strongly influences our *understanding* of how we think: our sense, however vague, that thinking tends to be linear and sequential, that it runs from left to right. In reality, however, we deal with many problems or decisions in a nonlinear way. Thinking, and especially scientific thinking, takes other pathways as well, as I've suggested in Figure 1.1.

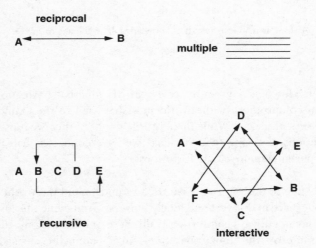

Figure 1.1. Directions of Thought

The classical case of reciprocity is the way a theory or hypothesis guides our observations and experiments, and how those observations and experiments may then alter our hypothesis (simply stated, A influences B, and B influences A). As for multiplicity, we can think of many occasions where there have been multiple causes or multiple effects of an event; we'll examine the patterns of multiple cause and effect in Chapter 5.

In recursiveness, we find ourselves returning to previous thought modes that may or may *not* be contiguous. We start with a problem, for example, gather information on it by observation or experiment, form an hypothesis, and test the hypothesis by experiment. At that point we may find that our hypothesis is not proved (and maybe not disproved). We may then need to gather more information, reformulate our hypothesis, do further experiments, and so on. "The method of science," suggest philosophers Cohen and Nagel, "is essentially *circular*. We obtain evidence for principles by appealing to empirical material, to what is alleged to be 'fact'; and we select, analyze, and interpret empirical material on the basis of principles" (1934, 396). The process is anything but linear, as Figure 1.2 illustrates.

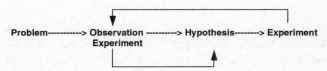

Figure 1.2. The Recursive Nature of Thinking

We can think of interactivity as containing elements of reciprocity and recursiveness, but somewhat differently patterned. From this our starting point, these elements appear as abstract and general. They will become clearer and more relevant, I hope, as we find examples of them in our inquiry.

In this chapter and throughout the book, I would like to examine the following thought modes, their interactions, and the role they play in scientific thinking:

- cause and effect
- classifying
- comparison
- definitions
- examples
- experiment

- figurative language and analogies
- induction and deduction
- observation
- quantifying
- theories and hypotheses
- visual thinking

I have divided this chapter into two parts. Part 1 examines the various thought modes as they appear historically. We will glimpse their development in the Lyceum of Athens and the library of Alexandria, the madrasas of Islam and the monasteries of early Christendom, in the great medieval universities, and out into the slowly secularizing world of the sixteenth century and beyond.

The Chinese, as well, made great advances in their empirical view of the universe—especially between the third and thirteenth centuries. But while Chinese technology began to appear in Europe from at least the 1500s, the Chinese probably had a limited influence on scientific thinking in the West (in his *History of Technology,* Charles Singer presents a long list of Chinese inventions and the dates of their appearance in Europe; 1956, 2:770ff.). Part 2 explores how the different thought modes interact with each other, in context, to create the language of science.

The Evolution of Scientific Thinking

We see most clearly in the past what is of most interest to us.

ROGER FRENCH

◆

There are dangers in imposing the standards of the present upon the past. One of these dangers lies in the assumption that the purpose of the past has been to prepare the way for the present.

HERBERT BUTTERFIELD

◆

The great discoveries . . . of science did not come suddenly out of the blue . . . each was prepared by a long evolution. . . . The mountaintops are exhilarating, but they could not exist by themselves.

GEORGE SARTON

◆

It began with a passion for understanding: the who, the what, the why of it. What caused the glittering lights in the brooding sky? What called them into being? And the strange white shape—a smile without a face—that we came to call the moon? Or the great unquenchable bowl of the sea? What governs the emanation and return of life? The coming and going of all things?

At first we looked outward for our understandings. And conjured up things in our own image, but far more powerful than us: things that would live when we no longer lived; things that could comfort us, console us, and in our abjection command us; things to help us understand our place in this boundless universe; to help calm our fears, assuage our terrors, and aid us in our restless search for understanding.

Thus there arose the gods and their chthonian reflections, from which we drew our first answers to the questions of birth and death, of fortune and misfortune, and to the less dramatic questions of how things worked and how we might improve upon them; in what ways we might dare our fate and cheat our destiny.

For some strange reason—perhaps partly from the restless intercourse in ideas common to maritime people—it was not until the sixth century B.C., among the Ionian islands off the coast of Turkey, that men began to look for other answers, to question the earlier solutions that, over time, failed to work . . . and never really did. And so it was that the Ionians began to think of the heavens and the stars as *material* things, as forces more impersonal, not to be supplicated by the sacrifice of animals or humans, or the offerings of the harvest. Instead, they turned to nature itself, directly, confronting it with their senses, recording their perceptions, and asking: How can we be certain of this? And so they began to compare, to look for patterns that recurred, to look for similarities, to name things and classify them, to probe more deeply into the earth and into the bodies of animals. And as these modes of thought develop and merge, we glimpse the early stirrings of science.

Facts and Theories

The history of science is a very large subject, but the history of super-stition is infinite.

GEORGE SARTON

✳

A theory is valued because it provides a clue on where to look for dis-coveries that have not yet been made.

MICHAEL GHISELIN

✳

All other religions are superstitions . . . except our own.

S. DARIAN

✳

The most crucial apposition in scientific thought is the distinction between *facts* and *theories*. It is a distinction that has been with us since the Ionians and one that will likely pursue us as long as there is language.

From the time of the ancients, people have always been curious about the world: first, about the world outside them; then more gradually, about the world within. Lacking the tools of modern science, they had to rely chiefly on speculation. Certain speculations, or "theories," were based on observation, others on intuition, imagination, and spiritual insights.

So the Old Testament begins with a theory on the origins of the world. In answer to the question "Why does man suffer such misfortune?" Genesis proffers the theory that he has forfeited his initial oneness with all things by eating of the tree of knowledge (thus was born his sense of differentiation, or *comparison*). Our theory here is clearly as well a statement of *cause* and *effect*.

Along with god, freedom, and love, the term *theory* is one of the least understood of words. A theory, in science, is a belief, a statement, an hypothesis that has been around for a long time and has accumulated a great deal of evidence to support it. When it has gained common acceptance in the scientific community, it becomes a *principle* or a *law*. Without that body of evidence, it remains a hunch, a guess, a *hypothesis*. By modern standards, most theories of early times were seldom more than hypotheses.

One of the best discussions on the difference between facts and theories (theories in the premodern sense) comes from the nearly forgotten nineteenth-century British philosopher William Whewell, whose writings were overshadowed by his famous contemporary John Stuart Mill. Following in the footsteps of Kant, Whewell draws a series of related contrasts between theories and facts, thoughts and things, necessary and experiential truths, deduction and induction, and ideas and sensations. As Whewell explains, the first member of each pair comes from our minds; it is more abstract and conceptual. The second member is from pure observation.

"Without thoughts," he urges, "there could be no *connexion;* without things, there could be no reality . . . Only when the two elements are united do we have [true] knowledge" (Whewell 1858, 1:25). In other words, we know facts only by thinking about them, and this thinking about them involves faculties of the mind different from observation. His example is instructive:

> The Fact that the year consists of 365 days . . . cannot be known to us, except as we have the Thoughts of *Time, Number,* and *Recurrence.* But these Thoughts are so familiar, that we have the Fact in our mind as a simple Thing without attending to the Thoughts which it involves. (Whewell 1858, 1:29ff.)

We can add to these a near endless list: spirit and matter, soul and body, the Hindu *sarga* and *pralaya* (latent and manifest). Ultimately, we can reduce it to a distinction between the observable and the unobservable.

In a sense, the development of science is the study of how people dealt with theories: how they created and evaluated them and what use they put them to. In this, there is no direct line of progress. For even the great luminaries such as Copernicus, Kepler, and Newton—while embracing observation, experiment, and measurement—accepted as given certain theories that had no basis in fact, theories that could not be proved and eventually turned out wrong.

Most early theories dealt with devils and deities as the causes of phenomena. One of the first to subject competing theories to scientific scrutiny was Anaximander of Miletus, the Ionian philosopher who drew what may have been the first map of the known world (de Santillana 1970, 27). Except for scraps, his work has disappeared. But enough of it comes down through later commentators, to help us understand the new modes of thinking that had begun to appear.

So that great chronicler Herodotus reconstructs Anaximander's speculations on the behavior of the Nile: why it begins to rise at the summer solstice, continues for a hundred days, then falls again at the end of that period, remaining low throughout the winter until the return of the solstice. Anaximander could find no one in Egypt to explain the reason. Accordingly, he consults several Greeks, all of whom offered various theories that the philosopher rejects, one by one, after evaluating the evidence directly: (1) "The Etesian [trade] winds cause the water to rise by checking the flow of the current towards the sea." But Anaximander points out that the Nile rises even when the winds do *not* blow (*observation* or reliable reports). He further argues by *comparison:* Other rivers opposed by the winds are not affected by them. (2) The second theory—in Herodotus's phrase—is legendary, and so cannot be verified. (3) The third is rejected from logical arguments based on geographic knowledge of the day.

By seeking answers in nature rather than in Providence, Anaximander ushers in a new way of thinking. His way of theorizing, suggests classicist George de Santillana, "is as much an innovation on the way of thinking that came before as the whole of science has been since, from Anaximander to Einstein" (de Santillana 1970, 36).

THEORIES AND HYPOTHESES. As we have seen, theories are hypotheses that are several steps closer to truth. But while hypotheses have been with us since man first began his speculations, the *topic* of hypotheses does not receive intensive treatment until the seventeenth and eighteenth centuries and the writings of Newton and Francis Bacon. As we will see in Chapter 6, the essence of hypotheses is their tentativeness—their degree of probability. For da Vinci and Galileo, Bacon and Descartes, no matter what their differences, there was agreement on one thing: that the methods of science yield conclusions that have nothing provisional about them but possess an absolute certitude. One of Newton's major contributions was the realization that *the results of science are always tentative* and subject to new evidence.

Observation and Induction

Science is the observation of things possible, whether present or past;
prescience is the knowledge of things which may come to pass, though
but slowly.

All our knowledge is in our perceptions.

LEONARDO DA VINCI

❉

Pussycat, pussycat, where have you been?
I've been to London to visit the Queen.
Pussycat, pussycat, what did you see there?
I saw a large mouse under her chair.

ANON., TRADITIONAL

❉

Before the rise of experimental science, the surest way to perceive and establish facts was through direct observation, a mode that has been with us since the beginning of language, and before. The question is: What happens to those observations? How are they processed, stored, and acted on? In man's questing mind, there has been a constant need for interpretation, for theorizing. In the ancient Near East, that theorizing usually took on a strong theistic flavor: both human and astronomical events were determined by the gods.

This frame of mind continues through the ancient and medieval world and is with us today. But from the time of the Ionian philosophers in the sixth century B.C., another perspective emerges: a focus on nature and natural, as opposed to supernatural, explanations. With this focus on nature comes the need to observe nature in its finer details. This is harder, of course, with things you could not put your hands on—like heavenly bodies, which, nonetheless, came to be viewed as solid material objects, not conscious beings. But other more terrestrial fields, like biology and medicine, were eminently well suited to direct observation.

And so we hear of the Pythagorean Alcmaeon of Croton, who, around 500 B.C., "is said to have discovered by dissection the optic nerves connecting the eyes with the brain and the Eustachian tubes linking the ears with the mouth" (Mason 1953, 19). We read in Hippocrates's treatise *The Sacred Disease* (on epilepsy), from the fourth century B.C., how the great physician completely rejects any divine or sacred causes for the illness and the thousand and one cures that offered no relief. It is under Hippocrates that medicine assumes its place as the *inductive* science par excellence.

Thus it is that the life sciences usher in a new mode of thinking. That mode of thinking—direct and careful observation—undergoes a long and tortuous history. It is derailed by Plato and championed by Aristotle. The change in Greek science from the speculative to the empirical was also influenced by the engineers and geographers, the naturalists and physicians, who returned from Alexander's campaign through Asia with a wealth of information on new plants and animals and the contours of the earth (Mason 1953, 33).

The empirical view is seriously neglected in the early Middle Ages, but taken up by Arab scientists, starting in the ninth century with Al-Hazen, who rejects the existing theory that the eye sends out light to view an object, proposing instead that the light reflecting from an object travels *to* the eye (Singer 1959, 152). It is embraced by the great Islamic physicians: Al-Razi, who contributed original observations in his diagnosis of smallpox and measles; and by Ibn Sena (Avicenna), who wrote over two hundred scientific works, and whose *Canon of Medicine* became a standard text in the hospitals of Christendom for five hundred years.

In other ways as well, Islamic science contributed to the role of observation, in both chemistry and astronomy. During their time, Moslem observatories were the most advanced in the world, and stretched from Toledo to Samarkand. They also made considerable improvement in the design of astronomical instruments.

But it is not until the thirteenth and fourteenth centuries that observation emerges in the great centers of learning at Oxford and Paris, where it begins to compete with the more Scripture-based theories as a source of hypotheses for explaining the world and its workings. It was men from the scholarly tradition—men like Adelard of Bath, William of Ockham, and Nicholas of Cusa—who set the stage for the later paladins of empiricism and the inductive approach to scientific inquiry.

Events and individuals continually strengthened the emphasis on observation as a primary mode of inquiry. The Age of Exploration in the fifteenth century brought with it the need for careful calculation and observation as indispensable aids to navigation. The Reformation in the sixteenth urged men to reject traditional authority and interpret the Scriptures for themselves. In the same manner, the new scientists turned from the theories of the ancients and of the schoolmen, and began to view the world in a more empirical way.

At the same time, the crafts tradition—always tied to observation and experiment—drew closer to the scholars' pursuit of "mental" theories and their growing use of mathematics. The development of modern science resulted from the confluence of these two very different traditions. We have, further, the great Renaissance artists, with their renewed interest in the human body. So Dürer and Boticelli, Michelangelo and Leonardo, all studied human anatomy through dissection.

From the sixteenth century, men of science turn more and more to observation as a major mode of inquiry: Copernicus, Kepler, and, of course, Francis Bacon—champion of the inductive method. Even Galileo and Newton, though they emphasize mathematical and experimental approaches, stress the central role of observation. By the nineteenth century, observation (along with mathematical analysis and experimentation) has become the chief tool of scientific research. We have only to think of Pasteur, the geologist Charles Lyell, and the two great proponents of observation, John Stuart Mill and Charles Darwin. Darwin's *Origin of Species,* suggests historian of science Rom Harré, was "probably the greatest work based almost wholly on observation" (Harré 1976).

As we will see in later chapters, observation and induction play a major part in many of our other thought modes, including classifying, hypotheses, and experimentation.

Cause and Effect

Nature is full of infinite causes that have never occurred in experience.

LEONARDO DA VINCI

❉

Final causes are like Vestal virgins, Dedicated to God and sterile.

FRANCIS BACON

❉

In a sense, cause, or causality, is different from certain other thought modes: Patterns like observation and experiment, comparison and analogy, are all means. Cause is both means and end: It is both a tool and a goal of scientific inquiry. As such, it is intertwined with many of our other thought patterns.

It is easy to understand how cause and effect may have been one of our earliest modes of thinking. Of all the questions in our language, the most provocative, the most persistent and open to endless speculation, is the question *why?* The range of answers to that question spans the universe: from the riddles of the mystics to the carefully reasoned arguments of philosophers and physicists. In Chapter 5, we will examine the language of cause and effect: its lexical, syntactic, and discourse features. Here, let us spend a moment glimpsing some of its historical expressions.

As we have seen, scientific thinking made great advances with the Greek experience. Yet, it never quite detached itself from divine etiologies—

belief that all things have a divine origin, or cause. Assuming for a moment that these theories were *correct,* the problem is: there is no way of verifying them. And so there was little *need*—except in practical technology—to develop such tools as mathematics, experimentation, or careful observation. With their more impersonal view of nature, the pre-Socratic philosophers open the door to a closer reading of phenomena—a reading that aided greatly in sharpening the tools of thought.

Let's return briefly to Anaximander and his problem of the rising waters of the Nile. His analysis of the various causes derives from (1) comparison, (2) logic based on existing geographic knowledge, and (3) a recognition that one of the theories was mythological. This is clearly a departure from earlier forms of analysis.

The most extensive classical analysis of cause and effect appears in Aristotle, who in his endless passion for classifying, lays out four types of causes: (1) *material cause:* "the primary matter out of which objects were made"; (2) *formal cause:* "the designs, patterns, and forms which were impressed upon the primary matter"; (3) the *efficient cause:* "providing the mechanism whereby such designs were realized"; and (4) *final causes:* "the purposes for which objects were designed." Aristotle himself was mainly concerned with formal and final causes (Aristotle 1984, "Parts of Animals," section 641b). Taking the example of a clay vessel, we have:

1. material cause: the clay;
2. formal cause: the design of the vessel;
3. efficient cause: the potter's wheel and hands;
4. final cause: the purpose that the vessel was intended for.

What shall we make of these permutations? As for (1) material causes, we would not normally consider the material something is composed of as a cause of that thing: clay is not the cause of a pot any more than bark is the cause of a tree. Likewise for (2) formal causes: design is a *feature* of the pot but not a *cause.* In fact, we would not normally think of man-made objects as having causes at all. Interestingly, however, Aristotle believes that formal causes are inherent in all natural objects and processes. This rings true for us, in the genetic sense: genes cause people to be people and butterflies to be butterflies.

On (3) efficient causes, we would likewise probably reject the potter's wheel and hands as a cause of the pot. Still, the potter's hands and tools do *produce* the pot. And as we will see in Chapter 5, sentences in our corpus do use verbs like *generate, influence,* and *promote,* and nouns like *product* and *reflection,* to indicate cause-and-effect relationships. What to make of (4) final causes? Was the vessel intended for carrying wine or water? Was it intended for drinking? Regardless of its purpose, though, we would reject this as a "cause" of the pot. In this variation, Aristotle is probably reflecting a theory of the times: that all things have some (hidden) purpose, or teleology—can we say . . . a certain destiny?

In one way or another, probably every scientist and philosopher has commented on cause and effect. There are volumes devoted to the topic. The most we can do here is identify a few of the milestones. One of those milestones—more than a millennium after Aristotle—is in the person of William of Ockham (1295–1349), one of the great medieval schoolmen who seized upon the new tools of science. William's important contribution to the topic is his emphasis on multiple causality: "The same species of effect can exist through many different causes" (cited in Crombie 1952, 232).

Later, Descartes was also to comment on the multiplicities of cause and effect. "There is no circularity," he exclaims, "in proving a cause by several effects which are known otherwise, and then reciprocally proving certain other effects by this cause" (quoted in Blake 1960, 95). (We will analyze the pattern of multiple causes in Chapter 5.) This same sense of *reciprocity* occurs in Galileo and Leonardo. "The scientist," Leonardo notes, may proceed inductively or deductively, "according to the nature of the subject," sometimes "deducing the causes from the effects in natural demonstrations; sometimes, on the contrary, deducing the effect from the causes" (quoted in Blake 1960, 17).

In a slightly different vein, Newton argues that "'True cause' was not one already known to exist, but rather one the existence of which was susceptible of independent corroboration" (Blake 1960, 133). True causes of phenomena are determining principles or laws (like the law of gravity), which we can discover by *observation* and *experiment* to be actually at work in the world (Blake 1960, 135).

The concept of reciprocity is central in the arguments of the eighteenth- and nineteenth-century geologists Hutton and Lyell, who emphasize the idea that one can reason from cause to effect *or* from effect to cause, depending on the type of evidence available. Geology in the eighteenth and nineteenth centuries was the chief battleground in the secularization of scientific theories. The two opposing camps, which later coalesced, were the Vulcanists, who emphasized the role of heat, and the Neptunists, who emphasized the role of water, in forming geological strata.

The Neptunists favored a secularized version of the Flood theory, which, regardless of its appeal, was basically untestable, based as it was on a primal ocean that disappeared in some unknown way when its job was done. James Hutton, on the other hand, argued that "only such forces as are seen in operation today should be used to explain the past formation of the rocks" (Mason 1953, 325). Hutton here is using observation as a basis for explaining causes from the distant past. Eventually, Hutton's view won out, but not before a century of furious debate, one that in several ways laid the groundwork for Darwin and the revolution he called into being.

Experimentation

The human mind has at different periods of its evolution passed successively through *feeling, reason,* and *experiment.* First, feeling alone, imposing itself on reason, created the truths of faith or theology. Reason or philosophy . . . brought on the birth of scholasticism. At last, experiment, or the study of natural phenomena, taught man that the truths of the outer world are to be found ready formulated neither in feeling nor in reason.

CLAUDE BERNARD

●

Apart from the origins of alchemy, which are shrouded in mystery, we begin to find references to experiment as a mode of inquiry as early as Alcmaeon, in his experiments through dissection. Aristotle as well, while more an observer than an experimenter, evidently performed a great number of dissections; at least fifty, by Mason's estimate (Mason 1953, 29). Dissection is mentioned in his books on animals. In fact, Aristotle often refers to a now lost treatise on anatomy; a term that, as classicist Robert French points out, is a translation of the Greek word for dissection (1994, 40).

And Strato (ca. 300 B.C.), Aristotle's later successor at the Lyceum, carries forward the experimental sense in his studies of the physical world. So in weighing a piece of wood before and after heating it, Strato finds that the remaining charcoal has the same volume as the original wood, but that it is lighter. His conclusion is that "matter" had departed from the wood, leaving small vacuous pores (Mason 1953, 31). Probably the foremost experimenter among the Greeks was Archimedes (287–212 B.C.), the son of an astronomer, and a man that historian of science Charles Singer calls the greatest mathematician of antiquity (Singer 1959, 69). As philosopher Arthur Ritchie points out, "all of the propositions in Archimedes' treatise *Statics* can be confirmed by experiment" (Ritchie 1958, 85).

As we have seen, medicine—because of its practical needs and tangible subject matter—began much earlier than astronomy to separate itself from the more theistic theories of causality. The most influential physician of the ancient world was Galen (130–200 A.D.), who was a keen observer and experimentalist, and whose theories dominated medicine down to modern times. Galen was born in Pergamum in Asia Minor and studied in Alexandria. When he was thirty, he returned to Pergamum and served as doctor to the gladiators—a position that gave him lots of experience with bones and bodies. Sometime during his thirties, he emigrated to Rome, where his fame as a doctor became so great that he was eventually appointed court physician in the reign of Marcus Aurelius (Thorndike 1923–1958, 1:224).

Galen was able, by experiment, to determine the general course of the veins and arteries, as well as their functions. His experimental inquiries were broad: "ranging from the production of the voice by the larynx, and the functioning of the kidney, to the medicinal properties of herbs" (Crombie 1952, 135). He even disagreed with the great Aristotle, by demonstrating experimentally that the nerves originated not in the heart but in the brain and the spinal cord. He also cautioned those who performed medical experiments on the extreme unlikelihood of ever observing "in even two cases, the same combination of symptoms and circumstances" (Thorndike 1923–1958, 1:146, 161).

True, some of his theories and prescriptions were wrong, such as his pronouncements on the movement of the blood, and the heart as the center of respiration. But it was his experimental method that set his intellectual descendants on the proper path.

CHEMISTRY. The history of chemistry mirrors the relationship between empiricism and theory. As in physics and medicine, it was originally tied to theistic or anthropomorphic ends and origins; then to alchemy and the quest for gold and immortality. At the same time, chemical investigations were of necessity grounded in observation and experiment. In this way, chemistry, like biology and medicine, was able to preserve the experimental viewpoint until its integration into the mainstream of scientific inquiry in the sixteenth century.

The experimental view was kept alive in the Islamic period. For we read of Al-Hazen's experiments with the magnifying glass, in which he approaches the modern theory of convex lenses (Mason 1953, 74). And of Al-Razi (865–925 A.D.) (Razes, to Europeans), the first original Arabic writer on medicine, who wrote over a hundred works and whose best-known compendium (The Comprehensive Book) included the whole of Greek, Indian, and Middle Eastern medicine then known (Crombie 1952, 32; Singer 1959, 146). He was also the greatest of Arabic-writing alchemists and devoted the early part of his life to alchemical experiments (Singer 1959, 146). It is interesting that five of the Islamic writers who most influenced European thought were physicians, and thus experimentalists. These are Al-Biruni, Avicenna, Averroës, and—as we have seen—Razes and Al-Hazen.

When the curtain rises on the later medieval world, we find a growing intellectual activity in the northern universities. One of the first to embrace the new methods of experimental science was Robert Grosseteste (1158–1253), who, in historian A. C. Crombie's words, "was the real founder of scientific thought in medieval Oxford, and in some ways of the modern English intellectual tradition." Grosseteste was a man of genius—born of humble parents—who went on to graduate from Oxford, where he later became chancellor. He was proficient in law, medicine, and mathematics, and learned in Greek and Hebrew. His most celebrated work was an attempt to explain the shape of the rainbow, using refraction of light by a spherical lens. His writings also reveal one of the earliest references to the use of glass containers for experimental purposes—itself a great breakthrough.

Grosseteste's famous disciple was Roger Bacon (1241–1294), who declaimed against those who "based their opinions on fallible authorities, or the weight of custom." The true student, he stresses, should know "natural science" by experiment. In Bacon's view, the first aim of experimental science is to verify the results of mathematical reasoning (in this he anticipates Galileo and Newton). The second is to complement deductive inquiry by adding knowledge that it could not determine by itself, a sentiment later emphasized by Descartes. The third is to discover realms of learning not yet known (Crombie 1952, 227).

Bacon seems to regard "experimental science" as something different from the other natural sciences, its purpose being directed toward practical ends. And though his science *may* not have been that far in advance of his times (as Thorndike suggests), Bacon's imagination was. For he envisioned cars that moved with great velocity and without animals; flying machines constructed "so that a man sits in the midst . . . revolving some engine by which artificial wings are made to beat the air"; and—anticipating Captain Nemo—machines that move along the bottom of seas (Thorndike 1923–1958, 2:654).

As interest in its new tools spread, science began to draw in those men of religious orders with the greatest intellectual curiosity. Typical of them was Nicholas of Cusa (1400–1464). Like Grosseteste, he was born poor and rose to a position of prominence—as a cardinal of the Church. In an experiment reminiscent of Strato, Nicholas describes weighing a piece of wood, burning it, then weighing the ashes, in order to determine its water content. Writing in "Statics Experimentis," from his work *Idiota* ("Everyman"), where he records his wood experiment, he suggests various experimental applications of the balance; comparing, for example, "the weight of herbs with those of blood or urine, in an effort to understand the actions of medicines. He also tries to calibrate the time a given volume of water takes to run through a given hole, as a standard for comparing pulse rates" (Crombie 1952, 265). We will meet him again in the sections on quantifying and comparison.

An even more accurate experimentalist was Leonardo da Vinci—the illegitimate child who became one of the most wide-ranging geniuses in the history of the world. In his notebooks, Leonardo mentions—among other things—having dissected more than ten human bodies (da Vinci 1939, 2:107): "removing the very minutest particles of the flesh by which the veins are surrounded, without causing them to bleed" (da Vinci 1939, 2:108). He describes "the anatomy of the bones, which have to be sawn to show which are hollow and which are not, which have marrow and which are spongy" (da Vinci 1939, 2:110). Leonardo is insatiable, and examines the structure and function of the veins and arteries, the nerves and sinews, muscles, skin, and bones (da Vinci 1939, 2:115). What is sneezing? he asks. And yawning? (da Vinci 1939, 2:114). He inquires into "the cause of breathing, the cause of the motion of the heart . . . the descent of food from the stomach, the cause of emptying of the intestines" (da Vinci 1939, 2:117).

But it is Galileo (1564–1642) who firmly establishes experiment (combined with mathematics) as a cornerstone of scientific inquiry. Galileo was the son of a minor nobleman who had seen better days. Where his passion for experiment came from, who can say? We know that he was not an ivory-tower scientist. From his *Dialogues Concerning Two New Sciences,* we can picture him dealing with the problems of shipbuilders in Venice, the handling of artillery, or the pumping of water in mines.

Galileo used experiments for both inductive and deductive purposes. In the famous inclined plane experiment—illustrating the Law of Descent (heavy bodies fall with increasing velocity)—he begins by setting up the experimental apparatus, then observes the acceleration of a ball along its metal grooves. From this, he draws a mathematical hypothesis, which he then tests with further experiment.

Another topic of contemporary interest was the flight path of projectiles, which Galileo was able to determine mathematically. In this he showed how one could demonstrate "what perhaps has never been observed, from phenomena already known." The demonstration thus provided an explanation for those phenomena, and the experimental discovery of the predicted facts verifying the explanation (Mason 1953, 123). In other words, *one could work backwards from the facts to unseen and unobservable causes,* then verify the causes mathematically and experimentally. On the role of experiments, Galileo remarks, in his *Dialogue Concerning the Two World Systems* (Copernican and Ptolemaic):

> One sole experiment, or concludent demonstration produced on the contrary part, sufficeth to batter to the ground . . . a thousand . . . probable arguments.

Descartes (1596–1650), like Galileo, was a mathematician and experimentalist. Like Galileo, he tended to use experiments to test hypotheses that were first determined mathematically. As he explains in a letter:

> I use that kind of philosophizing in which there is no principle that is not mathematical and evident, and its conclusions confirmed by true experiment. (Mason 1953, 166)

Despite himself, Descartes accepted certain *givens,* the foremost of which was God. Starting from the existence of God, the philosopher deduces the entire universe, step-by-step, in a series of clear, well-ordered mathematical propositions. In this way, Descartes—in some ways—harks back to the vision of the Schoolmen. He also embraces the analogy of *man as a machine,* subject to the same laws as the mechanical universe (thus Man the Machine replaces the long-prevalent analogy of Man the Microcosm). But the human machine is independent of any metaphysical forces and thus exhibits a "constancy of response under constant conditions, the *sine qua non* for experimental investigation" (Schiller 1973, 138).

The philosopher also helps establish the idea (along with the chemist Lavoisier) that the same laws applied to living and nonliving (organic and inorganic) matter. Descartes's most influential contribution was the concept of "scientific doubt," which, in the language of the laboratory, translated into the controlled experiment. And he was to have a major influence on Claude Bernard, the man chiefly responsible for establishing the experimental method in physiology. As Bernard was to remark two centuries later, "Descartes' conception dominates modern physiology. Living beings *are* mechanisms" (Schiller 1973, 138).

Isaac Newton (1642–1727). As we have seen, Galileo "legitimizes" the experimental method as one of the most important tools in scientific investigation. Newton takes experimentation one step further, and adopts it as the ultimate test for all the steps in the process. In Newton's view, many theories are derived from experience or can be deduced from first principles (givens). This fact, however, gives them no finality. "For the principles themselves, like all conclusions derived from experience, stand always open to the correction of further experimental investigation" (Blake 1960, 138). Even though one may formulate theories from observation or mathematical analysis, those theories "can be legitimately established by experimental evidence only, and then can be overthrown only (1) by showing the insufficiency of the evidence adduced in their favor, or (2) by producing adverse experimental evidence" (Blake 1960, 128). While the first test of Newton's Laws came from astronomical observation, these Laws were later elaborated in laboratory experiments.

True experimental method was established in different sciences at different times. For mechanics it was Galileo in the sixteenth century, for chemistry it was Lavoisier in the seventeenth, and for physiology it was Claude Bernard in the nineteenth.

Claude Bernard (1813–1878). From his mentor, the physiologist Magendie, Bernard derived the idea that the only true way to study living things is by experimentation. Such a viewpoint immediately eliminated—or at least minimized—the influence of unverifiable hypotheses. While Galileo often used experiments to *demonstrate* hypotheses he had previously worked out mathematically, Bernard used experiment strictly as a tool for discovery. Indeed, as he says in his classic *Principes de médecine expérimentale,* he often discovered phenomena he was not searching for. His disciplined process of observation, hypothesis, and experiment led Bernard to several conceptual breakthroughs and set new standards for experimental procedures. These included an emphasis on the control of variables and a more tangible measure of cause and effect: The experimental method, according to Bernard, "demonstrates that there is no effect without a cause and that the cause is material" (Schiller 1973, 156).

Still another insight was the relationship between theories and hypotheses—true and untrue. An hypothesis may stem from an existing theory, and its confirmation by experiment may add to the theory. But a disproven hypothesis may still lead to new information. French historian of science Joseph Schiller cites as a prime example the discovery of glycogen synthesis in the liver. The prevailing theory, according to Schiller (1973, 150), was that animals could not synthesize organic compounds. In searching for other locations in the body where glucose was destroyed, Bernard discovered the exact opposite: that it *was* synthesized by the liver. The discovery, exclaims Schiller, "revolutionized both physiology and biochemistry."

We will analyze Bernard's experimental method more closely in Part 2 of the chapter, when we examine the interrelationships of the various thought modes.

Quantification and Measurement

If it can't be counted, it's not science.

LORD KELVIN

❋

All of the great scientists were probably mystics.

GEORGE SARTON

❋

As with our other modes, the process of quantifying has probably been with us since the beginnings of human thought. The ancient Near East did not lack the passion. The Egyptians, judging from their measurements of land and the construction of the pyramids, had achieved extraordinary precision in their measurements. In the Great Pyramid of Cheops, for example, the fifty-six roofing beams over the chamber weighed an average of 54 tons. These limestone blocks had to be cut exactly before placing them in position. According to Egyptologist Sir Flinders Petrie, the mean error of the length of the sides was 1 in 4,000, "equal to that produced by a difference of 15°C in the temperature of a copper measuring bar. . . . On shorter lengths of 50 ft. the differences are only 0.02′" (Sarton 1959, 1:36, quoting *Wisdom of the Egyptians,* 89). There are at least sixteen Egyptian documents on mathematics that have come down to us from before 1000 B.C. The oldest is the Rhind papyrus, dating roughly to 1900 B.C., which discusses fractions, divisions, problems dealing with determination of areas and volumes, and other problems leading to equations of the first degree with one unknown quantity (there were no equations per se, but we do find symbols denoting unknown quantities) (Sarton 1959, 1:36). In their constant need to reestablish land boundaries effaced by the Nile floods, the Egyptians may well have invented geometry, a term referring to the measuring of the land.

Likewise in Mesopotamia. Despite their clumsy number system and lack of a medial zero until late in their history, the Sumerians achieved a high degree of mathematical abstraction. Their tablets contained a variety of tables: tables for multiplication, for squares and cubes which, when inverted, yielded tables of square roots, cube roots, and reciprocals. Though lacking the form of equations, they solved problems requiring linear equations, simultaneous equations with many unknown quantities, and quadratics as well. They also handled negative numbers, a concept that did not appear in Western mathematical thought until the time of Leonardo. "It is quite clear," emphasizes historian of science George Sarton, "that the Sumerians had as much natural genius for algebra as the Greeks for geometry" (Sarton 1959, 1:73).

Among the early Greeks, it is Pythagoras, of course, who unfolds the world of numeracy. With the Pythagoreans come the concept of *proportion* and relationships, and astronomy as we know it today. True, the Babylonians had done remarkable work in mapping the heavens, but it is the Pythagoreans who take us to the level of orbits and rotations, and the insight—for the first time—that the earth was a sphere. Eventually they are overawed by their own discoveries and come to deify them—in relating numbers and musical tones to the movement of the stars. These mystical associations echo through time and appear briefly in such figures as Grosseteste and Leonardo, Copernicus and Kepler. Still, the Pythagoreans sow the seeds for a concept that underlies the whole enterprise of science: that of quantifying and quantification. The theory that "all things are numbers" led inquiring minds to search for those numbers, and quantities, in the phenomena (Lloyd 1987, 277).

There have been serious criticisms that ancient Greek science was basically qualitative, and that both the physical and life sciences tended to avoid exact quantitative expression (for different points of view, cf. Lloyd 1987, 215). Classicist G. E. R. Lloyd examines this theory in terms of specific fields and concludes that while there is truth to it, quantitative methods played an important part—sometimes excessively—in many Greek inquiries into nature and the universe.

Even Plato, opposed as he was to observation and induction, stresses the centrality of mathematics; as, for example, in the *Philebus,* where he groups different branches of knowledge according to their use of mathematical concepts; or in the *Republic* (525 C–D) (Hamilton and Cairns 1971), where he urges that it be made a required part of the curriculum for future leaders. And finally, in his statement—showing a strong Pythagorean influence—that "God is primarily a mathematician" (Sarton 1959, 1:432, quoting Plutarch). Unfortunately, the neo-Platonists' influence in Renaissance times was manifested in more of a mystical reverence for numbers than in any practical applications of mathematics (Kearney 1971, 100).

As for Aristotle, while he was not a professional mathematician, numerical analysis plays a considerable part in his thinking. Sarton even states that "most of his examples of scientific method were taken from his mathematical experience" (Sarton 1959, 1:501). Under Aristotle, members of the Lyceum "improved the definitions and axioms and more generally the philosophical substructure [of mathematics]." One of its members even undertook the first study of conics (Sarton 1959, 1:506). Still, Aristotle's quantifying sense tends more toward *proportion* and *comparison*—in other words, relative quantities—than absolute numbers; e.g., "in natural motion the more there is of a heavy body the faster it moves downward" (Lloyd 1987, 217). (In the next section, we'll take a closer look at this relation between comparison and quantifying.)

But it is really Archimedes (287–212 B.C.) who is acknowledged as the greatest mathematician of the ancient world and one of its most famous engineers. Born in Syracuse (in Sicily), educated in Alexandria, he returned to his birthplace, where he died in a Roman invasion, while contemplating a problem of geometry. The Romans did not know much of his work in mathematics, which began to appear in Latin only in medieval times through the medium of Arab translations. As we will shortly see, however, it came to have—in unlikely ways—a major influence on the scientific revolution of the sixteenth and seventeenth centuries.

GEOPHYSICS. Among the Alexandrians and before, there was considerable speculation on the shape and especially the size of the earth. Aristotle argues that the size of the earth is small compared to the sphere of the fixed stars. He further indicates the circumference of the earth at 400,000 *stadia,* according to several different sources. However, he gives no details on the methods of their reckoning (Lloyd 1987, 231). Eratosthenes in the third century B.C., using his own calculations, estimates the circumference at 250,000. Although the length of the stadium was not standardized, Sarton reckons that Eratosthenes' *stadium* may have equaled 157.5 meters, thus yielding a value of 39,360 kilometers, less than 1 percent off the actual circumference of 40,120 km (Sarton 1959, 2:105)! We find other examples in the works of the Alexandrians. So Ptolemy (85–165 A.D.), in his *Syntaxis,* records the latitudes and longitudes of over a thousand stars in degrees and fractions of degrees. Ultimately, says Lloyd: "However hesitant in its beginning, Greek astronomy eventually achieved outstanding success in developing detailed, quantitative models to account for complex natural phenomena" (Lloyd 1987, 240).

The arrival of Indian and Arabic numbers and methods of calculating contributed greatly to the quantifying sense in Europe. By late medieval times, we find Nicholas of Cusa stressing the importance of measurement in studying the natural world—using the balance for weighing and the water clock and hourglass for timing (Thorndike 1923–1958, 4:389). Though his mathematical work was not fruitful—the cardinal became obsessed with the problem of trying to square the circle—he was to influence Leonardo, Copernicus, and Kepler, and his inquiries contributed to the seventeenth-century development of differential geometry (Taton 1964, 13).

By the time of the Renaissance, the number of books on mathematics— for laymen and scholars—had increased tremendously, due partly to the art of the printing press, partly to the growing need for applied mathematical knowledge among bankers and merchants, engineers and civil servants. As Alexandre Koyrè remarks, though, neither of these things can quite explain "the spectacular advances made by the early 16th century Italian algebraists, nor their systematic attempts to 'symbolize' arithmetical and algebraic operations" (Koyrè, in Taton 1964, 11). In Italy alone, some 214 mathematical books were published between 1472 and 1500, a period of less than thirty years (Sarton 1957, 28).

It was also a time of great theoretical advances. Trigonometry had been developed by the Arabs, on an Indian and Greek foundation. Unfortunately, the most advanced Arabic work was written after the Moslem and Christian worlds parted company, and so Western mathematicians had to pursue the same ends independently. The elements of modern trigonometry were established in a treatise of Regiomontanus, published in 1533 (Sarton 1957, 25). Algebra suffered the same fate, and it was not until the Renaissance that algebra come to flower, largely through the work of Scipione, Tartaglia, Farrari, and Geronimo Cardano, whom Sarton describes as "the most singular team in the whole history of science" (1957, 28). One of the great advances of Renaissance mathematics was the development of algebraic symbols. Though the use of mathematical symbols begins as early as Babylonian and Egyptian times, the chief progress was made during the Renaissance period (Sarton 1957, 38).

Some of the famous sixteenth- and seventeenth-century mathematicians were also physicians, physicists, or both—a fact which must have promoted the use of mathematical principles in these other disciplines. Cardano, for example, was recognized as the most illustrious mathematician, physicist, *and* physician in Europe (Sarton 1957, 34). Similarly, Copernicus (also a physician), Tycho, and Kepler had all taught mathematics at one time.

As we saw earlier, the Age of Exploration in the fifteenth century brought with it the need for careful calculation and observation, as aids to navigation. This and other developments led to the scientific revolution of the sixteenth and seventeenth centuries, a revolution that emphasized observation, experiment, and measurement as the keys to understanding the world of nature. And it was those branches of science conducive to measurement that experienced the most dazzling breakthroughs.

So it is that Leonardo emphasizes the indispensability of mathematics. Throughout his notebooks, we find statements like the following: "There is no certainty in sciences where one of the mathematical sciences cannot be applied" (da Vinci 1939, 2:289). And a little further on: "You deceive yourselves and others, despising the mathematical sciences, in which truth dwells" (da Vinci 1939, 2:289). Proportion also plays a major role in Leonardo's quantifying and appears in his comments on anatomy and botany, physics and mechanics. Leonardo had studied the stress coefficients of vertical pillars and had determined that "the carrying power of a pillar of a certain height and material varied inversely as the cube of the diameter" (Mason 1953, 117). His notebooks contain an entire chapter devoted to mathematical considerations ("The Proportions and the Movements of the Human Figure"). In a statement on the optics of the eye, one can almost hear the whispers of Pythagoras:

> We may give the degrees [distances] of the objects seen by the eye as the musician does the notes heard by the ear. I will found my rule on spaces of 20 braccii each [1 braccia = about 1.76 feet]; as a musician does with notes, which, though they can be carried on one into the next, he divides degrees from note to note, calling them 1st, 2nd, 3rd, 4th, 5th; and has affixed a name to each degree in raising or lowering the voice. (da Vinci 1939, 1:60)

But the threshold is crossed with Nicholas Copernicus, a versatile genius of the age, who was lawyer and prelate, physician and diplomat, in addition to being an astronomer. Nicholas was born in the small trading town of Torun, located between Prussia and Poland, the son of a wholesale copper dealer, which may have accounted for his name (Koppernigt). Copernicus's new system proposed that (1) the earth revolved on its axis and (2) the earth and the other planets revolved around the sun, which was the center of the universe—a revolutionary theory first proposed by Aristarchus *almost two thousand years before*. Copernicus's arguments are chiefly mathematical, and it is from this time that existing theories begin to be subjected to mathematical analysis.

The final touch comes from Galileo, who tied mathematics firmly to scientific method. The irascible genius stresses size, shape, and quantity as the key elements when examining physical bodies. Apart from the telescope, suggests historian Taylor Sherwood, all of Galileo's physical discoveries involve measurements or numbers. In Crombie's words: "It was Galileo who was chiefly responsible for carrying the experimental and mathematical methods into the whole field of physics and for bringing about the intellectual revolution by which at first dynamics and then all sciences were established in the direction from which there was no return" (Crombie 1952, 289).

From then on, most of the scientific luminaries of the seventeenth and eighteenth centuries employ mathematics as their most important tool: Kepler and Descartes, Lavoisier and Newton. As historian Herbert Butterfield remarks: "The problem of gravitation would never have been solved— the whole Newtonian synthesis would never have been achieved—without, first, the analytical geometry of Descartes, and secondly, the infinitesimal calculus of Leibnitz" (Butterfield 1985, 101).

With the publication of Lavoisier's *Elements of Chemistry* in 1789, that field breaks with its alchemical past and begins to adopt quantitative methods in its inquiries. As for Newton's approach to science, his induction—in Blake's words—"proceeds throughout in quantitative terms; it employs exact measures, and its propositions are cast in numerical and mathematical forms" (1960, 141).

Comparison

We have noticed in several previous sections how comparison interacts with other modes of thought. In this way, it is similar to cause and effect in the sense that both are integral to many other thought processes. For example, comparison plays a major role in observation and experiments, in classifying and defining, in metaphor and quantifying. It is therefore interesting to examine it in connection with some of our other thought patterns.

As we have seen, Adam's eating of the apple was one of the earliest stories acknowledging human beings' abilities to analyze phenomena—specifically, to differentiate, or make comparisons. We observed some early attempts at this, including those of Anaximander in examining the three theories given him for the rising and falling of the Nile, and how he employed a comparative approach in evaluating them. Indeed, the ability to compare theories (hypotheses) in meaningful and rigorous ways is the central tool of scientific inquiry.

Comparison in Observation and Experiment

It is in the physical sciences, in contrast to the astronomical sciences, that the comparative sense first emerges. And though it does not develop in an unbroken line, it seems to grow stronger over time. One of the first references to comparative embryology appears in Alcmaeon (ca. 500 B.C.), who studied the development of young animals, examining incubated eggs of chicks and watching their bodies develop. Likewise in Aristotle, who probably dissected animals from more than fifty different species and studied their anatomical structure. The philosopher's *History of Animals* seems to be, at times, one long extended comparison (Aristotle 1984, 2:485a, 534b, for example). Historian of science Charles Singer refers to Aristotle as the founder of comparative anatomy (Singer 1959, 17; Sarton 1959, 1:540). We noticed earlier—in the section on experiments—how Strato compares the weight of a wooden block before and after heating. We have also seen how Nicholas of Cusa does the same, in order to determine its remaining water content, and how he uses comparison as a basis for other experiments.

Apart from Galen (130–200 A.D.), investigators in Europe showed limited scientific interest in biology, human and otherwise, until nearly Renaissance times. With the coming of the Renaissance, there appear the great artist-engineers, who deepened their knowledge of the human body through dissection. The most prominent was Leonardo, whose work gave a great stimulus to human and comparative anatomy. Leonardo compares the intestines of humans and apes, lions, bovines, and birds (da Vinci 1939, 2:118). He examines "the legs of a frog, which have a great resemblance to the legs of a man, both in the bones and in the muscles" (da Vinci 1939, 2:119). The following passage offers an insight into da Vinci's comparative approach to analyzing phenomena:

> I have found that in the composition of the human body as compared with the bodies of animals, the organs of sense are duller and coarser. . . . The eyes in the Lion tribe [e.g.,] have a large part of the head for their sockets, and the optic nerves communicate at once with the brain; but the contrary is to be seen in man; for the sockets of the eyes are but a small part of the head, and the optic nerves are very fine and long and weak, and by the weakness of their action we see by day but badly by night, while these animals can see as well at night as by day. The proof that they can see is that they prowl for prey at night and sleep by day. (da Vinci 1939, 2:121)

In the study of the human body, Leonardo had made a start. But the real father of modern anatomy was Vesalius (1514–1564), who frequently compared human structures with those found in animals and whose adherence to comparative method can be found throughout his work (Singer 1959, 204). By the end of the seventeenth century, partly through the influence of the Paduan school of anatomy that Vesalius had founded, the comparative method of investigating animal structures had become well established.

Vesalius's work in comparative studies finds echoes in Goethe, who, suggests Singer, "was the first since Aristotle to point out explicitly that the structure of animals exhibits uniformity of anatomical plan." That work comes to further flower in men like William Harvey, who founded the modern science of physiology largely on the basis of comparative method (Singer 1959, 112), and in Cuvier (1769–1832), who virtually called into being the field of paleontology.

The comparative method was firmly established by the time of Darwin's voyage down the coast of South America and his observations of how species on the Galapagos resembled those of the mainland but differed even from island to island.

Comparison in Classifying

The very *basis* for classifying is a comparison of two or more things: determining their similarities and differences. Again we turn to Aristotle, who classified over five hundred animal species by the gradation of their forms. In his studies of comparative embryology, he used an animal's degree of maturity at birth as a main criterion in his classification system (Mason 1953, 30).

As their names indicate, entire fields—comparative anatomy, embryology, zoology, and others—are based on comparison. This becomes apparent in Leonardo and later comparativists. We find it in Vesalius's great work *The Fabric of the Human Body,* which includes comparisons of human and animal structures (Singer 1959, 204).

Nowhere is it clearer than in the work of Geoffroy St. Hilaire (1772–1844), professor of zoology at the Paris Museum of Natural History. St. Hilaire developed the idea that all animals have the same organs. An organ might be enlarged, atrophied, or even eliminated, but its function does not change. St. Hilaire sought out homologous parts of different animals, noting that "the forelimb in the higher vertebrate animals was adapted to a variety of functions: running, climbing, swimming, or flying, but the arrangement of the bones in the forelimb was always the same" (Mason 1953, 302).

In Chapter 10—"The Language of Comparison"—we will observe how central the comparison of life forms has become in modern biology texts.

Comparison in Quantifying

Professor of Operations Research Russell Ackoff lists three functions of measurement: (1) comparing the same properties of different things, (2) comparing the same property of the same thing at different times, and (3) describing how various properties of different things are related to each other (Ackoff 1961, 179). All three involve comparison.

We saw earlier, in the section on quantifying, how Aristotle and his followers tended more toward proportion and comparison in their quantitative judgments. The comparative sense of number appears throughout Greek thought. We find a similar outlook in Strato, who directed the Lyceum after the master's departure. Anticipating Galileo, he observes: "If one drops a stone or any other weight from a height above the earth of about a finger's breadth, the blow made on the ground will not be perceptible, but if one drops the object from a height of a hundred feet or more, the blow it makes will be a powerful one" (Lloyd 1987, 223).

This comparative sense extends to other disciplines: in the medical writer Galen (130–200 A.D.), for instance, who notes degrees of difference (comparison) rather than specific measurement when discussing grades of hot and cold, wet and dry. This quality of comparison comes to influence

Greek quantitative thinking into the Alexandrian period and beyond, and may well have contributed to the development of comparison as an element of scientific thinking. It is prominent in the Roman architect Vitruvius, Nicholas of Cusa, and da Vinci. Even Newton's Law of Gravity—the greatest discovery in physics before Einstein—was formulated as a proportion (the force of attraction between two bodies is proportional to their masses, and diminishes with the square of their distances). As we will see in Chapter 9—"The Language of Quantifying"—the majority of quantitative statements in our biology text tend to be relational rather than numerical.

The emphasis on proportion over exact measurement came partly from the fact that, for matters of time at least, people in the ancient world had no exact means of measuring short intervals. As Lloyd explains: "The day was divided into hours of variable length; an hour being a proportion of daylight or darkness. Shorter periods were measured by the water clock or sundial." But as for intervals like a second or a number of seconds, there was nothing available (Lloyd 1987, 226).

Comparison in Analogy

As we will see in Chapter 4, "The Role of Figurative Language," an analogy *is* a comparison. Analogies in science have two functions: *explanation* and *discovery*. As a tool of discovery or speculation since ancient times, analogies have taken on forms ranging from the improbable to the fantastic. The strangest and most influential was the theory (an analogy) of Man the Microcosm—the idea that in countless ways, man was a miniature replica of the universe.

The idea appears early, at least from the time of Alcmaeon in the sixth century B.C., who believed than man and the universe were built upon the same plan (Mason 1953, 19). The image is championed by Plato and finds its way down the centuries, occurring in the twelfth-century Muslim philosopher Averroës, one of the most influential medieval thinkers. We find it in the speculations of the experimentalist Robert Grosseteste, and in that least theistic of scientists—Leonardo da Vinci (da Vinci 1939, 2:111, 149). Even Harvey—who discovered the circulation of the blood—speaks of the heart as the sun of the microcosm, and of the spirit in the blood as similar to that found in the stars (Thorndike 1923–1958, 7:516).

THE MECHANICAL UNIVERSE. The analogy that finally dethroned the idea of Man the Microcosm was another: the universe as a giant machine. And so, by some strange consistency, man as well comes to be viewed as a little machine. Notice here: It is not the idea of Man the *Microcosm* that changes, but the image of the *universe*—to which the image of man changes to conform.

The mechanical universe was embraced by Galileo and Descartes, Newton and Laplace, Boyle and Kepler; and in the nineteenth century by the physiologist Claude Bernard. Kepler's writings "teem with analogies," some playful, some integral to his thought process. In a letter to a colleague, he writes: "My aim is to show that the celestial machine is to be likened not to a divine organism but rather to a clockwork" (Gentner 1997, 408). We even find both themes existing side by side in the physiologist William Harvey.

Why is it that Galileo seized upon the new metaphor with such a passion? Mechanical analogies had been floating around earlier. The chief influence, suggests historian Hugh Kearney, was the first Latin translation (in 1543) of Archimedes, who—like Galileo—was a mathematician and mechanical engineer (Kearney 1971, 44) and whose view of the world did not factor in the theistic assumptions of the ancients.

The mechanical universe also evolves from the crafts tradition and its convergence with the scholastics, starting in the sixteenth century. We can also trace its origins back to the Atomists of Ionia (Democritus, Lucretius, Epicurus), who held that everything in the universe was composed of atoms. Their cosmology was basically mechanistic, and they avoided the human analogy as a basis for understanding the world. Atomic theory began to reappear in the sixteenth century, along with this new vision of the universe.

How did Man the Machine come to replace Man the Microcosm? There are never single answers to big questions. And this is a giant one. In all likelihood, the change resulted from the confluence of the three forces we have observed: (1) the crafts tradition, (2) the reappearance of atomic theory, and (3) the influence of Archimedes' writings on his kindred spirit Galileo.

As a final thought, we might note the effect of analogy on Darwin's Theory of Evolution. In his travels on the *Beagle* (1831–1836), Darwin had observed the modifications that different species had undergone. What he could not figure out was *how* it happened. After returning home, he began his investigations: working, as he says, "on true Baconian principles, and without any theory," collecting an enormous quantity of facts, including studies of animal breeding. "I soon perceived that selection [the modification of traits] was the keystone of man's success in making useful races of *animals* and *plants*." But how that selection could be made in *nature* continued to elude him. The answer came from a wholly unexpected source. As he relates in his notebooks:

In October 1838, 15 months after I had begun my systematic enquiry, I happened to read for amusement Malthus on Population, and being well prepared to appreciate the struggle for existence which everywhere goes on from long continued observation of the habits of animals and plants, *it at once struck me* that under these circumstances favorable variations would tend to be preserved, and unfavorable ones to be destroyed. The result of this would be the formation of a new species. *Here then I had at last got a theory by which to work.* (1958 [1892], 42)

In short, we have Darwin's recognition that survival in nature is analogous in its effects to the domestic practice of selective breeding.

Classifying

Our next topic is classifying, which, as we will see in Chapter 3, represents man's attempt to create order out of the chaos and multiplicities of existence. Classifying is integral to other modes, requiring comparisons, definitions, and, at its inception at least, observing. Like causality and measurement, it in all likelihood began quite early in the human horizon. Even perhaps before the shape of language, people needed to decide if an animal was friendly or hostile, if a plant was edible or poisonous.

PLATO AND ARISTOTLE. As in so many things, the process is systematized and elaborated by Aristotle, who was, together with his many other passions, drawn to classifying. We can glimpse its antecedent in his master Plato, whose vision, though rigidly deductive, foreshadows a sense of hierarchy in things, which comes to full flower in Aristotle and the birth of classification. It is not only physical phenomena but concepts that Aristotle wrestles into categories; in fact, he devotes an entire treatise to the subject. Recall his various types, or classes, of causality that we examined earlier. Starting with the physical world, Aristotle develops—in classicist de Santillana's words—"a natural history leading to a system of Ideas, thanks to the power of classification" (1970, 210). As a bridge between the material and the immaterial, he classifies three types of soul: the vegetal, animal, and human (Aristotle, *On the Soul*), a distinction that is found again and again in the literature of later ages.

We noted earlier that Aristotle had classified over five hundred animal species; in so doing he pointed out, for example, that whales were mammals because they bore their young alive. But the most striking thing about Aristotle's biological work is his effort to establish the *relationships* between living things. This he arranges in a serial order, a *scala naturae,* or ladder of nature, that starts with inert material (believing that life sprang from lifeless matter), proceeds through the lower and higher plants, and up through the various levels of animals, until it reaches man (Singer 1959, 41ff., citing Aristotle's *Historia animalium*).

Though Aristotle does not present a formal classification of animals, there are enough terms scattered throughout his work to suggest such a system, which would include, among the vertebrates:

Man

Cetaceans (marine mammals)

Viviparous quadrupeds (horses, sheep, oxen)

Birds

Amphibians and most reptiles

Serpents

Fish

In modern classification systems, we use the terms *genus* and *species,* both of which are Latin translations of Greek words used by Aristotle. Even our concept of species in modern biology is directly attributable to him. The master's work in classifying is carried forward by Theophrastus, who utilized it in his botanical studies. It is from Theophrastus that we get the botanical definitions of *fruit* and *pericarp,* and of *metra*—a word he used to signify "the central core of any stem whether from wood, pith, or other substance" (Singer 1959, 47).

ARAB SCIENCE. In Europe, little important work was done in classifying until the full return of science in the sixteenth century. During that time, the Arabs continued with the systematization of knowledge. Our modern division of substances into animal, mineral, and vegetable was probably first suggested by Al-Razi, whom we met in the section on observation and induction. This was carried forward by Avicenna, whose *Canon of Medicine,* according to Singer, is the culmination of Arab classification. Singer describes the text as excessively complex and partly responsible "for the passion for subdivision which afflicted Western Scholasticism." Avicenna may well have contracted the habit from Aristotle, for we know that he had studied the great philosopher, in addition to Euclid, Ptolemy, and Galen, by the time he was twenty (Sarton 1959, 67). Singer further notes that the *Canon* was probably the most widely read medical work ever written (Singer 1959, 148). It is interesting that one of the more characteristic genres of Arabic thought was a number of treatises dealing with the topic of classification in the sciences.

With the explosion of European science in the sixteenth century come men like Vesalius, whose work in comparative anatomy relies heavily on classifying. "Skulls are systematically measured and individuals and races are classed as broad-headed, long-headed, and round-headed" (Singer 1959, 204). In Germany, the study of botany received heightened attention. By the seventeenth century, with the rapid increase in the number of species known, a growing need was felt for a more systematic way of grouping them. This need found expression in men like John Ray (1627–1705), the English naturalist who helped develop the orderly arrangement of animals and plants.

But the father of modern classifying was Carl Linnaeus (1707–1778), who seems to have developed a classificatory passion that surpassed even Aristotle's. Linnaeus developed systems for classifying animals, minerals, even diseases. He was the first to introduce the term *mammal* (Latin *mamma,* meaning udder), signifying animals that suckle their young (Singer 1959, 92). His main focus was in the realm of botany and his grouping of plants into classes, orders, genera, and species.

Others contributed to the scientific development of classifying, joined as it was to comparative studies. In the last section, we came across men like St. Hilaire, who, as a professor of zoology, combines observation, comparison, and classification in his studies. Similarly, the paleontologist George Cuvier, whose work *Le Règne Animale,* remarks Singer, "describes a species from almost every genus then recognized" (1959, 231) and led to the further development of animal classification. Then, too, we have the Encyclopedists, advocates of deism and scientific rationalism and identified with the Enlightenment. Classifying was central to their weighty tomes, which attempted to bring all human knowledge under a single cover.

In chemistry, classifying received a further stimulus in the work of Robert Boyle (1627–1691) and what has become the modern definition of chemical elements:

> I mean by elements, certain primitive and simple, or perfectly unmingled bodies, which not being made of any other bodies . . . are the ingredients of which all those called perfectly mixed bodies are immediately compounded, and into which they are ultimately resolved. (Quoted in Mason 1953, 190)

By this time, the subject of classifying had become a topic in its own right and received extensive treatment by men like the astronomer John Herschell and John Stuart Mill. The fifth chapter of Herschell's *Discourse on the Study of Natural Philosophy* (1842) deals with classifying and offers some keen insights into the process. The variety of objects to observe in nature is so vast, suggests Herschell, that we will be lost in them unless we limit ourselves to a few facts or to a number of facts joined together by common resemblance; in other words, unless we classify them. Moreover, to give something

> a name which shall at once refer it to a place in a system, we must know its properties; and we must have a system, large enough, and regular enough, to receive it. (Herschell 1842, Section 132)

> When the cause of a phenomenon neither presents itself obviously on the consideration of the phenomenon itself, nor as it were is forced on our attention by a case of strong analogy . . . we have no recourse but . . . to the formation of a class of facts, having all the phenomena in question for a head of classification; and so search among the individuals of this class for some other common points of agreement [comparison], among which the cause will necessarily be found. (Herschell 1842, section 144)

The Interrelation of Thought Modes

> Why should there be *a* method of science? There is not just one way to build a house, or even to grow tomatoes. We should not expect something as motley as the growth of knowledge to be strapped to one methodology.
>
> IAN HACKING
>
> ❋
>
> Styles of scientific research vary almost as much as human personalities.
>
> JAMES WATSON,
> *The Double Helix*
>
> ❋

As Martin Goldstein observed at the beginning of our chapter, the essence of science is in the testing of theories by examining facts—facts that are established through observation, experiment, or measurement. As for the ways we arrive at these theories or establish these facts, there is no fixed sequence. The initial question or problem can be physical or mental. It can be a question, an anomaly, an inconsistency. Beyond this, there is a variety of paths one may follow to solve the problem, answer the question, or resolve the anomaly.

Approaches may differ *between* sciences—between scientists in the same or different fields. Approaches may differ for different problems or branches in the *same* discipline—for example, evolutionary and cell biology. We can think in terms of inductive and deductive sciences, though presumably the distinction is more a matter of degree than of kind. "Science," to quote philosopher Mortimer Adler, is primarily inductive. "Its primary arguments are those that establish a general proposition by reference to observable evidence—a single case created by an experiment, or a vast array of cases collected by patient investigation" (Adler 1929, 259).

Mathematics, by contrast, is wholly deductive. "Its fundamental principles are neither based upon experience nor necessarily in conformity with it" (Stebbings 1933, 301). In some ways, early astronomy—before the development of accurate measuring instruments—also tends to be more deductive, in the sense that men's perceptions of the heavens were so dominated by existing theories (Kuhn's paradigms) that there was little room for more objective observation. Worldviews greatly influenced approaches to science: In early medieval times, suggests A. C. Crombie, "the primary interest in natural facts was to find illustrations for the truths of morality and religion. The study of nature was not *supposed* to lead to hypotheses and generalizations of science" (1952, 7).

THE LANGUAGE OF DISCOVERY AND THE LANGUAGE OF THE TEXTS. As I mentioned in my Introduction, the language of discovery is quite different from the language of texts—both research reports and textbooks: Neither of these captures the false starts and failed experiments, the sudden flashes of insight and inspiration. The essence of the research report is to convince the reader of the author's results. In this sense, its underlying structure is one of persuasion, in the guise of objectivity. As Charles Bazerman reminds us: "The popular belief of this past century that scientific language is simply a transparent transmitter of natural facts is, of course, wrong" (Bazerman 1989).

Our textbooks differ again in purpose—their function is not persuasion but explanation. By the time a concept finds its way into a textbook, the battles have pretty much been won. It is not a matter of controversy, but of understanding. Occasionally a textbook will include an analogy or metaphor that was instrumental in a discovery, such as Kekulé's dream of a snake biting its tail, which prefigured his discovery of the benzene ring. But this is not the norm.

But the steps in the process of discovery—the progression of thought modes involved in the observations, speculations, and experiments—are not usually found in our textbooks or research reports. For this reason—before we dive into our analysis of the texts—let us trace, as best we can, the paths of discovery that were taken by some of the great inquiring minds of the past.

Aristotle (384–322 B.C.)

Except perhaps for Hippocrates, Aristotle appears as the first true man of science. In him, we begin to sense a coalescence of the many varied thought modes: cause and effect, observation and experiment, comparison and classifying, measurement and visuality. Let us admit at once that many of his theories—on both physical and heavenly phenomena—were ungrounded, unproven, and eventually refuted. Earlier philosophers had been long on theories and short on observation. Aristotle alters the balance. His focus— and his best work—deals with the world of physical reality, the world of physical organisms.

We noted earlier that Aristotle had *classified* over five hundred animal species, a process that required, above all, *observation* and *comparison*. His technique was to look for *differentiae* between animals and their parts, that would help him explain the various functions of those parts (French 1994, 44). It is also clear that he worked *experimentally*. In this, he followed the existing method of choice in animal experiment, which was dissection, a procedure often mentioned in his books on animals. In fact, Aristotle refers to a now lost treatise on anatomy (the English version of the Greek work for "dissection") (French 1994, 41). As for the use of *quantifying,* no less an authority than Sarton, as we have seen, feels that "most of his examples of scientific method were taken from his mathematical experience" (Sarton 1959, 1:501). Evidently he was also the first scholar to use *illustrations* in a biological treatise, for he makes reference, in his *History of Animals,* to diagrams of organs in the lost treatise.

Leonardo Da Vinci (1452–1519)

We have examined Leonardo's role in the development of experiment and observation, comparison and quantifying. Let us tie together the various strands in an effort to better understand his approach to scientific investigation. In a note on method, he writes:

> In dealing with a scientific problem, I first arrange several experiments, since my purpose is to determine the problem in accordance with *experience* and then to show why the bodies are compelled so to act. That is the method which must be followed in all researches upon the phenomena of Nature. . . . We must consult *experience* in the variety of cases and circumstances until we can draw from them a general rule [i.e., a theory] that is contained in them. (In Mason 1953, 84)

In the passage Leonardo is equating *experience* with *experiment*. Does this mean that to him experiment is a form of experience? This seems to be the case, judging from comments like the following, in his notebooks: "Experience never errs; it is only your judgments that err by promising themselves effects such as are not caused by your experiments" (da Vinci 1939, 2:288).

In a problem on vision and linear perspective, da Vinci hopes to find out "how much a human image diminishes at a certain distance and what its length is; and then at twice that distance and at 3 times, and so make your general rule" (da Vinci 1939, 1:61). Leonardo illustrates the problem with the following drawing (Figure 1.3).

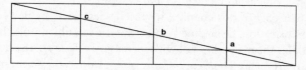

Figure 1.3. Linear Perspective in da Vinci

He then measures and makes the following observation: "If a second object (b) is as far beyond as the first (c) is from the eye, although they are of the same size, the second will seem half the size of the first and if the third object (a) is of the same size as the second, and the third is as far beyond the second as the second from the first (c), it will appear half the size of the second; and so on by degrees . . . But beyond 20 braccii [1 braccia = about 1.76 feet] figures of equal size will lose ¼ and at 40 braccii they will lose ⁹/₁₀ and ⁹/₂₀ at 60 braccii, and so on by diminishing degrees" (da Vinci 1939, 1:59).

To Leonardo, the ideal approach seems to be experience, leading to inductive observations—through experiments and measurement where possible—and resulting in a general theory. The scientist *may* proceed inductively or deductively, depending on the nature of the subject; at one time, "deducing the causes from the effects in natural demonstrations," another time, "deducing the effect from the causes by mathematical demonstrations" (quoted in Blake 1960, 17). Thus we have:

problem ➤	experiment ➤	theory
	observation	
	comparison	
	measurement	

Galileo (1564–1642)

Things come first and names afterwards.

Beyond the stars of the sixth magnitude, you will behold through the telescope a host of other stars . . . so numerous as to be almost beyond belief.

GALILEO

❋

Galileo was a man of conflicting qualities. On the one hand, the brilliant mathematician and physicist. On the other, a man of republican tastes:

fathering three children by his mistress, writing his most important work in the vernacular—to be understood by the layman, arguing with shipwrights on problems of navigation and design.

In the first part of this chapter, we briefly described Galileo's most famous demonstration: his inclined plane experiment, illustrating the Law of Falling Bodies (heavy bodies fall with increasing velocity). The drawing in Figure 1.4, from his *Dialogues Concerning Two New Sciences* (Galilei 1974, 176, simplified), illustrates the experiment. In it, a ball descends in a groove from A to P. The lapse of time is indicated on the right, in seconds (AC = 1, AI = 2, AO = 3). And the speed is reckoned as the square of the times, as 1, 4, and 9.

The experiment was done for the purpose of learning, not just for demonstration, as illustrated by the fact that it was performed at least a hundred times (Galilei 1974, 179).

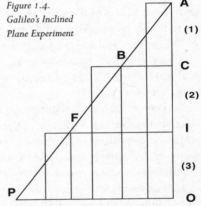

Figure 1.4.
Galileo's Inclined
Plane Experiment

From his experiments, we can gain some understanding of his approach to scientific investigation. As Crombie describes it:

> He tried to arrange things so that he could study the problem under simple and controlled experimental conditions, such as a ball rolling down an inclined plane: (1) He made a few preliminary observations, (2) and analyzed the mathematical relations obtaining between two factors only, space and time, excluding all others. Then (3) he tried to invent what he called a "hypothetical assumption," which was a mathematical hypothesis from which he could (4) deduce consequences that could be (5) tested experimentally. (Crombie 1952, 296)

Presumably, it all starts with observation; for everywhere in Galileo's work, we find a keen observer. With his newly invented telescope, he pierced the heavens:

> On the seventh day of January in this present year 1610, at the first hour of the night, when I was viewing the heavenly bodies with a telescope, Jupiter presented itself to me . . . besides the planet there were three starlets, small indeed, but very bright. Though I believed them to be among the fixed stars, they aroused my curiosity. (*The Starry Messenger,* in Galilei 1957, 51)

By observing their change of positions on successive nights, Galileo was able to determine that they were *not* stars, but in reality the satellites of Jupiter (*Starry Messenger,* in Galilei 1957, 51–56), as we see in Figure 1.5.

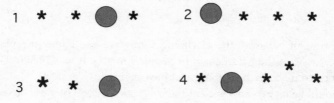

Figure 1.5. A Drawing of the Satellites of Jupiter

Until this time, there had been no concrete evidence for Copernicus's heliocentric theory. It was little more than a plaything for mathematicians. But Galileo's observations of Venus showed that Ptolemy was wrong—that the planet moved, not around the earth, but around the sun (Galilei 1957, 74).

In summing up Galileo's approach to scientific inquiry, we find that science begins with observation. We then arrive at general theories by induction from experience. One then varies the conditions (experiment) and isolates causes (hypothesis), then verifies or falsifies theories by experiment (Crombie 1952, 292):

problem →	observation →	experiment →	hypothesis →	experiment
		measurement		

The image of Galileo's time is an image of questing minds laboring under the rod of religious conservatives with the power of life and death over ordinary citizens. In Galileo's day, it was the Church that had the power to limit scientific inquiry. But before we become too self-righteous, we should realize that the same tendency exits today, except that it derives more from governmental policies, on such issues as cloning, fetal tissue, and the applications of DNA technology.

Newton (1642–1727)

Newton is one of the men whose ideas have made philosophers necessary.

H. S. THAYER

✱

Posterity does not care how difficult it was to make a discovery—only how important the results were. Had Columbus made a more daring and difficult trip to the North Pole, he would not be the object of parades and statues.

HAROLD SHARLIN

❋

By the time of Newton, the mechanical universe had come to replace the analogy of Man the Microcosm in people's minds. It was Newton's great challenge to discover how that machine operated.

It would be nice to have a clear record from Newton on how he worked, as we do with Kepler and later from Darwin. Unfortunately, we don't. But there are enough comments from his letters, from the *Opticks* and from his masterpiece the *Principia mathematica*, to piece things together. We might wonder how closely he followed these pronouncements in discovering his Laws. Lord Keynes, in his readings of Newton, suggested there was something mystical about even his scientific thoughts: "that he solved a problem intuitively and dressed it up in proofs afterwards." Thorndike quotes the famous economist on Newton: "His experiments were always, I suspect, a means, not of discovery, but always of verifying what he already knew" (Thorndike 1923–1958, 8:591).

Newton's two most important tools were mathematics and experiments. In a well-known passage from the *Principia,* he states:

> In experimental philosophy we are to look upon *propositions (3)* inferred by *general induction (2) from phenomena* (#1) *(1)* as accurately or very nearly true . . . till such a time as *other phenomena* (#2) *(4)* occur by which they may be either made more accurate or liable to exceptions [i.e., by *observation* and *experiment] (5). (Principia*, Rule 4, in Thayer 1953, 5 [emphasis mine])

Thus, we have:

Problem →phenomena → induction → proposition → phenomena → experiment → hypothesis
Question   #2
#1   observatio

In expounding his views on hypotheses, he states in a letter to a colleague, Roger Cotes: "[The concept of hypothesis] is not to be taken in so large a sense as to include the first principles or axioms, which I call the laws of motion. These principles are deduced from phenomena and made general by induction, which is the highest evidence that a proposition can have in this philosophy" (in Thayer 1953, 6). In other words:

Question/Problem ➤	phenomena ➤	induction ➤	final principle
			axiom
			laws of motion

Continuing in the same letter, he says: "Experimental philosophy proceeds only upon phenomena and deduces general propositions from them only by induction" (Thayer 1953, 6, quoting a letter to Prof. Cotes):

Question/ Problem ➤	phenomenon #1 ➤	induction ➤ inference	proposition ➤	> phenomenon #2	> observation experiment

Writing to another colleague, he explains: "For the best and safest method of philosophizing seems to be, first, to inquire diligently into the properties of things and to establish those properties by experiments; and to proceed later to hypotheses for the explanation of things themselves. For hypotheses ought to be applied only in the explanation of the properties of things, and not made use of in determining them; except in so far as they may furnish experiments" (letter to Oldenberg, in Thayer 1953, 5):

Question/ Problem ➤	phenomena ➤	experiment ➤ (quantifying)	properties ➤	hypothesis ➤	experiment ➤ (quantifying)	hypothesis

We should note that, according to Newton, the only experiments really worth performing were those that were amenable to quantification, so that we may justifiably add measurement in the places where he mentions experimentation. As for the role of hypotheses, Newton was famous for his hostility to them—defining hypotheses as any proposition "which is not a phenomenon or not deduced from the phenomena" (letter to Cotes, 28 March 1713, quoted in Butts and Davis 1970, 15). This did not keep him from embracing several untestable hypotheses such as God's influences on the laws of physics, and a belief in an interstellar substance—or ether—that transmitted the force of gravity.

The eighteenth century has been rightly called the Age of Newton. But it was not so much for his physics or metaphysics as for his views on the aims and methods of science (Butts and Davis 1970, 104). Indeed, most of the major figures in nineteenth-century England who were concerned with the role of science—including Herschell, Whewell, and Mill—spent a great deal of time discussing Newton's methodological ideas (Butts and Davis 1970, 106).

Apart from Aristotle, our three "case studies" to date all lived roughly in the two centuries from 1500 to 1700, a period recognized as the engine of the scientific revolution and a turning point in world history. This period—according to historian Hugh Kearney—saw a change from traditional modes of thinking that accepted authority as natural and desirable to a "modern" view that encouraged critical assessment of all assumptions (Kearney 1971, 7).

By 1500, the great "authorities" of the past—Aristotle in physics, Ptolemy in astronomy, and Galen in medicine—had been integrated into the Christian worldview. By 1700, they were replaced by Galileo, Newton, and Harvey. The "modern" view is even more evident in our last two figures, Claude Bernard and Charles Darwin, men of the nineteenth century, and the first to completely abandon divine theories and hypotheses in their thinking.

Claude Bernard (1813–1878)

We must never make experiments to confirm our ideas, but simply to control them.

CLAUDE BERNARD,

An Introduction to the Study of Experimental Medicine

❋

Earlier we read of Claude Bernard as the man who established the way of experiment in the field of physiology. Bernard's *An Introduction to the Study of Experimental Medicine* has probably done more than anything ever written to set experimentation in its fuller context of scientific thinking.

In comparing observation and experiment, he quotes from his predecessor Cuvier: "The observer *listens* to nature; the experimenter questions and forces her to *unveil* herself" (Bernard 1961, 32). He goes on to explain that we call someone an observer who examines the phenomenon but does not *vary* or change it; an experimenter is someone who does. The observer notes a fact, the experimenter tests it (1961, 41ff.). He points out, however, that there are two kinds of observation in his experimental method: one at the beginning and one at the end. The first is that of the naturalist: in other words, observing phenomena in nature, not their laboratory state. The second is created by the experimenter. The significance of the second is its comparison with the first. The first observation presents a fact; the second, by experiment, tests the validity of the hypothesis suggested by the first. As Schiller puts it, rather tantalizingly: "The second fact *intervenes* when the first has exhausted its possibilities" (Schiller 1973, 159).

On the topic of comparison, Bernard stresses that comparative experimentation is the "true foundation of experimental medicine," urging that most errors in experiments "come from neglecting comparative judgments of facts or from thinking cases comparable when they are not so" (1961, 158). The very essence of experimenting involves comparing two facts: one normal (in nature), the other abnormal (contrived).

Turning to the role of hypotheses, Bernard places great emphasis on a priori ideas (hypotheses), which he regards as a "stimulant to experiment." "The starting point," asserts the scientist, "always rests on hypotheses or theories [that are] *more or less imperfect.*" As for the origins of hypotheses, it is feelings, he holds, "that give rise to the experimental idea, or hypothesis," what Bernard calls "the *previsioned* [pre-imagined] interpretation of natural phenomena." At times, he describes "the feeling" as an anticipative idea: "An anticipative idea or hypothesis is . . . the necessary starting point for all experimental reasoning" (1961, 58). Elsewhere he says: "The greatest truths . . . are at bottom simply a *feeling* in our mind" (1961, 55). In the following insightful passage, we see our modes of thought coalesce:

> *Feeling* alone guides the mind and constitutes the *primum movens* of science. Genius is revealed in a delicate feeling which correctly foresees the laws of a natural phenomenon; but this we must never forget, that correctness of feeling . . . can be established and proved only by experiment. (Bernard 1961, 69)

Here is no ivory-tower philosopher but one of the foremost men of science, examining as clearly as he can the process that has helped him make some of his great discoveries. The author further offers some keen insights into the relationship between hypotheses and observations, inductive and deductive reasoning:

> An idea that comes to us at the sight of a phenomenon is called *a priori* . . . This *a priori* idea, which rises in us *à propos* of a special fact, always contains . . . without our knowledge, a *principle* to which we refer the special fact, so that when we think we are moving from a special case to a principle, i.e., making an induction, we are really making a deduction. (Bernard 1961, 74)

Bernard also introduces two important terms: *experimental method* and *experimental reasoning,* which I will say a few words on before we turn to a specific case. In the author's experimental method, the "true scientist": (1) notes a fact; (2) associates that fact with an idea (a feeling, or hypothesis); (3) designs an experiment. (4) by various means, including comparison, deduces conclusions from the experiment, (5) subjects those conclusions to new experiments, and so forth (Bernard 1961, 50).

Experimental *reasoning* functions a similar way. It is based on comparing two facts, except that in "observational sciences" such as astronomy, both of these facts are gained from observation, while in the "experimental sciences," at least one fact is based on an experiment. For example, a physician observing a disease in different circumstances reasons about the influences of these circumstances and deduces consequences from the various observations. He is reasoning experimentally, although he makes no experiments. But if he wants to learn the inner mechanism of the disease, he needs to experiment (Bernard 1961, 42). Likewise:

> an astronomer first makes observations and then reasons about them [or does calculations] to deduce a system of ideas which he controls by observations. . . . The astronomer reasons like an experimenter because the experience which he gains implies . . . comparison between two facts bound together in the mind by an idea. (Bernard 1961, 43) [such as Galileo's observations of the moons of Jupiter—SD]

> A naturalist observing animals in all the conditions necessary to their existence, and deducing from these observations consequences verified and controlled by other observations—such a naturalist uses the experimental method even though he performs no experiments, properly speaking. (Bernard 1961, 43)

Here is a specific case, which I have borrowed intact, from Schiller's excellent article (1973, 155):

Observed fact: CO (carbon monoxide) is toxic	Hypothesis 1: The venous blood in question is hyper-generated, since its color is the same as arterial blood.	Experiment 1: The blood is treated with hydrogen, which normally displaces oxygen.
Phenomenon: Venous blood (normally black) is shining red like arterial blood.	Result 1: No oxygen is displaced. Hypothesis 1 is invalidated by Experiment 1. A new question is raised: If oxygen was not present to be displaced, where had it disappeared?	
The Problem: Why?	Hypothesis 2: Oxygen was displaced by another gas.	Experiment 2: Blood is treated *in vitro* with CO in confined air.
	Result 2: CO in blood is not displaced.	

Conclusion: "The immediate cause of CO toxicity is the suppression of the oxygen-carrying capacity of red blood cells. The shining red color of the venous blood in question is due to the presence of CO instead of oxygen. Oxygen is normally exchanged for CO_2, causing the change of color from shining red to black. The shining red venous blood has not been able to pick up CO_2; CO, fixed and not able to be displaced, offers the counterproof" (Schiller 1973, 155).

Figure 1.6 illustrates the recursive nature of Bernard's thought.

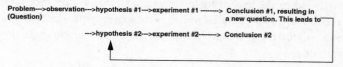

Problem--->observation--->hypothesis #1--->experiment #1 -------> Conclusion #1, resulting in
(Question)   a new question. This leads to

--->hypothesis #2--->experiment #2-------> Conclusion #2

Figure 1.6. Recursive Thought Modes in Claude Bernard

Charles Darwin (1809–1882)

The course of evolution shows no more evidence of foresight than a
river's flow to the sea.

MICHAEL GHISELIN

◉

Though Darwin was a contemporary of Bernard, his approach to scientific
investigation was rather different. For one thing, he was not an experimentalist, though he did rely greatly on observation. Theory and analogy
also played a crucial role in his inquiries, as did comparative study. For we
read in his autobiography: "Hardly any point gave me so much satisfaction when I was at work on the *Origin,* as the explanation of the wide difference in many classes between the embryo and the adult animal, and of
the close resemblance of the embryos within the same class" (Darwin 1958
[1892], 46). We can observe the comparative sense eagerly at work in his
explorations on the *Beagle.*

Far from being a revolutionary, Darwin had actually started at Cambridge with the thought of becoming a minister. As he relates in his autobiography: "I did not then in the least doubt the strict and literal truth of
every word in the Bible" (Darwin 1958 [1892], 18). But the young squire
was so influenced by his professors in geology and biology that he decided
to pursue his studies in natural history. He so impressed his tutors that he
was recommended for a post as naturalist on the H.M.S. *Beagle.* And it was
on his 'round-the-world voyage, from 1831 to 1836 along the coasts of
South America and out into the Pacific, that he received his true education.

Darwin's three major theories concerned: (1) the formation of coral
reefs, (2) the origin of species, and (3) natural selection. The development
of those theories all follow a similar pattern, and accordingly, it is well
worth analyzing the process. Early in his journey on the *Beagle,* Darwin
had read Charles Lyell's *Principles of Geology* and was deeply influenced
by it. In a region near Valparaiso, according to his diary, he found a no-
ticeable lack of birds and animals, and the presence of shells at 1,300 feet.
"It seems a not very improbable conjecture," he concludes, "that the want
of animals may be owing to none having been created since the country

was raised from the sea" (quoted in Ghiselin 1984, 36). This geological hypothesis led to the first of his three major theories—on the creation of coral reefs. For as he explains in his autobiography, commenting on the elevation and lowering of land and the depositing of sediment on the Latin American coast:

> This necessarily led me to reflect much on the effects of subsidence, and *it was easy to replace in imagination* the continued deposition of sediment by the upward growth of corals [analogy]. To do this was to form my theory of the formation of barrier reefs and atolls. . . . No other work of mine was begun in so deductive a spirit as this, for the whole theory was thought out on the west coast of South America, before I had seen a true coral reef. (In Ghiselin 1984, 23)

As the *Beagle* proceeded along the west coast of the continent, the young naturalist observed how closely-related species succeeded each other, and how the same species on the Galapagos had developed slight variations from those of the mainland. In the infinitude of time, he reasoned, they became dispersed and separated by barriers—mountains and oceans, for example—and had developed differently: some evolving, others becoming extinct. The pattern of their distribution thus depended on their means of locomotion and the nature of the barriers they encountered. Later he was to write in the *Origin of Species:*

> All the individuals of the same species . . . are descended from common parents [Hypothesis #1]; and therefore, in however distant and isolated parts of the world they may now be found, they must in the course of successive generations have traveled from some one point to all the others. (Darwin 1859, 355)

But Darwin could not quite account for the differentiation in like species that occurred in animals on nearby islands. This led to his third and most influential contribution—the theory of natural selection. This theory, like the other two before it, resulted chiefly from two sources: (1) observation and, especially, (2) appropriating a theory from another field and fitting it to his own inquiries. For, as he states in the *Autobiography:*

> It was evident that such facts as these . . . could only be explained on the supposition [Hypothesis #2] that species gradually became modified, and the subject haunted me. . . . My first notebook was opened in 1837. I worked on true Baconian principles [induction], and without any theory collected facts in a wholesale scale . . . by conversation with skillful breeders . . . and by extensive reading. . . . I soon perceived that selection was the keystone of man's success in making useful races of animals and plants. But how selection could be applied to organisms living in a state of nature remained for some time a mystery to me. (Darwin 1958 [1892], 42)

The answer (theory), as we saw earlier, came from a casual reading of Malthus's *Essay on Population* and reflections on the struggle for existence:

> It *at once struck me* that under these circumstances favorable variations would tend to be preserved, and unfavorable ones . . . destroyed. The result of this would be the formation of a new species [Hypothesis #3]. *Here then I had at last got a theory by which to work.* (Darwin 1958 [1892], p. 42; emphasis mine)

Summarizing, we have: (1) Darwin starts with an existing (geological) theory, based on the fossil record, that there was an evolution of organic species. (2) This theory guided his observations of modified animal forms. (3) He adopts Malthus's theory, in the form of an analogy, to explain how selection works in nature. (4) He continues to gather information (induction) to substantiate his theory of natural selection. Viewing it diagrammatically:

Existing Theory (Lyell's) ➤	Observation Comparison (on the *Beagle*)	Hypothesis #1 ➤	• Observation (data collection) ➤	Hypothesis #2
			• analogy (Malthus's theory)	
Hypothesis #2 (continued) ➤		Observation (data collection) ➤		Hypothesis #3

Summing Up

What conclusions can we draw, from our brief journey into the minds of past travelers? Perhaps the best we can do is sketch out a general approach to scientific thinking and discovery; realizing that the sequence is not fixed, and that, in the end, there is no certainty:

Perhaps, as sociologist Steven Shapin has asserted, there *was* no scientific revolution, no moment at which the world was made modern. As he put it: "The lives and thoughts of Galileo, Descartes, and Boyle were hardly typical of 17th century Italians, Frenchmen, or Englishmen" (Shapin 1993, 7).

With some notable exceptions—such as Hippocrates, Leonardo, and Galileo—most men of science clung to supernatural and other unprovable forces as causes of things. It was not until the late nineteenth century that scientific thinking *began*—and I use the word advisedly—to influence the way people looked at things. Even today, at the start of the twenty-first century, we carry with us the images and metaphors of an earlier age. We have still not grasped Galileo's adage that "things come first and names afterwards."

1	2	3	4	5
A physical or mental problem	Gathering Info	Hypothesis	Experiment	Proving Hypothesis
	Observation	Probability	Variables	Solving the problem
	Speculation	Prediction	Comparison	
	Written records	C&E	Measurement	
	Defining	Analogy		
	Classifying	Visualizing		

Yet, in the past two thousand years or so of our inquiries, the tools—or ways of thinking—that we are about to examine have helped us attain a far greater understanding of and control over nature; and since we are part of nature, control over ourselves.

As we enter the brave new world of quarks and quantums, DNA and cloning, the horizon shifts before our eyes. Who can say that new thought modes will not emerge, to aid us in our paradox: that of a finite animal grappling with infinity.

Let us turn now from this historical excursion and analyze some of our various thought modes as they appear in their modern context. But first, as Confucius was heard to say: "We must define our terms."

Chapter 2

The Language of Definitions

I was walking in Central Park when I came upon a lady with a small boy of seven or eight, who was holding on to a big, very furry old English sheepdog. I said to the boy: "That's a lovely beast you have there."

The boy's mouth scrunched up, and he said to me with an injured tone in his voice: "He's not a beast."

"What do you mean by a beast?" I asked him.

The boy replied: "A big furry animal."

Imagine a world where there were no definitions. What effects would it have—on your thinking? On your perception? On your ability to communicate with other people? The question is not completely academic, for it was a problem that confronted some of the early scientists and philosophers (who, as we have seen, were one in the same). It was not until things began to be defined—and classified—that a true knowledge of the natural world could grow. Definitions tell us what a thing is. Classifying tells us how it relates to other things. As we will see in this chapter, the two are intimately connected.

Definition and agreement on terms provide the basis for communicating in all walks of life: science and politics, economics and law. Defining words and concepts is one of our most important analytical skills, yet a skill that is taught haphazardly, if at all. We can define in many ways, not all of them appropriate for the same word.

Defining is best understood as a series of interlocking systems: dominated by the semantic system, which interacts with the subordinate syntactic, lexical, and typographic systems to produce a broad range of definition formulas. Consider, for example, one way of defining: the semantic feature of restatement, or paraphrase. This can be expressed by an appositive phrase (syntactic), set off between two commas (typographic):

Pterodactyls, *birdlike reptiles with scaly feathers,* lived in the Lower Jurassic Period.

In this chapter, I would like to explore these systems and their interrelationships, starting with the concept of audience, which includes such topics as: presupposition, intended purpose, situation (context), and conciseness (specificity). Following this we will examine some of the components and general properties of definitions: the term and class word, limiting features, relaters, typographics, and formal definition markers. A section on semantic features analyzes the commonly accepted ways of defining: for example, by classification, synonym and antonym, paraphrase, connotation; and semantic modes such as contrast, types, function, reason, and origin. A final section details certain syntactic features: the grammatical formulas used in framing both written and spoken definitions.

A Few Preliminaries

In the history of thought, definition has fallen chiefly to the philosophers. More recently we find it a significant topic for students of technical and scientific writing. The two perspectives stand poles apart. While philosophers tend to explore implication and consistency in and of themselves, the technical writer focuses on clarity and communication. Moreover, topics seldom overlap. The technical writer deals more with denotative items; the philosopher, more with connotation or connotative implications.

Still, knowledge is indivisible. Philosophic considerations may prove the ultimate arbiter of a definition, as in philosopher Richard Robinson's example of the term "collision." "If a man's car is insured against collision," he asks, "and is then damaged by running into a body of floodwater pouring across the road, must the insurer pay? Can one collide with water?" (1954, 1).

Here we have a hard dollars-and-cents determination based on a definition. Another value of definition is its insistence on clarifying the writer's thoughts. Henri Bergson suggests that we can never be sure of understanding something until we express it in words. We may carry the point one step further: verifiable knowledge of a concept depends on our ability to formulate or define it.

Definitions may provide an actual vehicle for new scientific and technological advances, as when familiar words are combined to form new *concepts (audio-lingual, time-space, radio-telescope, anti-matter).* The term *aerospace* illustrates the process. The word *air* refers to the earth's atmosphere; *space,* to the region beyond. Until recently, as Professor Sigfried Mandel points out, the two regions were quite distinct. But with the advent of rocketry, this distinction no longer holds, so that the U.S. Air Force coined the new word *aerospace*. As physicist P. W. Bridgman remarked, Einstein's chief contribution may have been his redefining the concept of simultaneity.

Preliminary Definitions

In technical and scientific discourse, a term may come up before the writer is ready to examine it in depth. For this reason, an author may provide a preliminary definition: a brief explanation that clarifies its meaning in the immediate context. For example:

> Further reactions occur when solar radiation encounters *the gaseous envelope that surrounds the Earth,* the atmosphere.

As a preliminary definition this does fine; as a technical description, it doesn't take us very far. And indeed the author goes into greater detail further on in the book (a college geology text). Such explanations, however, do have their place as primary definitions in the reporting of scientific phenomena appearing in newspapers and popular magazines. The depth and detail of a definition depend, of course, on the speaker's or writer's audience.

The Audience

The complexity of a definition depends on the age, interests, purpose, and background knowledge of the audience. The less expert the audience, the greater your need to define, but the less technical your definition can be. When writing for the layperson, words used in defining should be more common than the term being defined. Once you have the reader going back to the dictionary, you've lost her.

Clearly, one would define things differently when writing for *Popular Science, Harper's,* or the *Journal of Astrophysics.* Here are some contrasts:

Genres and Type of Audience

1. Popular magazines, newspapers	Uneducated layperson
2. *Scientific American* and popular books	A reader conversant in the general area (e.g., business or social science)
3. High school text	Layperson: Limited general knowledge and technical background information
4. Introductory college text	Layperson: Educated to college level of general knowledge
5. Scholarly journal, specialized and book-length study (e.g., a volume on optics)	Specialist, advanced graduate student

Presupposition

For each of the categories above, the writer assumes a different level of presupposition, or background knowledge, on the reader's part. Obviously, technical matters are discussed in popular magazines, but terms are defined immediately, often by an appositive, as in the following *Time* magazine article:

> . . . lymph glands and lip cancer, as well as leukemia and multiple myeloma (a form of bone cancer) occurred up to three times more frequently among farmers.

Compare this with a definition from an introductory chemistry text:

> When the lightest of all atoms, hydrogen, loses its lone electron, the ion produced is a fundamental particle called the proton.

Here, the writer presupposes knowledge of the terms *electron, ion,* and *fundamental particles,* which are, however, defined earlier in the text. This contrasts with an article from a scholarly journal, containing the highest presupposition level, so high that a report is often unintelligible to all but the specialist, as in the following descriptive information:

> *Flagellar basal bodies* have not been reported previously *for cuticle-secreting epidermal cells* in insects. They are described here for *larsal, pulvillar . . . and tracheal diploid epithelial cells* in the fly Sarcophaga bullata. The pair of *basal bodies* OR *kinetosomes* is positioned in all of the cell types, with the exception of tracheal cells, near the base of a fine *cuticular covered process* OR *microtrichium.* [emphasis mine]

Whew! Understanding of all the italicized words is based on presupposed knowledge. We can extricate two definitions, both signaled by OR: (1) that kinetosomes are basal bodies, and (2) that microtrichium is a cuticular covered process. But the definitions are only for the specialist. To the uninitiated, they offer little understanding.

Length and Specificity

Another audience-related problem involves length and specificity of definition. There are arguments for and against lengthy definitions. For one thing, a short definition is easier to remember. For another, longer definitions may contain unessential items. In reality, conciseness appears more in informal discourse, where a definition acts to clarify an unfamiliar expression. The most technical and detailed definitions are found in contracts where a product must conform to the strictest tolerances and test standards, as in different types of cement on a construction job. Single-word definitions are seldom sufficient because a person unfamiliar with the dimensions of the term being defined (the *definiendum*) would probably have a similar problem with the word defining it (the *definiens*). The more words in the definiens, the greater chance that meaning will come through to the reader, as in this example from a later section:

> Whenever one material is oxidized, another is reduced. *Reduction* refers to the gain of electrons. . . . In other words, the electrons which are lost when a substance is oxidized are accepted by the substance which is reduced.

Stipulative Definitions

A further perspective on audience is found in the concept of stipulative definitions, in which the writer attributes a unique or specialized meaning to a term. All definitions, in Ogden and Richards's words, "are essentially ad hoc. They are relevant to some purpose or situation and consequently are applicable only over a restricted field, or universe of discourse" (1946, 111). If *you* provide the definition (instead of having the reader consult a dictionary), you can focus on the meaning that emphasizes your purpose. This is especially true in technical writing, where a common word may take on specialized meaning. If needed, the field itself may be noted in the definition. To borrow Mandel's example:

> A pitch circle is the locus of points, *in gear terminology*, describing the mating path of two meshing gears. (1970; emphasis added)

Components and General Properties of Definitions

A formal definition (DEF) contains a term (T), a genus or class word (CW), and one or more limiting features (LF):

$$T = CW + (LF_1 + LF_2 + LF_3 + LF_n)$$

Let's examine the nature and behavior of these elements, plus other properties such as relaters, typographics, overt and covert markers, and the sequence of components.

Term and Class Word

The term to be defined (the species, or definiendum) speaks for itself and needs no elaboration. The class word (class, genus, or definiens) is usually at a higher level of abstraction than the term (a man is an *animal* that uses language). At the same time the CW should be as narrow as possible, so that the limiting features need not include an excessive amount of information.

A class word may be *general* or *specific,* depending on the term being defined:

General		Specific	
structure	device	metal	instrument
substance	method	machine	fruit
concept	a science	tool	animal
policy	process	furniture	container
means	activity		

The list invites comment. It is hard to *visualize* a general CW. On the other hand, you can easily close your eyes and picture examples of the specific CWs. In distinguishing them, we could say that general class words have far more connotations and a broader *coverage* across fields, so that people might refer to both a science of physics and a "science" of love. Either type (general or specific) may be suitable, depending on the nature of the term being defined.

Enter here the philosophical argument of whether we define *words* or *things.* Sometimes we can only define words: in cases where the term has no demonstrable referent, or denotation (like God or unicorns). In such instances, the CW may be very general. Moreover, certain terms do not benefit from inclusion of a class word. Consider the term *function,* best defined as a type of relation. As Abelson suggests, "Whatever can be said about relations in general can also be said about functions in particular" (Abelson 1967, 323). The *American Heritage Dictionary* defines function as "the natural or proper action for which a person, office, mechanism, or organ is fitted or employed." Here the CW is already known and only the limiting features are needed. In teaching definitions, guard against the habit—common among unsophisticated language users—of choosing such class words as *thing, something, object,* that add nothing to the understanding.

General and Specific Definitions: Repetition of Term

Definitions can be general or specific. In a general definition the class word lies at a higher level of abstraction and does not repeat the term. The term, however, *is* often repeated in a specific definition. Compare the following:

a. bonding: "the interaction that holds atoms together to form a stable structure" (general definition)

b. metallic bonding: "As for metallic bonding, as its name implies, it is the type of bonding that holds together the atoms of metals such as copper, silver, and so forth." (specific definition)

Sentence b presupposes knowledge of the term *bonding* and is thus concerned with a specific type instead of the general class. Sentence b could be rewritten with a general class word:

c. Metallic bonding is a (chemical) interaction that holds together the atoms of metals such as copper, silver, and so forth.

With a common word as part of the term (e.g., *swordfish*), it makes no sense to choose a more obscure CW. The word *one* often appears in place of the common word in a two-word term ("A throttling process is one in which a fluid, originally at a constant high pressure, seeps through a porous wall . . . into a region of lower pressure").

Limiting Features

After the term and the class word, our third basic element of definitions is the limiting feature or features: those items that differentiate the specific term from other members of the class. There are many properties, qualities, functions, that define and differentiate terms; similarly, a certain restricted number of grammatical forms or formulas for presenting those attributes. The detailed types of limiting features (LFs)—and their interaction with other systems—are examined in the sections on semantics and syntax.

In addition to term, CW, and limiting features, definitions reveal certain other optional properties.

Relaters

A relater is a word or phrase that joins the CW to a specific property of the limiting feature; for example, *used for,* in the sentence: "A plane is a tool used for shaving down the edges of wood." The phrase *used for* indicates the semantic mode of purpose (other types appear in the section "Semantic Features," item #13, below). Relaters can be viewed as an independent entity or as part of the LF. The relater dominates the choice of what is to come and thus has a semantic function.

Typographics

Certain typographic marks serve as vehicles of definitions. These include:

1. the equal sign (=): "In formal definitions, T = CW + LF."
2. colon (:): "Some substances are compounds: they are capable of being decomposed into simpler substances."

3. pairs of commas: ". . . large rotating air masses, known as mesocyclones, which frequently spawn twisters."
4. parentheses: "Operant conditioning refers to conditioning in which the organism . . . emits a response, or *operant* (a sentence or utterance)."
5. pairs of dashes (— . . . —): "Locke's notion of the mind as a *tabula rasa*—a clean slate—has influenced later thinkers in a wide variety of fields."
6. quotation marks: The use of quotation marks around a word that is not being quoted suggests it is being used with special (stipulative) meaning, as in the following:

Technically, a theory of a particular language is a "grammar" of the language. This use of the term "grammar" bears little resemblance to the popular concept of the term or to the section on "grammar" found in most secondary-school textbooks of English.

The writer goes on to define grammar as "a collection, first, of those elements which comprise the language (the sounds, words, and so on) and second, of those rules which combine the elements in sentences."

7. italics: Often used in conjunction with items #1–3 above:

A more effective reaction can be obtained with hydrogen three, *known as tritium,* a radioactive but long-lived isotope.

In this example, the writer could have used pairs of commas, parentheses, or pairs of dashes interchangeably, since all three often serve the same purpose: setting off an appositive.

Overt and Covert Definitions

An overt definition contains a formal marker (lexical, typographic) identifying it as a definition. A covert definition is one that does not, as in the following example:

Frederick Soddy proposed the name *isotope* (from the Greek, meaning "same place") for atoms of the same element that differ in mass.

As Professor Charles Stratton notes, the use of formal syntactic markers improves clarity of writing in general. This is true of definition writing in particular. However, marked definitions have their good and bad points. On the one hand, a formal marker signals an important term is being presented, one the reader should make special note of. At the same time, constant repetition of the same markers leads to a heavy style that can diminish a reader's interest. Following the dictum "Good art is concealed art," I would advise (1) varying the definition markers where possible, and (2) using subtle covert definitions fairly often.

Sequence of Components

In actual texts, the sequence of definition components is often shifted around, seldom appearing in "pure" form. Notice the following example:

> (1) The molecules of a gas have very little attraction for each other. (2) The individual molecules have great motility and these molecules will move farther and farther apart until the gas completely fills the space available to it. (3) This movement of molecules from one area to another is termed (4) *diffusion* and is (5) the result of the continuous inherent movement of all molecules.

In positions 1, 2, and 5, we find the semantic modes of reason, behavior, and result (as in "Semantic Features," item #13, below), with the CW and term appearing in positions 3 and 4, respectively.

While definitions often occur after the term, they are sometimes placed before it, especially when the term represents an unfamiliar or intricate concept. This way, the reader will not be confused or slowed down by the obscure term, but instead be ready for it:

> Certain atoms are unstable combinations of the fundamental particles. These atoms spontaneously emit rays and are thereby transmuted into atoms of a different chemical identity. This process, *radioactivity,* was discovered by Henri Becquerel in 1896.

This is particularly true for mathematical notation, where a formula or equation—introduced cold—may be meaningless until explained.

Synthesis

The quote on radioactivity, just above, provides an example of synthesis. Here the CW *process* condenses, or summarizes, a considerable amount of previous material. While chiefly a feature of definitions, the technique is frequent and complex enough to deserve attention. One way of testing comprehension (of any discourse material) is to have a person rewrite the proposition. The above quote could then be rewritten as follows:

> Radioactivity is a process in which an unstable combination of fundamental particles spontaneously emits rays and is thereby transmitted into atoms of different chemical identity.

Semantic Features

We characterize words by a near endless variety of semantic properties. Obviously, only a limited number of those properties apply to any one word, and so we search for those essential qualities or operations that define a term and differentiate it from others. Below is a detailed list of semantic features used in framing definitions. The most elaborate entry is semantic modes (#13), a set of properties-relations-measures found both in short formal definitions and in longer expanded ones. The semantic features list is suggestive, not definitive, and is not watertight. We can detect an overlap among collocation, synonym, and even connotation, for example. Yet, these do provide distinct resources for defining, and accordingly, are best entered separately:

1. classification/category	dog: animal (kingdom); a mammal (class); canine (family)
2. limiting feature 1	A dog is a *domestic* animal.
3. limiting feature 2	A dog is a domestic animal sometimes used for *guarding property and tending sheep.* (Syntactic Features #4)
4. level I example (species)	Retriever
5. level II example (subspecies)	Golden Retriever
6. level III example	Sheba (a specific dog)
7. coordinate classification	cat—dog (pets); sparrow—robin (birds)
8. synonyms	Fido, Rover, hound, man's best friend
	car: auto, rod, wheels
9. paraphrase/restatement	Teacher: "What's a licking?"
	Student: "He would get spanked."

a. lexical items: *that is, or, in other words*

(1) The problem of a budget deficit, *or/in other words* spending more money than is received in taxes, is basically one of an unmanageable debt service.

(2) Sieve tubes are the most prominent, *appearing as* rows of rather large living cells that have thin walls and protoplasm but no nucleus.

10. antonym/contrast	hot—cold
(minus a feature)	arid (= minus water)
11. collocation (words that the term might occur with)	Dogs bark, wag their tails.

	Associations with desert: *waste, sand,* or be associated with, *oasis, camel.*
12. connotations	dog: no good, messy, comforting
13. semantic modes	

a. condition

b. contrast/elimination

c. etymology

d. example

e. function/use

f. location

g. operation/process/behavior

h. origin/source

i. parts/ingredients/contents/
   composition

j. reason and result

k. relation

l. similarity/comparison

m. types

n. behavior

o. others (illustrative): color, degree,
   shape, texture, value, velocity, etc.

Semantic modes can appear in a one-sentence definition or a multiple-sentence expansion. Here are some examples and a few comments on individual items:

- Definition by Nonexample. Reduces potential confusion with other similar items: "The term laminated timber is used to describe a wooden member built up of several layers of wood whose grain directions are all substantially parallel. *It must not be confused with plywood,* in which the layers have grain running at right angles to each other" (R. Smith 1973, 25; emphasis added).

- Degree. "To provide for a high enough resistance, Edison used a wire, or filament, made of carbon. However, if this filament is heated until it emits light—that is, *to incandescence*—it burns up in the air."

- Etymology. Often cites Greek or Latin terms: ". . . light and heat are electromagnetic waves, which span only a small part of the spectrum

(Latin 'an appearance'), a collection of waves of different lengths usually covering a considerable range."

- Location: A tiger is a large striped cat. It is found only *in Asia.*
- Example. An example is *not* definition. It is not desirable to define
  something simply by giving an example of it. An example may follow
  a definition but should not replace it:

An acid is a compound which neutralizes a solution of sodium hydroxide.
Common examples are sulfuric acid and nitric acid.

Here are some further cases:

1. T followed by example:

Groundfish, *including cod, hake, and halibut,* are found on the Atlantic coast.

Condiments, *such as cinnamon, nutmeg, and paprika,* were once too expen-
sive for most people.

2. Example followed by T:

Rats and mice are among the most common rodents.

The cow, bison, camel, and llama are all ruminants.

- Operation or Process. The physical movement or operation of the
  item. It is often marked by a *process word* in the form of a class word
  (noun) or verb. Omitting a process word from a definition that takes
  one may result in a poor definition. For example:

The digestion of a complex starch molecule to sugar molecules actually uti-
lizes water and thus is a type of *hydrolysis*—one molecule of water is added
for every molecule of sugar that is produced.

Adding the process word *conversion* provides a focus for the definition
(hydrolysis is the *conversion* of a compound into simpler compounds involving the uptake of water).

- Origin: "The ancient people of the world had a 'magic.' Digging in
  the earth or along seashores, they sometimes found yellow, glasslike
  pebbles. These pebbles consisted of amber, a fossilized form of resin
  which had oozed from a certain type of now-extinct pine tree."
- Parts/Composition:

Masonry cement has been especially designed to produce better mortar than
that made with normal Portland cement [comparison] or with a lime-cement
combination.

It is made by grinding together (1) a carefully proportioned mixture of normal clinker and (2) high-calcium limestone. To the finely ground product (3) an air-entraining agent, (4) a plasticizing agent, and (5) a retarder are added.

- Relational definitions. Also called locant definition or definition by synthesis: defining things by relating them to other things in time and space. To borrow Robinson's example: "Big Ben means the biggest bell in the House of Parliament."

- Multiple Modes and Features. I have included the following for two reasons: (1) to illustrate the use of multiple modes, and (2) as a model for student exercises, in which passages would be presented and the student would label the modes and features. I have done the first two. Why not try the third yourself?

Alpha rays consist of particles that are composed of two protons and two neutrons [PARTS]. These alpha particles are ejected [BEHAV] from the radioactive atom at speeds around 10,000 miles/sec [SPEED], carry a 2+ charge [BEHAV] . . . and have a mass [SIZE] approximately three times that of the proton [COMPAR].

The loose, surficial materials—the noncemented rock fragments, and mineral grains derived from rock [TYPES and RESTATEMENT], which overlie the bedrock in most places [LOC], are known as regolith [Gr. *regos,* 'blanket', and *lithos,* 'rock'] [ETYMOL]. Bedrock and regolith are closely related [COMPAR]. Regolith originates in the destruction of bedrock [ORIGIN]. Regolith, whether on land or on the sea floor, is of two kinds, residual and transported [TYPES].

Particles of solid matter from outer space [   ] that fall to the ground through the atmosphere [   ] are meteorites. They reach the ground in a wide range of sizes [   ] and in quantities estimated to be as large as 2.4×10^9 tons annually [   ]. Meteorites consist of four major groups [   ]. . . . All meteorites . . . are thought to have originated within the Solar System [   ], from the broken bits of former planets [   ].

Syntactic Features

Syntax does not function apart from semantics and other levels of language. We can see this in the following list, where the syntactic, semantic, and lexical features in items #1–7 are mutually interactive. Entry #8 contains a limited number of *equational verbs* that provide definition markers.

These verbs can be considered parts of the *lexical* (in contrast to the semantic) system. To distinguish: we can define the semantic system as *categories* of meaning, the lexical system as actual words that function in the semantic system and whose choice is dominated by it. For example, the semantic category of *parts* and *composition* may be expressed by the lexical items *contains, consists of*. The appositive noun phrase (in #9), as we have seen, interacts with the typographic system, while the expanded definition of two or more sentences (in #10) depends for its content on the various semantic features. Here is a list of formal and semiformal formulas that are usually found in writing. Items #1–7 are added to TOPIC + CW:

1. An engineer is a person who designs machines, systems, or public works.	relative/subordinate clause with verb+s (third-person singular present)
2. Aluminum is a metal which is produced from bauxite.	which/that + past participle
3. Aluminum is a metal produced from bauxite.	past participle
4. A utility knife is a tool for cutting hard, thin surfaces.	for + verb+ing
5. A tangent is a straight line touching a curve at one point.	verb+ing
6. A drill is an instrument with which you bore holes.	preposition + WH word (in/for/by which/whereby)
7. A pentagon is a plane with five sides.	with 1 noun phrase (with/with the property of)
8A. N1 + VL + N2: is read, means, refers to, is concerned with, is considered:	linking verb (VL) (except be) used for defining
• is read: "The symbol ? is read 'not equal to.'"	
• means: "The term set means a group or collection."	
• is considered: "The archaeopteryx is considered the first bird."	N1 = Term
• is concerned with: "Thermodynamics is concerned with energy relationships involving heat, mechanical energy, and other aspects of energy and energy transfer."	N2 5 known word(s) (definiens)

8B. N2 + VL + N1: known as,
    is called

   • are known as: "Fish that feed
     at the bottom of the ocean
     are known as ground fish."
   • is called: "Moving particles that
     carry an electric charge are called
     current carriers."

9. ". . . restrictions were eased   appositive noun phrase (separated by
   to permit experiments in such   commas, parentheses, or dashes)to-treat
   hard-illnesses as interstitial
   cystitis (a painful bladder
   inflammation).

10. "Whenever one material is   expanded definition: two-or-more-
    oxidized, another is reduced.   sentence definition
    Reduction refers to the gain of
    electrons. . . . In other words,
    the electrons which are lost when
    a substance is oxidized are accepted
    by the substance which is reduced."

Some terms and concepts are many-faceted and cannot be encompassed by a one-sentence definition. Their implications, applications, critical types and examples, or other features require an expanded form of explanation. Moreover, words in isolation seldom have a single meaning. Instead, meaning is absorbed from the context a word appears in. Even dictionary meanings are determined by context. A word may remain ambiguous even in a sentence; for example, "He couldn't reach the *bank* in time." The two possible results: (a) He couldn't get his money; (b) he drowned. Ultimately the fullest meaning of a word lies at the discourse level, which allows for an extended definition and deeper exploration.

Spoken Formulas

We find a great many differences between spoken and written language. These differences apply to ways of defining. For example, spoken definitions are usually more informal and tend to use different structures. Here is a sampling of spoken formulas:

1. *you know:* "There's a great diversion [SD: diversity] in this class. *You know,* it's heterogeneous."
2. *gesture:* Definition by gesture; e.g., defining the word *grasp* by the gesture of grasping.

3. *realia:* bringing in realia (corresponds to pictures in written form).
4. *Ostensive/Extensional Definition.* Pointing to the object being defined.
5. *be + when:* "Fatigue *is when* you're too tired to do anything." "Coasting *is when* you're able to move without using any energy." (an infelicitous form)
6. *this is called/known as:* "Some animals move to a warmer place in the cold weather. *This is called* migration."
7. *meaning:* a. People live and learn. b. You hate to think they don't; learning *meaning* profiting from things you do right and don't do right. (STIPULATIVE)

Hypothesis: There is more restatement and paraphrase in spoken definitions.

Hypothesis: Children's definitions tend to be more operational and verb-centered than adults, as in this example from "Semantic Features," item #9:

Teacher: What's a licking?
Student: He would get spanked.

Different Grammatical Forms

Just as a term is defined by certain dominant semantic features, it tends to be expressed by a particular syntactic form. At the same time, as I. A. Richards suggests, "A choice of grammatical form very often seems to impose the use of a logical form" (1973, 391). To develop flexibility of mind as well as potentially new insights, we should practice defining a thing in different ways: varying its grammatical form, and if possible its semantic features and other resources.

In the thread of discourse, definitions are not always apparent. They may be unmarked and so effortlessly woven into the text that neither reader nor writer is aware of the act of defining. We benefit by elevating this awareness to consciousness, at the same time developing our own abilities to explain and clarify meaning. Ultimately, definitions provide us one of the finest analytical skills for thinking, understanding, and communication.

Let's turn now to one of the key elements of formal definition, and to the pattern of thought that—more than any other—helps us make sense of the seemingly endless variety of things that compose our world: the mode of classifying.

Chapter 3

The Language of Classifying

The ultimate paradox of the intellect is that of the part trying to understand the whole.

S. DARIAN

✻

We were visiting a Tibetan monastery, to order some paintings and just to have a look around. The Tibetans were incredibly hospitable; you could refuse them nothing. So it was that the abbot offered us a cup of tea. Tibetan tea . . . which, I had forgotten, is made from rancid yak butter and salt. I took a first sip and nearly choked. My companion was of more solid stuff and managed to down two cups.

As we were walking down the path leading from the monastery, I turned to her and said: "It wasn't the tea. It was really a matter of classifying. If I had thought of it as *soup,* there would've been no problem drinking it."

In this chapter, I would like to explore the syntactic, lexical, and graphical features of classifying as they appear in two university-level introductory science texts, one in biology (Starr 1984) and one in chemistry (Hein 1993). We will also look at several other markers and features of classifying, including: plurals, relaters, and quantifiers. We will close with a section on problems in classifying, for learning and teaching, for both native and non-native speakers.

Let's begin with a few observations on the role, or functions, of classifying. In addition, we will briefly examine the *concept* of classifying and its development in Western thought, especially as it bears on our analysis of introductory science texts. This section will also contain a short treatment of induction and deduction, which is central to the classifying process. It also explores the graphical representation of classifications, especially classification trees, sentence lists, and pictures. Quotes from the biology text will be designated as B, those from the chemistry text as C.

The Role, or Functions, of Classifying

Far from a dry, mechanical operation, classifying is one of the most important mental skills we have for understanding our world; perhaps, as geographer David Harvey says, the basic procedure for finding order in that world. It is also critical to our survival. Categorization, in Bruner's words, "serves to cut down the diversity of objects and events that must be dealt with uniquely by an organism of limited capacities" (1956, 235). This need to classify, suggests biologist Alec Panchen, "also applies to other animals and is by no means confined to animals closely related to man." Panchen continues: "It is literally vital for any animal to have a series of metaphorical compartments in which to place perceived phenomena—food, drink, shelter, danger, own species" (1992, 1).

In addition, urges psychologist William Estes, "classification is basic to all of our intellectual activities" and is a major concept in contemporary thought (1994, 4). It is central to text-based research, which tends to be a constant interaction among the preliminary outline (classifying), gathering information, reworking the outline (reclassifying), gathering further information, and back and forth until a final form is achieved.

The very purpose of scientific inquiry itself is not simply finding unique instances of things, but, as philosopher of science Max Wartofsky states, discovering "relations or patterns among the facts, to order them or to link them to each other in some intelligible way" (1968, 129). Our chief tool for achieving this is classifying. The process, according to Harvey, may be considered the "beginning point or the culmination of scientific investigation" (1969, 326). And while, as philosopher of science Harold Larrabee says, "we are born into a world where most of the familiar things are already pretty thoroughly classified" (1945, 247), breakthroughs in science often result from the discovery that something we thought belonged to one category actually belonged to another. Apart from the world of aphorisms, original classifications are rare:

> I like women with a past and men with a future.
>
> OSCAR WILDE
>
> ✱
>
> There are two kinds of people: those who kill themselves because they are not Ernest Hemingway or Marilyn Monroe, and those who kill themselves because they *are.*
>
> ANON.
>
> ✱

In the last analysis, classifying is at the very core of language. It is our chief means of establishing levels of linguistic meaning, since, to borrow Mill's phrase (1950, 90), "by every general name which we introduce, we create a class." As Harvey reminds us: "If language were restricted to proper names only, communication would be impossible" (1969, 324).

The Concept of Classifying

A Brief Historical Note

A taxonomy is "a system by which categories are related to one another by means of class inclusion" (Rosch and Lloyd 1978, 30). It is based on the mode of thinking that we call classifying. That mode of thought, or analysis, was crystallized by Aristotle in his *Organon* and *Metaphysics* as he worked free from the more Eastern, mystical, synthesizing world of the pre-Socratic philosophers, and from Plato, arriving at a midpoint between the two. And it has come down to us as our most influential way of organizing knowledge. Classification, and its correlate, inductive-deductive reasoning, have attracted some of the best minds of the ages—Bacon, Locke, Darwin, Russell, to name but a few.

It was given a considerable boost by the encyclopedic tradition in France and the desire to organize all of human knowledge under one cover. The need for classifying increased greatly with the birth of modern science. For as philosophers Cohen and Nagel remark (1934, 243), "all sciences in their early days are classificatory." Apart from its use as a tool of science, classification as a legitimate subject of research began only in the twentieth century, with Émile Durkheim's publication of "De quelques formes primitives de classifications," in the *Année Sociologique* for 1901–1902.

Induction and Deduction

We will avoid the philosophical debate on inductive and deductive reasoning. The argument has filled volumes. Instead, we will limit ourselves to a few comments on the role of these methods in classifying. Psychological studies suggest there is a basic word in a classification hierarchy, an *exemplar,* that corresponds to the level of generic classes in biological taxonomies (Estes 1994, 56). The exemplar is normally a word for which there are distinctive perceptual features; for example, a word such as dog rather than canine or animal. It may also be simply the most common word in the classification set. Superordinate terms tend to lack the perceptual associations of the basic generic term (Miller 1978, 81–82). Let us keep an eye out for exemplars as we examine the classifications in our corpus.

HYPONYMY RELATIONS. Hyponymy is the relationship of inclusion, of organizing words into taxonomies in treelike diagrams. In a hyponymy relationship, the word *diamond* is a *hyponym* of *precious stones.* The term *precious stones* is *superordinate* to *diamond.* Words at the same level as *diamond (ruby, sapphire, emerald)* are *co-hyponyms,* while the entire list of co-hyponyms is called a *lexical set. Precious stones* is a hyponym of *stones,* which is in turn a hyponym of *minerals,* while the broader category of *min-*

erals would be a *lexical field*. The tree would resemble the diagram in Figure 3.1.

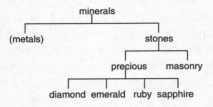

Figure 3.1. A Taxonomy of Minerals

Intimate Connections:
Observation, Definitions, and Examples

Nothing exists by itself, from the smallest to the largest of things. This is equally true for the skills of thinking. What do we do when we classify? We observe (but not necessarily). We define. We compare. We contrast. We provide examples. We generalize. We measure. How do some of these thinking skills or modes of perception bear on the act of classifying? Let us spend a moment on the question.

OBSERVATION. There is no such thing as unbiased observation. As someone once remarked, we see things through our categories. In Wartofsky's words: "In observation, we already classify" (1968, 154). Or to quote Nietzsche: "Everything that reaches consciousness is utterly and completely adjusted, simplified, schematized, interpreted" (in Medawar 1969b, 27). We observe a tree, a boat, a human being—and various properties of trees and boats and human beings spring up to guide our perceptions. Even the evidence of the senses, prompts Nobel laureate Peter Medawar, "does not enjoy a necessary . . . authenticity" (1969b, 41).

DEFINITION. Classifying and defining are so bound up together that it is hard to imagine one without the other. Indeed, a formal definition requires the presence of a class word (term = class word \ + limiting feature or features). Consider the following examples:

> A mixture is a material containing two or more substances [definition] and can be either heterogeneous or homogeneous [classification]. (C50)

In this example, *mixture* is the word being defined, *material* is the class word, and the limiting feature is *two or more substances*. In this case, an additional classification is built into the sentence. One of the more common patterns in our texts is a separate definition, followed by an elaborating classification in the ensuing sentence:

> Those forces that hold oppositely charged ions together or that bind atoms together in molecules are called chemical bonds. The two principal types of bonds are the ionic bond and the covalent bond. (C229)

Notice how definition and classification are intertwined in the next example:

> The sum of all chemical reactions that occur within a living organism is defined as metabolism. Many hundreds of chemical reactions occur in a typical cell. To make sense of this myriad of reactions, biochemists have subdivided metabolism into two contrasting categories [classification], anabolism and catabolism. Anabolism is the process by which [definition] . . . Catabolism is the process by which [definition] . . . (C900)

EXAMPLES. The example, or species, is the only real entity in a classification. The higher levels (taxa) "represent our perceptions of relationships among the groups of species" (Starr 1984, 209). Dogs per se do not exist, nor even spaniels, but cocker spaniels and springer spaniels do. Dogs and spaniels are still abstractions, though admittedly, more tangible than canines. The use of examples is so closely related to classifying that it is sometimes hard to distinguish the example (the species) from the class word. One indication (though not definitive) is the use of the singular for the species. Notice the following use of the word *example,* which in fact indicates a class rather than a species. The actual individual species is the specific cyanobacteria, *Anabaena:*

> There are thousands of diverse eubacteria. Here we will consider a few examples. . . . Cyanobacteria are an example. . . . Many species grow as chains of cells that surround themselves with a mucous sheath. Some cyanobacteria, including *Anabaena,* produce . . . (B227)

A frequent pattern is a definition, followed by a classification—at one or more levels—terminating in specific examples:

> The phenomenon of two or more compounds having the same number and kinds of atoms is isomerism. There are two types of isomerism. In the first type, known as structural isomerism . . . For example, butane and isobutane, ethanol and dimethyl ether . . . are structural isomers. (C709)

Patterns

As with many of the tools in scientific thinking, the language of classifying results from an interplay of various syntactic, lexical, and discourse elements. In this section, I would like to explore these elements in separate but clearly related treatments.

Syntactic Patterns

Our texts reveal six syntactic and discourse-based patterns used to express the idea of classification. I will list them, with examples, and offer a few comments where appropriate. In our notation, the term *classifier* will be used for generic words that signal a classification; e.g., *class, group,* or *category* for nouns, or *divide, classify,* or *group* for verbs. CW indicates a class word (a member of the lexical field) either above *(super,* for superordinate) or below *(hypo,* for hyponym) another class word. The term *subord* (for subordinate) indicates an item at the next lower level in the hierarchy.

(1) Degree Word: Some, Most, All	+ CW (super)	+ be	+ CW (hypo)
Some of	the proteins	are	enzymes (B49)
All	cells (except bacteria)	are	eukaryotic (B45)
About half	of all flowering plants	are	polyploid species (B187)
Most	monerans and protistans	are	microbes (B222)
The vast majority	of bacteria	are	heterotrophs of one sort or another (B225)

Notice that all of the superordinate class words are plurals. As we will see shortly, plurality can be a classification marker. The degree words indicate that there are other items in the lexical set (*co-hyponyms:* closely related words at the same classification level) that are not being discussed in the immediate context. Notice also that the *directionality* of the pattern is from general to specific: the superordinate term appears first.

(2) CW (hypo)	+ be	+ CW (super)
A carbohydrate	is	a simple sugar or a large molecule composed of sugar units (B28)
Carbohydrates	are	the most abundant biological molecules (B28)
Enzymes	are	proteins with enormous catalytic power (B61)
Ribose and deoxyribose	are	in this category (B28)

Directionality is from specific to general: the hyponym appears first. The phrase *the most abundant* is a quantifier, a concept discussed later in the chapter. Sentences two and three have a certain "definitional" or descriptive "feel" to them rather than a "classificatory" feel: While there are other biological molecules and other abundant biological molecules, and other proteins with catalytic power—the discussion is not concerned with these distinctions, but rather with the qualities of the specific molecule and enzyme. The last example contains the anaphoric phrase *in this category* (it refers to a previously mentioned item) and thus relates somewhat differently to its discourse environment.

(3) CW (hypo)	+ be	+ classifier	+ CW (super)
Steel	is	a type	of alloy
Maple		is classed	as a softwood

Directionality is from specific to general.

(4) CW (super)	+ classifier (Vpass)	+ CW (hypo)
Electrolytes	are classified	as strong or weak, depending on . . . (C373)

Though the last two sentences *(Maple . . . Electrolytes . . .)* each contain a passive verb as classifier, their directionality is opposite. In the first example, *Maple* is a subclass of *softwood* (the sentence goes from specific to general). In the second, *strong or weak* are subclasses of *electrolytes*. The sentence goes from general to specific. One could arguably place the "Maple" sentence in Pattern #3 or 4. The reason for including it in Pattern #3 is my sense that directionality is a more powerful organizing device than the classifier (in this case, the passive verb).

(5) CW (super)	+ be	+ (either)	+ CW or CW (hypo)
Covalent bonds	may be	either	polar or nonpolar
Overall, the main metabolic pathways	are		degradative or biosynthetic (B60)
Most antigens	are		protein or polysaccharide molecules (B394)

We can classify a sample of matter as		either	homogeneous or heterogeneous (B49)
A substance	is	either	an element or a compound (C49)
A mixture	is		a material containing two or more substances and can be *either* heterogeneous or homogeneous (C50)
Properties	are		the personality traits of substances and are classified as *either* physical or chemical (C67)

(6) Sentence		+ enumeration of classes.	
These events	fall into	5 broad categories: [followed by a list]	(1) . . . (2) . . . (3) . . . (4) . . . (5) . . . (B177)
There are	3 general categories	of variables: [followed by list]	independent variables, dependent variables, controlled variables (B11)
Chemistry	may be broadly *classified*	into two main *branches:*	organic and inorganic chemistry (C5)
Trees	are generally *divided*	into 2 *groups,*	hardwoods and softwood (R. Smith 1973, 3)
Compounds	fall into	two general types,	molecular and ionic (C56)

In this pattern, syntactic features are subordinate to discourse features. Specifically, the first three slots form an independent sentence by themselves. The series of hyponyms that follows is appended by colons (examples one, two, and three) or by commas (examples four and five). In examples one and two, the series is presented in the form of a list.

We might arguably place sentences three, four, and five in a class of their own, with the pattern: CW (hypo) + classifier (V) \ + classifier (NP). One could also include sentence one, although the CW here is anaphoric (it refers to an item in a previous sentence). It is a matter of classification. As science educator Peter Gega reminds us, classifying is done to fit a purpose. "What works to fulfill the intent of the classifier is what counts. Objects can be classified in many ways" (1994, 73). If our purposes are purely linguistic, we might establish a separate pattern. If they are pedagogical, this more inclusive discourse-based arrangement might be preferable, since it reduces our list of patterns by one.

There are four feature differences in our six patterns. The primary feature is directionality ($\downarrow$) or ($\uparrow$). Four of the six patterns go from general to specific (superordinate to hyponym). The other three features—let's call them secondary—are the existence of (2) a degree word, (3) a classifier (adjectival or verbal), or (4) the pattern (either) . . . or. Our own classification encounters some difficulty with the secondary features.

For example, Patterns #1 and 5 have the same directionality. Pattern #5 is differentiated from #1 by the existence of (either) . . . or. However, it also contains two sentences with degree words. How to resolve the overlap? There are two solutions. First is to accept the overlap—some scientific classifications do overlap at certain levels (see, for instance, Figure 3.8). The other is to decide whether one secondary feature is more significant than the other. In the case of Pattern #5, the terms *overall* and *most* acknowledge that there are two major hyponyms in the class, and that other pathways and antigens are not significant.

Lexical Considerations

The lexical elements in classifying can be arranged in four groups:

- nominal (nounlike) classifiers
- verbal (verblike) classifiers
- multiple classifiers and concordances
- words in multiple forms

NOMINAL CLASSIFIERS. Our corpus reveals fifteen or sixteen nouns or noun phrases used to indicate a classification. The list includes: *branches, category, class, classification, example, division, families, a form of, group, grouping, kind(s) of, set, sort of, subdivision,* and *type of.* Of these, the most common words are: *category, class,* and *type of.*

VERBAL CLASSIFIERS. We also find eight or nine verbal forms used to indicate a classification. They include: *class, classify, be classified, distinguish, divide, fall into, grouped,* and *separated.* Of these, the most frequent by far is the passive *be classified* (Pattern #4), followed by the verb *fall into* (as in "They fall into three categories").

MULTIPLE CLASSIFIERS AND CONCORDANCES. The most common concordances between our nominal and verbal classifiers are:

classified (pass) into	branches, groupings
fall into	types, categories
divided into	groups

WORDS IN MULTIPLE FORMS. The following words appear as different parts of speech:

class (n), class (v), classification

division, divide

group (n), grouping, group (v)

Other Discourse Features

In this section, I would like to discuss three additional features of classifying as they appear in our texts: (1) Relaters, (2) plurals, and (3) what we might call "The Etcetera Factor."

Relaters

Relaters indicate a special way that different items at the same level (cohyponyms) relate to each other. Though several items may be at the same level in a hierarchy, there may be an unequal relationship among them, some type of sequence or priority relationship; for example, one of time, cause and effect, and so forth. These relationships are not indicated in classification trees, since such graphic devices are schematic rather than elaborative.

Our first example deals with the structure and function of neurons. The text lists their various tasks, then explains that there are:

different *classes* of neurons, called sensory neurons, interneurons, and motor neurons . . . We can define each class in terms of its role in a control scheme . . . by which the nervous system monitors and responds to change. The scheme has *receptors, integrators,* and *effector components* . . .

Sensory neurons are receptors that can detect specific stimuli, such as light energy. *They relay signals to the spinal cord—the integrators* . . . In the brain and spinal cord are interneurons, which integrate information arriving on sensory lines and then *influence other neurons in return*. Motor neurons *relay information away from the integrators* to muscle cells or gland cells. (B427; emphasis mine)

A classification tree of the information would look like Figure 3.2:

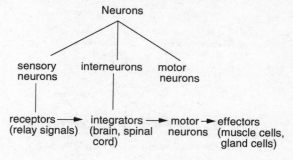

Figure 3.2. Classification Tree (Neurons)

While the three neurons belong to the same lexical set, their relationship is clearly sequential. Impulses are relayed from sensory neurons → to interneurons → to motor neurons. Presumably for this reason, the text represents the relationship as a sequential diagram—as I've shown in Figure 3.3—rather than a classification tree:

Figure 3.3. Sequential Diagram

Our second example is drawn from information on the immune system. The text, in the form of a sentence list, describes the six kinds of white blood cells responsible for immune responses. This would yield a classification tree with the concept White Blood Cells Responsible for Immune Response as superordinate, and the six specific kinds of cells as co-hyponyms. The text follows this with:

> The cells just listed belong to *two* fighting *branches* of the immune system. Both are called into action during most battles. T cells *dominate* one branch; they carry out a "cell-mediated" response. B cells *dominate* the other branch; they carry out an "antibody-mediated" response. (B393; emphasis mine)

The implication here is that there are several other cell-mediated and antibody-mediated kinds of responses and that T cells and B cells *are the most significant*. Indeed, the chapter mentions some of the others later in the text. Figure 3.4 is a tree diagram of this and related information from the text:

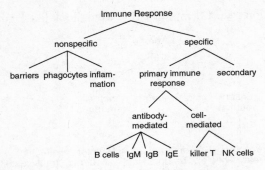

Figure 3.4. Classification Tree (The Immune Response)

Our third example comes from the same source. Notice, in the tree diagram above, the level of primary and secondary immune responses. While these are co-hyponyms, they are of unequal power. For the text goes on to state:

> A secondary immune response to a previously encountered antigen *occurs more rapidly* than a primary response, and it is *greater and of longer duration*. (B396; emphasis mine)

Quantifiers

Relaters shade over into quantifiers, a subclass of relaters that indicates a quantitative difference among members of a lexical set. Our second and third examples above could probably fit this category, inasmuch as they state a greater magnitude of certain hyponyms over others. Many of the degree words in Pattern #1 are further examples of quantifiers:

> *Most* antigens are protein or polysaccharides. (B394; emphasis mine)

> *The vast majority* of monerans and protistans are microbes. (B225; emphasis mine)

> *All* cells (except bacteria) are eukaryotic. (B45; emphasis mine)

> *About half* of all flowering plants are polyploid species. (B187; emphasis mine)

> There are 280,000 species of plants . . . *Most* are vascular plants. (B245; emphasis mine)

Plurals

In classification statements, the use of a plural in a word that might be read as a species indicates that the example is a member of a class rather than a species. Notice the following:

> Bryophytes are nonvascular land plants . . . Bryophytes include *mosses, liverworts,* and *hornworts.* (B248; emphasis mine)

The plurals indicate that there are different species of mosses, etc.; that mosses are not a species.

> *Enzymes* are *proteins* with enormous catalytic power. (B61; emphasis mine)

> *Sugars* and other *alcohols* have hydroxyl groups attached to the backbone. (B27; emphasis mine)

Interpretation: There are different kinds of proteins, sugars, and alcohols.

> Different animal viruses infect invertebrates and vertebrates. Among them are the *Herpes viruses* and the *viruses* that cause recurring, worldwide epidemics of influenza. Between 1918 and 1920 alone, a Spanish influenza virus killed more than 20 million people. *Influenza viruses* infect tissues of the upper respiratory tract. (B225; emphasis mine)

Interpretation: There are several types of Herpes and influenza viruses.

> There are thousands of diverse eubacteria. . . . Cyanobacteria *are* [plural] an example. . . . *Some* cyanobacteria, including Anabacteria, produce a nitrogen-fixing enzyme. . . . *Many* species grow as chains of cells that . . . (B227; emphasis mine)

Comment: The plural suggests that *cyanobacteria* is not a species. This is reinforced by the following markers: *some* and *many species.*

The Etcetera Factor

What I have called the Etcetera Factor refers to various words that indicate there are other unstated members of a class. These words can be *overt,* i.e., specifically stated *(other, some other),* or *covert,* i.e., implied (*Three kinds of* X, suggesting there are other kinds of X). Some quantifiers also have a similar effect ("Most antigens are . . ." "About half of all flowering plants . . ."). Here are some examples of "etcetera words" or phrases. I have divided them into the following classes: Other, Enumerators, Quantifiers, Tacit Classes, and Miscellaneous.

OTHER. An overt marker:

> Chloroplasts of mature leaves contain chlorophylls, cartenoids . . . and *other* pigments, each of which absorbs certain wavelengths of light. (B73; emphasis mine)

Meaning: There are other kinds of pigments.

> Sugars and *other* alcohols, . . . (B27; emphasis mine)

. . . fungi and *other* decomposers . . . (B241; emphasis mine)

As we saw . . . crossing over and recombination put new mixes of alleles (variant genes) in chromosomes. We also saw that the structure and number of chromosomes can change through nondisjunction or *some other* abnormal event. (B155; emphasis mine)

ENUMERATORS. Covert:

Three common lipids (the glycerides, phospholipids, and waxes) have fatty acids, stretched out like tails. (B29; emphasis mine)

Implication: there are other lipids as well.

Three kinds of nucleotides . . . are adenosine phosphates, the nucleotide enzymes, and the nucleic acids. (B227; emphasis mine)

When that happens, *three types* of white blood cells . . . make precise counterattacks. (B393; emphasis mine)

There are *thousands* of diverse eubacteria. Here we will consider a few examples. (B227; emphasis mine)

Let's now look briefly at *two* anaerobic routes. Both are fermentation pathways. (B87; emphasis mine)

Note the absence of the definite article in sentence five (*two*, not *the two*). This implies there are more than two anaerobic routes.

QUANTIFIERS.

Overall, the *main* metabolic pathways are degradative or biosynthetic. In degradative pathways, carbohydrates, lipids, and proteins are broken down in stepwise reactions. (B60; emphasis mine)

The *main* degradative pathways are aerobic respiration . . . and fermentation. (B80; emphasis mine)

TACIT CLASSES.

When only one class is mentioned, there is a tacit assumption that other classes also exist. For example:

Four classes of psychoactive drugs are problems in our society. (B439)

Tacit class: psychoactive drugs that are *not* problems in our society.

MISCELLANEOUS.

Bacteria are the *smallest* cells. (B45; emphasis mine)

Implication: There are other larger cells.

There are *several* different classes of antibodies (Ig) . . . that enlist the aid of different immune cells or chemical weapons [overt]. When bound to antigens, *for example,* IgM and IgG antibodies enlist the aid of macrophages . . . and IgE antibodies call histerame-secreting cells into action [covert]. (B395; emphasis mine)

For example here suggests there are other Igs as well and is thus being used as an implied etcetera marker. Here is another case in which the word *example* functions as an etcetera marker:

Photosynthesis and aerobic respiration are *examples* of metabolic activity, which occurs only in living things. (B5; emphasis mine)

Implication: There are other kinds of metabolic activity.

Our final example is from a classification table (not reproduced here) (B35) with the column headings *Category, Main Subcategories,* and *Examples.* The phrase *main subcategories* suggests there are other subcategories omitted from the table.

Contiguous, Extended, and Nested Classifications

Contiguous and Extended Classifications

As we have seen, many classification statements are unmarked or implicit. For this reason, classifying may seem less significant in written discourse than are other modes of organization. This is not the case in our science texts, which draw heavily on classifying. In addition to a variety of patterns, we find passages in which classifying statements follow one upon another in series. Notice the following example:

. . . proteins [level 2] are the most diverse of all biological molecules [level 1]. They include *enzymes,* which . . . they also include molecules concerned with cell movements, storage, and transport. Many hormones are proteins; so are antibodies [level 3]. (B31; emphasis mine)

The passage above includes three classifying statements, at three levels of classification. In this way, classifying can be seen more as a discourse-level than a syntactic-level phenomenon. While there are discrete sentence-level patterns, the process of classifying often involves a passage of several sentences, for the writer to present the various levels of the classification. Here, for instance, is a passage containing six levels of classification:

Four classes of [2] psychoactive [1] drugs are [3] problems in our society [tacit class: psychoactive drugs that are *not* problems in our society]. They are [4] stimulants, depressants and hypnotics, narcotic analgesics, hallucinogens and psychedelics. . . . Stimulants include [5] caffeine, nicotine, amphetamines, and cocaine. . . . [6] Coffee, tea, chocolate, and many soft drinks contain caffeine. (B439)

Here in Figure 3.5 is what the passage would look like as a classification tree.

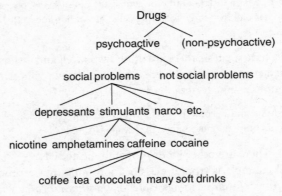

Figure 3.5. *Classification Tree (Psychoactive Drugs)*

Nested Classifications

We also find sentences containing *nested classifications:* single sentences containing classifications at more than two levels. For example:

Many hormones, including sex hormones, are steroids. (B31)

In this sentence, *steroids* is superordinate to *hormones,* which is superordinate to *sex hormones.* The following passage also contains a sentence with three levels of classifying, plus a fourth level in the following (contiguous) sentence:

Among [1] the lipids [2] that have no fatty acid tails, we find [3] the steroids. . . . You have probably heard of [4] cholesterol. This steroid is a key component of animal cell membranes. (B29)

As a classification tree (Figure 3.6), the passage would look like this.

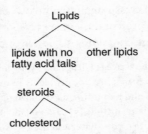

Figure 3.6. *Classification Tree (Lipids)*

Graphical Representations

In addition to text, there are several graphical formats in our corpus that are used to represent classifications. They include:

1. Classification trees and flowcharts
2. Diagrams
3. Line drawings
4. Sentence lists
5. Pictures/Photos
6. Classification tables
7. Charts

The most common device is the classification table (twenty-seven instances), followed by photographs (eighteen instances), classification trees and flowcharts (seventeen instances), and sentence lists (thirteen instances). Here are a few observations on these items:

PICTURES. Pictures may seem an unlikely way to represent a classification. But judging from their frequency, they are quite popular. Pictures function in three different ways: (1) The superordinate concept is discussed or mentioned in the text but *not* the species or item, which appears only in the photograph (B244, 246, 275, 287; C31, 208). For example:

> Figure 18.5 illustrates some of the diversity that exists among the club fungus. (B243) [SD: This is followed by photographs of three different species.]

> Spiders generally are eight-legged many-eyed predators (Figure 19.26). (B274) [Note: followed by photos of three different species. Note also that there is a numerical but no verbal reference to the pictures.]

(2) Both superordinate and hyponyms are discussed in the text, and several hyponyms are illustrated in pictures (B252, 275). For example:

> Seedless vascular plants once dominated the land (Figure 18.14).

> Existing members of this group include the lycophytes, horsetails, and ferns. (B249) [SD: followed by photos of the three existing species plus an historical reconstruction.]

(3) Superordinate and hyponyms are discussed in the text, but at considerable length, sometimes over several pages (B218, 288; C208). In this case, the pictures of specific species serve as *visual summaries*.

CLASSIFICATION TABLES. The tables in our corpus contain between two and five levels of classification in addition to a superordinate term in text or heading. About half the tables do *not* include specific species or examples. This is true even for one that contains five levels of classification

(B251). In addition to classifications, some tables also offer other kinds of information.

FLOWCHARTS AND CLASSIFICATION TREES. The use of flowcharts and classification trees differs markedly in our two volumes. The chemistry text uses flowcharts four-to-one, with all of them flowing downward ↓. The biology text, on the other hand, with its emphasis on evolutionary processes, makes greater use of trees (six compared to one), which are all directed upward ↑. It has only one flowchart, used to describe the branches of the immune system. The reasons for the difference are not apparent. Since biology is more time-oriented than chemistry (evolution, physical development) and since language is partly metaphorical (Lakoff and Johnson 1980), one can logically conceive the process of evolution and growth in an upward direction, especially since, as Lakoff and Johnson point out, *up* connotes positive change, as does evolution.

SENTENCE LISTS. The sentence list is a halfway house between text and visuals and is the fourth-most-common graphic.

Problems in Classifying

Directionality

As we have seen in our study of patterns, a potential problem in the reading (or writing) of classifications is *directionality:* it may not always be clear whether the direction of a classification statement is general to specific or specific to general. Patterns #1 and 5 are general to specific. Patterns #2 and 3 are specific to general. And Pattern #4 contains an example of each.

Division and Classification

Along with numerous classification statements, our corpus contains many instances of composition (parts, partition, division): describing the relation of parts to wholes. It is sometimes hard to distinguish the two concepts. We can normally identify division by key words—nouns such as *parts, components, section* or *subsection;* or verbs such as *composed of, consists of, constructed of, contains.* However, we find cases where some of these partition words are used for classifying:

> Even the most complex animal *is constructed of* only *four kinds of* tissues, called epithelial, connective, muscle, and nervous tissues. . . . Nearly all of the cells in these body tissues are collectively called somatic cells. . . . The exceptions are the germ cells, the only cells in the animal body that give rise to sperm and eggs. (B337; emphasis mine)

The verb *constructed of* is normally considered a division marker, but here it is followed by the phrase *kinds of,* which usually indicates a classification. A clue to the status of the word *tissues* is its plurality, indicating it is above the species, or example, level. This is borne out by photos on the following page, showing different kinds of epithelials, etc.

The next example further illustrates the connection between the two modes. The classifying word *classes* actually *is* a part of the superordinate *nucleic acids:*

> Nucleic acids are complex chemicals that combine several different *classes* of smaller molecules [definition] . . . We will start the examination of nucleic acids by learning about a critical *part* of these molecules, two *classes* of heterocyclic bases, the purines and the pyramidines.
>
> There are five major bases commonly found in nucleic acids—two purines (adsenine and guanine) and three pyramidines (cytosine, thymine, and uracil). (C843; emphasis mine)
>
> A DNA unit *is composed of four kinds of* nucleotides, the *subunits* of nucleic acids. A nucleotide *consists of* a 5-carbon sugar, a phosphate group, and one of the following nitrogen-containing bases: adenine, guanine, thymine, cytosine. (B145; emphasis mine)

Ultimately, division is a relationship of parts to whole, while classification is one of class to subclass. The characteristic clause type in division is possessive, with the verb *have* (All vascular plants have well-developed roots, stems, and leaves). In terms of graphical representations, division tends to rely more on diagrams and labeled pictures (Halliday and Martin 1993, 174–175).

Overlap and Inverted Sequences

Classifying is an attempt to make sense of the seemingly infinite number of things in the universe—to *find* or *create* order. In both cases, a degree of arbitrariness creeps into the process. For in the last analysis, classifications are not things at all, but our efforts—based on memory, reasoning, and fallible perceptions—to organize that universe. In this we are influenced by the Western passion for symmetry that is encouraged by mathematicians and fathered by Aristotle. Unfortunately, such patterns do not necessarily correspond to the natural world. Thus it is reasonable to expect inconsistencies in the classifications from our corpus.

Accordingly, we find cases in our texts of overlapping categories, as well as inverted sequences (in which a hyponym appears above its superordinate). Here are a few examples. The first illustrates the problem of ambiguity, or overlap—in which a hyponym may belong to more than one superordinate (category). It comes from a chapter on immunity that describes the body's various kinds of defense responses, some of which are nonspecific (occurring when any kind of invasion is detected) and others specific (the mobilization of white blood cells to specific kinds of invaders). The text goes on to describe various kinds of nonspecific defense responses, as we can see in Figure 3.7.

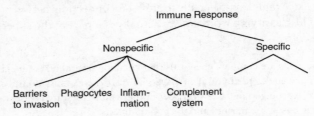

Figure 3.7. *Classification Tree (The Immune Response)*

A subsequent section on the complement system states:

When certain bacterial . . . cells invade a tissue, about 20 plasma proteins interact as a system—the complement system—*with roles in both nonspecific and specific responses.* (B391; emphasis mine)

Thus the anomaly (overlap) of the complement system as a partly specific, partly nonspecific response. A second example deals with metabolism and the concept of *metabolic pathways* (L1), which are defined as:

an orderly series of reactions, the steps of which are quickened with the help of specific enzymes. *Most* sequences are [L3] *linear;* some are *cyclic.* Branches often link different pathways, with products of one pathway serving as reactants for others. Overall, the main metabolic pathways are [L2] *degradative* [catabolic] *or biosynthetic* [anabolic]. (B60; emphasis mine)

The highest superordinate, *metabolic pathways* (Level 1), is followed by *linear* and *cyclic sequences* (Level 3), which, as the following tree illustrates, occurs *below* the actual names of the main metabolic pathways (Level 2). The tree includes the terms *aerobic* and *anaerobic,* which are mentioned in a previous passage. The logical sequence, as I've sketched in Figure 3.8, is:

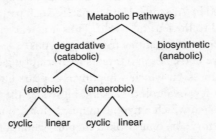

Figure 3.8. *Classification Tree*
(Metabolic Pathways)

Our last example illustrates an inverted sequence, in which the hyponym appears above its superordinate:

[Level 1] Most of the *substances* we encounter in our daily lives are [L2] *mixtures*. Often they are [L3] *homogeneous mixtures,* which are called *solutions.* When you think of a solution, [L5] juices, blood plasma, shampoo, soft drinks, or wine comes to mind. These solutions all have [L4] *water* as a main component. However, many common items, such as [L5] air, gasoline, and steel are solutions [L4] *that do not contain water.* (C326; emphasis mine)

Here's what the passage would look like as a classification tree (Figure 3.9):

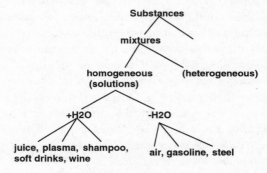

Figure 3.9. Classification Tree (Substances)

Conclusions

Several theoretical issues were raised at the beginning of the chapter. Let us examine them in terms of our texts and the examples chosen for illustration and analysis. An initial matter is the actual function or functions of classifying. Psychologists Bruner and Panchen suggest that one of the *functions* of classifying is to reduce the overwhelming number of items that must be processed by creatures of limited capacities, humans and otherwise. One of our excerpts, on the immune system, indicates that this function operates at the microscopic level as well: as when the immune mechanism classifies an invader as either specific or nonspecific (Figure 3.4) and chooses a form of defense accordingly.

Crowson and Harvey reformulate the theory slightly as: our primary thought process for understanding, or finding order in, the world. Or, as Wartofsky says: discovering "relations or patterns among facts . . . to link them to each other in some intelligible way" (1968, 129). The matter of order, or intelligibility, of course, may be culture-bound or culture-independent (Bergenholtz and Tarp 1995, 85). Recalling our classification tree of minerals and stones, we can logically imagine a culture where diamonds are *not* considered precious stones. Or take the excerpt on psychoactive drugs that cause social problems in our society. These include narcotics and caffeine products such as coffee, chocolate, and many soft drinks. In certain traditional societies, narcotics were not a social problem and even formed part of accepted religious ritual. The author of our biology text is careful to stipulate, however, that the classification applies to "our society" (B439).

A final example is from the text and classification tree explaining the term *substance*. To the nonspecialist, items like blood plasma, shampoo, air, and steel would not be perceived as related. To the scientist, they are all examples of homogeneous solutions. Can we say that the gulf between specialist and nonspecialist from the same culture is a culture-bound difference? To a certain extent, the answer must be yes.

As for Estes's thesis that classification is basic to all of our intellectual activities, we have observed its interactions in our corpus. Here are just a few of the thought patterns associated with it. The very essence of a *formal definition* is its classifying function *(Enzymes are proteins . . . Many hormones are steroids . . .)*. In addition, classifying is one of the chief means of *expanding* a definition *(The forces that . . . bind atoms together in molecules are called chemical bonds. The two principal types of bonds are the ionic bond and the covalent bond.)*.

We have also seen how the process of *exemplification* flows naturally from the act of classifying. Examples provide the ultimate "anchor"—the specific species or "instantiation"—for the superordinates of the lexical field: endpoints in the semantic journey from immune responses to Killer T cells, from drugs to coffee, from lipids to cholesterol.

GENERALIZATION. Generalization also plays its part here, as one of the most basic processes of thinking in general and scientific thinking in particular. Hypotheses are generalizations. The uppermost term in the lexical field is a generalization. Per se, minerals, proteins, drugs, tissues—as we have seen—are concepts, ideas, and not things. As such, they are built on one or more levels of hyponyms beneath them. We can never know for sure whether an early cave dweller called that big orange cat with black stripes a tiger or an animal. From the standpoint of survival, he would have been safer calling it a tiger. But whichever it was, the process of classifying was central to his perception.

Another theory is the concept of *exemplars*—words that correspond to the level of generic classes in biological taxonomies. Estes and Miller suggest that exemplars are words that normally have distinctive perceptual features or are possibly the most common word in the classification set.

One problem with the perceptual nature of exemplars: in fields such as biology, chemistry, and especially physics, an exemplar might be microscopic or submicroscopic and so not *have* distinct perceptual features. Quite the contrary, several exemplars from our corpus appear at the highest level of abstraction (the lexical field), including *metabolism* (B5), *neurons* (B12), and *virus* (B14).

On the other hand, the term *cholesterol,* in the discussion of lipids (B18), probably qualifies as the exemplar because of its considerable popularity. A final example is the explanation of the term *substance* (B24), which lacks both perceptual qualities and widespread use. And we have to descend three further levels before we reach the most common words of the set *(juice, wine, gasoline).* In this case, these common everyday words could be part of a variety of lexical fields and so do not especially exemplify substances.

Finally, let's touch on geographer David Harvey's assertion that classifying may be considered the beginning point or culmination of scientific investigation. The three variables in the sentence are: *beginning point, culmination,* and *scientific investigation.* Unfortunately, scientists often dislike the phrase *scientific method,* perhaps because it suggests a rigid sequence of steps, whereas certain steps in scientific investigation tend to be sequential while others are not. Hypotheses, for example, may result from experiment, observation, *or* an internal thought process. Let us take as a working definition of scientific investigation: the systematic examination of natural phenomena. What support for Harvey's claim do we find in our corpus?

From the standpoint of "top-down" analysis (↓), each step down the ladder leads to a more specific item and ultimately to the smallest working part or process in the organism, if we are dealing, say, with biological phenomena. Apart from applications, in medicine, for example, this might be considered the culmination of the scientific investigation, to use Harvey's phrase. However, the terms *beginning point* and *culmination* are not necessarily synonymous with the highest (↑) and lowest (↓) points of a taxonomy (lexical field and hyponym). In our botanical excerpt (B19), people began to study ferns before they classified them as seedless vascular plants. In this case, the beginning point is at the species (hyponym) level, and the culmination is the lexical field at the "top" of the taxonomy. By contrast, the tree diagram of the immune response (Figure 3.4), plus studies in the history of science (Conant 1950–1954), suggest that the concept of immunity appeared long before knowledge of its specific responses (B cells, etc.).

We might learn a great deal more about the starting point (↓↑) of classifications by comparing the folk taxonomies studied by anthropologists with those in formal branches of science, but that would take us too far afield from our study.

Exercises and the Teaching of Classification

Linguist Louis Trimble suggests three kinds of classifications: *complete, partial,* and *implicit.* A complete classification contains three kinds of information: (1) the name of the class (the set), (2) members of the class (the subset, or hyponyms), and (3) the *basis* for classifying (how members are similar and different from each other). A partial classification includes the members and name of the class but *not* the basis, while an implicit classification has all the classifying elements, but they are not labeled as such (Trimble 1985, 8off.).

According to this scheme, the best place to start in teaching classifications is recognition of complete classifications, beginning with two levels (one superordinate and one hyponym). This means designing activities to help students recognize and define the class word and the members, and be able to state the basis for differentiating *and* relating them. Trimble warns that unless students grasp the concepts stated in complete classifications, partial classifications will be hard to understand, and implicit versions almost impossible (1985, 152). We should keep in mind that this framework involves discourse-level descriptions. Accordingly, it is important that the instructor work with discourse-length material, at least for comprehension purposes.

A more robust or canonical form of classification would contain additional features: items we have seen in examples throughout the chapter. Notice this passage and the drawing illustrating the two types of boats (Figure 3.10):

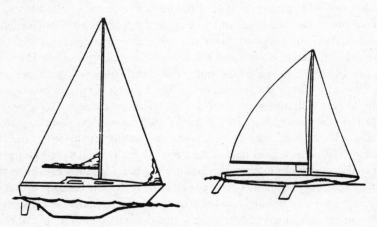

Figure 3.10. Displacement and Planing Boats

(1) Sailboats (2) may be divided into (3) two (4) categories: (5) planing boats and displacement boats. (6) A planing boat rests on the surface of the water. A displacement boat has part of its hull (or body) under the water.

We can recognize here six specific classifying elements:

1. the name of the class (sailboats)
2. a verbal classifying term (may be divided)
3. the number of class members mentioned (two)
4. a plural classifying word (categories)
5. two or more members of the class (planing boats and displacement boats)
6. the basis for classification (on the surface versus under the water)

In teaching classification, one should emphasize those classifying words—nominal and verbal—that help students recognize and understand the discourse pattern.

Implicit classifications are the hardest to spot, since, by definition, they lack the lexical markers that help identify them. One way of helping students extract the information is presenting a passage in incomplete mode, followed by the items you would like them to identify (Trimble 1985, 91). A handout would look something like this:

Three general categories of softwood lumber are cut, depending on their eventual uses. They are yard lumber, factory lumber, and structural lumber. Yard lumber is used for light construction such as flooring, roof planks, and siding. It comes from the middle part of the tree and is not especially strong. Shop lumber is used for making items such as doors and cabinets. It comes from the outer part of the log and has medium strength. Structural lumber is used for heavy construction and supporting heavy loads. It comes from the heartwood of the log (near the center) and is the strongest material possible. (R. Smith 1973, 9)

Class:	Softwood lumber
Members of the class:	Yard lumber, shop lumber, structural lumber
Basis for classification:	Strength, part of the tree

Here are some other ways to help students understand the complexities of classification discourse in general. They draw on two of the visual modes used by our texts to express them: trees and tables. Have students take a passage—complete, partial, or implicit—and outline it in the form of a classification tree. Our recent passage would look like Figure 3.11:

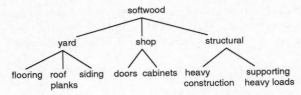

Figure 3.11. Classification Tree (Softwoods)

Or you might include a skeleton classification table (Table 3.1) and have students fill it in. As we saw earlier in our analysis, other information is sometimes included along with classification. In this case, the table might look like this:

SOFTWOOD	USE	ORIGIN	STRENGTH
Yard	light construction	middle of tree	low
Shop	doors, cabinets	outer part of tree	medium
Structural	heavy construction	center of tree	high

Table 3.1. Softwoods

Here are a few final penciled-in suggestions for teaching classifications:

1. Chapter Outlines. Have students do a classification tree for those chapters that lend themselves to it.
2. Start in the middle and have students go in both directions: ↑ and ↓. Push it to the limit. For example, have students start with their country or city and go by steps to *the universe* and to their own home. *Levels.* Have them start with two levels, then increase to three, then four, or maybe five.
3. Definitions. As we have seen, classifying and defining are closely related. When teaching formal definitions, point out the interaction between the two modes. Apparently, it is very easy for students to grasp the relationship between formal definitions and classification statements (Trimble 1985, 86).
4. Games. There are a thousand things in the mind and in the world waiting to be classified. And a thousand ways of classifying them. The game Twenty Questions can help students develop classifying questions (both broad and narrow). How many ways can you think of to classify the capital letters in the roman alphabet? (There are literally thousands.) Have students classify familiar things (orally or in writing): things in class, things they are interested in. Above all, remember: classifying can be fun. It is a true intellectual challenge, at any age. And to make it less than that is to turn the palace of the intellect into a dusty attic. May we never do this to our students. Or to ourselves.

Chapter 4

The Role of Figurative Language

Language is a machine for manufacturing falsehoods.

IRIS MURDOCH

❋

La veritè ä sola figliola del tempo. (Truth is the only daughter of time.)

LEONARDO DA VINCI

❋

The story is told of a man who set out to find the secret of life. After years of travel and hardship, he was told of a wise man who lived on top of a mountain. There were no well-worn paths and the climb was difficult, but he finally reached the top—where he found the wise man sitting on the ground, meditating.

"Tell me, O wise man," the seeker said, "what is the meaning of life?"

The wise man looked at him and smiled. Then, after a moment, he replied: "My son, life is a river."

"What!" the other man called out. "I've spent my life searching. I nearly killed myself getting up here. And all you can tell me is 'Life is a *river*'?"

The wise man looked at him, perplexed, and said: "You mean, life *isn't* a river?"

A Brief History of the Topic

The last twenty-five years have brought a growing interest in metaphor and metaphoric language. This interest appears in a variety of disciplines, including philosophy of language, philosophy of science, linguistics, cognitive and clinical psychology, and artificial intelligence (Ortony 1993, xiii). Of special concern for us is the function of analogy and metaphor in science. But while a great deal has been written on the topic, most major works have focused on their role in scientific discovery and as a source of theories and hypotheses in particular. Far less has been done on the place of figurative language (or *tropes*) in the explanation and teaching of science, especially its functions in science texts. For our analysis, I have taken the same two chemistry and biology texts that we used in Chapter 3 (Starr 1984 and Hein 1993).

While writers on the topic deal almost exclusively with analogy and metaphor, I would also like to examine such figures as personification and simile, animation and reification—some of which play a surprisingly prominent role in our corpus.

As we will see throughout the book, many thought patterns, such as hypotheses and cause and effect, contain *markers*—lexical and otherwise—that cue the reader to the existence of the pattern. Likewise, our analysis also reveals the existence of markers—lexical and typographic—for several figures, specifically analogies and metaphors, personification, and, of course, similes. We will also explore certain discourse-level features, such as: (1) dominant metaphoric themes associated with some of our figures—topics such as war, hunting, family and other relations; (2) thematic clusters and their collocations (e.g., passports, journeys, embarking on a journey); (3) the expansions of various figures to *extended metaphors* (those found in several sequential paragraphs) and *recurring metaphors* (those found in different places throughout the text), and (4) clusters of different tropes in proximate paragraphs.

Let's start with a short historical treatment of the topic, followed by a brief definition of terms. I would also like to say a few words on the uses of metaphor, in science, and for thinking in general. After that, an observation or two on the *operation* of metaphoric thinking. The subsequent section will provide a detailed analysis of our corpus. And finally, a few suggestions on the uses of figurative language in teaching science.

A Short Historical Note

Most contemporary writers on metaphor point the way back to Aristotle, as the start of it all. The philosopher, chiefly in his *Poetics* and *Rhetoric*, conceives of metaphor as an implicit comparison based on the principles of analogy. To Aristotle, the purpose of metaphor was chiefly ornamental (Ortony 1993, 3). But the use of metaphor in scientific speculation goes back even further, at least to Alcmaeon, one of the pre-Socratic philosophers, who defined health as a *balance* among various bodily qualities. It is interesting that Mark Johnson, writing in 1988, cites bodily balance as one of the two dominant schemas that provide the basis for our analogical understanding, especially in psychology (balanced/unbalanced) and law (checks and balances, equal rights, and other legal arguments) (Johnson 1988, 25–40).

Historically, metaphoric reasoning has played a major role in biological thought. So Galen, in the second century A.D., compares the veins of the portal system, which carries chyle to the liver, with the streets of a city, which carry food to the city's shops and bakeries. But the dominant analogy—still prevalent today in New Age speculations—is of man, the microcosm. As we saw in Chapter 1, the theme goes back to the pre-Socratics in the West and the Upanishads in Indian thought (Brahman-Atman). We find it in the Old Testament and in Plato. Basically it says that in countless ways—qualities, behaviors, actual physical properties—human beings resemble the universe. Galen himself imagined the body as created by a Divine Craftsman (Temkin 1949, 178ff.) (the Indian counterpart, Vishvakarman, is translated by the exact same term).

The theme, in different forms, has appeared among philosophers and scientists as varied as Descartes and Boyle, who viewed the "machine" of the body as part of the great machine of the universe. This, despite the general rejection of the concept and of its chief proponents the alchemists, by the new empirical philosophers of the seventeenth century, led by Francis Bacon.

From this reorientation came a changed role of metaphor and analogy in science, as we see from the giants of the age—Kepler, Galileo, and Newton—who make important use of analogy, but with a difference: They recognized it as a source of hypotheses, not as a reality, and insisted on subjecting it to experiment. So Kepler exclaims: "I cherish more than anything the Analogies, my most trustworthy masters. They know all the secrets of Nature, and ought not to be neglected in Geometry" (in Gholsen 1989, 297). The turning point in Kepler's discoveries, suggests Arthur Koestler, was an analogy between the sun, the fixed stars, and the intermediate spaces, on the one hand, and the Father, Son, and Holy Ghost, on the other.

The examples are legion: Newton's sudden insight that the force that caused an apple to fall—gravity—was the same force that kept the moon from spinning off into space. Or, as we have seen, Darwin's recognition that survival in nature is analogous in its effects to the domestic practice of selective breeding. With this all-too-synoptic background, let us turn to our next section, on definitions.

Some Definitions

The figures of speech found in our texts include similes, metaphors, and analogies, as well as personification, animation, and reification. A few definitions are in order:

PERSONIFICATION AND ANIMATION. Personification occurs "when an animate (or, almost always, human) feature is ascribed to an inanimate object or to an abstract concept" (Thomas 1969, 48). Personification and animation seem to derive from a common core. I have made perhaps an overly fine distinction, defining animation as attributing animal qualities to inanimate things. One surprising result of our analysis was discovering how prevalent both of these were in our corpus.

REIFICATION. We can define reification as attributing a physical quality to a nonphysical object.

METAPHOR. Metaphor, in its simplest form, states that A is B, or is a B. But that B is normally something *very* different, often *quite* dramatically or implausibly so, creating, in I. A. Richards's words, a *tension* between the two terms (Richards 1965). Yet, writers from Aristotle to the present have often treated analogy and metaphor together (Schon 1967, Chapter 3 *passim*), sometimes considering them as comparable terms (Pepper 1942); and Leatherdale, in his well-known study, argues that "any discussion of the cognitive aspects of metaphor works by means of analogy" (1974, 11). Discussion of analogy and metaphor in science has filled volumes. My main point here is simply to draw, for our purposes, a distinction between them.

ANALOGY. Analogy compares two different things that contain one or more similar features. In scientific discourse, those features tend to be a process rather than a physical property. Formal analogies take the form A is to B as C is to D (Gilbert 1989, 315), such as comparing the bark of a tree to the skin of a person (bark: tree:: skin: person). Here, as Smadar Kedar-Cabelli points out, the only similarity is "the outer protective covering of some object" (Kedar-Cabelli 1988, 66).

As we will see, this four-part relationship is not always present in our texts, in which one part of the equation may be implied or left to the reader's knowledge of the world. Still, as the word is often used loosely in the popular literature and even academic writing, it is well to keep in mind the original meaning of the term as *proportion* (Arber 1964, 36), which was one of the chief tools of the fathers of modern science—Galileo, Tycho, Kepler, and Newton.

SIMILE. Similes are widely held to be elliptical metaphors (Leatherdale 1974, 177; Buchanan 1962, 84). Owen Thomas describes a simile as a *restricted* metaphor which says A is *like* B (Thomas 1969, 47). Likewise, Fogelin argues that "metaphors differ from similes in only a trivial grammatical way" (1988, 25). He cites Aristotle to the same effect: "The simile . . . is a metaphor, differing from it only in the way it is put" (Fogelin 1988, 27, quoting from the *Poetics* [1410b, 11–12]).

The one dissenting voice is Stanford, who claims they are quite different. In a simile, the argument runs, "every word has its normal meaning and no semantic transference is incurred" (Stanford 1972, 29–30). In our corpus, as we will see, the regularly assumed terms *like* and *as* are not even found in the rendering of similes. In reality, there are over twenty terms that can be used as *connectives* between the two parts of the trope. I have examined similes, per se, in an earlier article (Darian 1973).

What are some of the ways these figures of speech differ? Consider the following examples from general discourse:

- personification: "Overhead, I could feel the sun laughing at me."
- animation: "The moon crept across the water."
- reification: "His words have followed me down the years."
- metaphor: "He was a lion among men."
- analogy: "The amount of information NASA handles in a year is equal to 100 million Sears catalogs."
- simile: "His words had the force of an electric shock."

For one thing, the first three do *not* involve a comparison. They do not compare anything. The last three *do:* A man is compared to a lion. The amount of information at NASA is compared to Sears catalogs. And finally, the person's words are compared to an electric shock. In addition, the first four are literally untrue: The sun does not laugh. The moon does not creep. Words do not follow people. And men are not lions. In contrast, the last two—an analogy and a simile—*are* true approximations: The amount of information is, roughly speaking, as great as 100 million catalogs. The speaker's words had an effect similar to an electric shock. By this criterion, we can distinguish the first four figures from the last two.

Some Uses of Metaphoric Thinking

Among the many uses of metaphoric thinking, the most serious "challenge," for our purposes, is its normal function in everyday language. P. K. Saha states the matter boldly: "Metaphor pervades natural language the way blood pervades the body" (1988, 41). The position is widely accepted (Richards 1965; Lakoff and Johnson 1980; Polya 1954; Adler 1929; Urban 1961). Some studies suggest that we produce about four figures of speech every minute in free discourse (Honeck and Hoffman 1980, 6). How, then, shall we make a case for the special use of figurative language in science?

As we saw historically—in our sinfully abridged sample—metaphoric thinking is acknowledged as an essential tool for scientific thinking in general, and as a source of new hypotheses in particular. Biologist Agnes Arber goes as far as to say that the whole of science has been built upon analogy. She explains:

since only a few of the countless phenomena in the universe can actually be observed, reliance must . . . be set upon the belief that the relations, which we are debarred from observing, are analogous to those . . . open to our perception. (Arber 1964, 36)

The number of those things is far fewer in the thirty-odd years since Arber's book appeared—due to developments in physics and electronic microscopy. But many of them remain as concepts, sometimes hard to grasp, and hard to teach. Metaphor, as philosopher Morris Cohen reminds us, "is necessary for the apprehension *and* communication of new ideas" (1965, 83).

UNDERSTANDING. Enter metaphoric language as a major tool for understanding and learning—which is what the readers of our texts are trying to do. Vosniadu emphasizes its role in the acquisition of new knowledge, while Leatherdale stresses the use of analogy and metaphor in making "things, processes, or structures *intuitable*," by relating them to ordinary experience (1974, 200). This function of going from the known to the unknown is a basic principle of learning, whether one is a scientist or a student studying science. In physicist J. Robert Oppenheimer's words: "We cannot, coming into something new, deal with it except on the basis of the familiar" (1956, 129). The thought echoes from Hutton's article "The Role of Models in Physics" (1953, 289, 293), tracing its way back to Bacon (*Novum Organum*, quoted in Leatherdale 1974, 14), and earlier still, to Aristotle (Upton 1961, 76).

REMEMBERING. Figurative language also helps the reader remember things, by providing a more tangible representation. Most figures of speech relate to one of the five senses, especially the visual. In our comparative list of sentences, five of the six examples had a visual component. It is well known that ideas associated with the senses are more easily remembered. The topics in our corpus that receive the greatest metaphoric treatment are: evolution, immunology, DNA, and certain cell functions, all of which are subjected to a range of figurative types. Why are these singled out? What do these topics have in common? One shared feature is that none of them is physically perceivable. While micrographs of cells are available, their operations are a process and are thus hard to portray in the static medium of a textbook. This process-nature also characterizes the other three topics.

Our chief metaphoric themes are war, hunting, family (and other) relations, and libraries—all of which *select* certain topics. The theme of libraries, for example, occurs only in discussions of DNA, and includes—in various places throughout the text—an entire range of figurative terms, from libraries, books, books of instructions, and copies, to proofreading, sentences, words, and alphabets. Here is an example (quoted again further on). Let us use B to designate quotes from the biology text, and C for those from chemistry. I have also used boldface in the quotes to indicate figurative elements:

> DNA is like **a book of instructions** in each cell. The alphabet used to create the **book** is simple enough: A, T, G, and C. But how is the alphabet arranged into the **sentences** (genes) that become expressed as proteins? How does a cell **skip through** a book, **reading** only those genes that will provide specific proteins at specific times? (B150)

In immunology, the overwhelming metaphor of choice is the theme of war. It is so prevalent and elaborate that we will examine it in detail in our analysis of the corpus. The metaphorics of war also occur in discussions of certain chemical and evolutionary processes. Like war, the theme of hunting also appears in sections on immunology and certain chemical processes; also when dealing with various bacterial and cell functions, including those of single-celled organisms. The theme of family relations comes into play in descriptions of evolutionary processes—especially among plants—and in different gene and chromosome relations. We will examine these themes in greater detail when we analyze the corpus.

The effectiveness of these themes in explaining the various topics depends on their freshness. "Our comprehension of an idea," suggests Owen Thomas, "fades in direct proportion to the loss of metaphoric effectiveness" (1969, 69). Or to put it more forcefully: "Most lexical items prove to be dead metaphors which were alive and kicking at some time in the past" (Sadock 1993, 44). This being the case, it is important for the authors of science texts to be aware of their "primal" metaphors. As these themes lose their metaphoric power, it is necessary to replace them with fresh ones.

It would be interesting to speculate on the point at which a metaphor ceases to be "fresh." Presumably, we reach that point when a phrase has become so commonplace that it no longer provides new insight into a relationship, when it no longer provides a different way of viewing or understanding the phenomenon.

There are a host of other uses for metaphoric thinking, in addition to the many arguments against its use, none of which we can explore within this short compass.

A final thought: Figurative language has a strong *iconic* quality to it. In other words, the second term in the proposition is almost always visual, or at the very least, related to one of the senses. Apart from invoking interest, two of the main functions of visuals are the stimulation of remembering and understanding. It is this *understanding* function that, I would suggest, is the chief function of figurative language in our texts, followed closely by the interest factor.

The Operation of Metaphoric Thinking

The *process* of going from the known to the unknown says as much about the formation of metaphors as about their use. There are, of course, whole schools of thought on the formation of metaphoric language, a topic we have little space to touch on here. So figures of speech may be regarded as: (1) a progression from normal vocabulary, (2) the *association* of two unlike matrices (I would subsume I. A. Richards's *tension* theory under this, as it also involves an interaction between two unlike matrices, as dissonant as that interaction may be), (3) an act of *visualizing,* (4) a projection of bodily forms and functions, and (5) a manifestation of the subconscious.

This is not the place to choose a theory. MacCormack's 1985 volume offers a detailed discussion (1985, 23−53). Our question is: What can we find in these divergent theories that adds to our understanding? We will explore their implications in the rest of the chapter. I would just say here that one of the functions of teaching science at the university level is imparting not only the facts and concepts of a discipline, but training students to think as scientists. This includes developing their abilities to formulate theories and hypotheses, a process which seems greatly aided by enhancing students' metaphoric powers. Such skills have been developed successfully as well at the primary and secondary school levels by W. J. J. Gordon and his associates.

Let us turn now to our texts and see what secrets they may hold for us.

Analysis of the Texts

Both chemistry and biology texts use a wide range of figurative language types. Their occurrence is far more prevalent in the biology corpus, and there are several possible reasons for this: (1) The difference could be idiosyncratic: authors' styles may differ. This we might determine by comparing several biology texts, which would take us too far afield. (2) What is more likely: the field of evolutionary biology has strong historical and speculative components (both conceptual), which lend themselves more to metaphoric language than do the facets of chemistry. (3) Likewise, the image of the human body and its bodily functions, as we have seen, has a long tradition of being analyzed, described, and understood in metaphoric ways.

In this section, I would like to examine the various tropes found in our texts, along with the several kinds of markers that alert the reader to their use. The most common figurative forms in our texts, in order of frequency, are: (1) metaphors; (2) personification, animation, and reification; (3) analogies; and (4) similes.

Metaphors

Metaphors in our texts appear in three patterns: (1) "one-liners," in which an image appears in an isolated sentence, (2) extended metaphors, and (3) recurring metaphors. The following are examples of one-liners:

> Imagine the many millions of chloroplasts in just one lettuce leaf, each a **tiny factory** for producing sugars and starches. (B71)

> A ribosome has two subunits, each composed of RNA and protein molecules. In all cells . . . ribosomes are **workbenches** for making proteins. (B45)

EXTENDED METAPHORS. We also find common use of extended metaphors: one or several sequential paragraphs that embellish on an original metaphor and carry it through several permutations. This level is absent in our chemistry text but appears in abundance in the biology corpus. The following example, with its strong "reifying" quality, extends over three paragraphs:

> We now have a **DNA library**—a collection of DNA fragments produced by restriction enzymes and incorporated into plasmids. We can insert the **DNA library** into bacteria or other host cells for amplification . . . we end up with cloned DNA—**multiple, identical copies** of DNA fragments . . .
> . . . Any DNA molecules "**copied**" from mRNA is known as cDNA.
> . . . With this method, the gene of interest is split into two single strands, which enzymes then **copy over and over to produce millions of copies** of DNA containing that gene. (B165)

From the original metaphor of *the library* (and its implied contents), the author extends the image to *identical copies,* the act of copying, and the process of ultimately producing millions of copies (volumes). Notice also the use of quotation marks ("copied"), indicating the word is being used figuratively (we will examine metaphor markers later on). As sometimes occurs with extended metaphors, an occasional infelicity appears: in this case, the incongruity of inserting the library into "other host cells."

RECURRING METAPHORS. The most striking use of metaphors is the recurrence of the same image at different places in the text, especially in our biology corpus, which returns again and again to the themes of *war, hunting,* and *relationships,* particularly *family relationships.* Let us take a closer look at these themes.

WAR. War—and the appurtenances of war—are the central metaphor in discussions of the immune system. Chapter 27 of the biology text (pp. 390–406), devoted to the immune system, is essentially an extended metaphor on war and its nomenclature. The metaphor occurs, however, in other places throughout the text, where discussions of immunization take place. We also find it, occasionally, with other topics. Notice the strong flavor of animation in the excerpts:

> Shown here is a photomicrograph of Volvox—each sphere a **colony** of microscopically small cells able to **capture** sunlight energy. (B58)

> [Nitrifying bacteria] have a role in the global cycling of nitrogen, a component of all amino acids and proteins. Nitrifying bacteria **attack** ammonia or nitrite in soil and water. (B228)

> The fossil record suggests that many aquatic fungi and plants had entered into symbiotic **partnerships** before **the invasion** of the land, many millions of years ago. (B244)

All in all, the text uses nearly forty different words and phrases borrowed from the vocabulary of war, some of which have a surprisingly modern ring to them, including *locking onto* and *chemical weapons;* or terms of strategy: *counterattack, strategically, infiltrate,* and *foreign agents;* plus the more tradition lexical associations, such as weapons and targets, attacking and defending, invading and destroying.

COLLOCATIONS. We also observe some of the collocations normally found in the language of war. Cells "**take up stations** in lymph nodes" (B391). Certain types of white blood cells "**mount a rapid attack** if the same type of **invader** returns" (B393). Other cells are "**called into action during most battles**" (B393). There are also examples of dubious collocations—words that don't normally occur together. So certain white cells "**engulf and destroy foreign agents**" (B392). Foreign agents are not engulfed and destroyed. Other cells "mount an immune response" (B394), but one does not *mount* a response. Another example describes a lichen as "a fungus and a captive photosynthetic partner" (B224), but the same entity is not normally a captive and partner at the same time.

A final example takes us down a slightly different road: "Complement proteins **coat the surface** of invading cells—and phagocytes **zero in on** the coat" (B393) (the homing device used in cruise missile technology). In fact, the metaphor of missile technology appears quite often (five or six times) in discussions of the immune system. We read of:

> B-cells: lymphocytes responsible for producing molecular [SD: atomic?] weapons, antibodies that **lock onto specific targets** and **tag them** for destruction. (B393)

> The main **targets** of an antibody-mediated response are bacteria and extra-cellular phases of virus. . . . In other words, antibodies can't **lock onto** antigen if the **invader** has entered the cytoplasm of a host cell. (B396)

> . . . it is not that you or any other individuals inherited a **limited genetic war chest** from your ancestors . . . Even if you encountered an entirely new antigen . . . , DNA recombinations in one of your maturing B-cells may have produced the exact chain configuration that can **lock onto the invader.** By happy accident, you have the **precise weapons needed.** (B398)

One key to understanding the process is Schon's observation that "the technology and social structure of an earlier era are reflected in the formal theories of a later one" (Schon 1967, 197). That technology, as we can see, also provides a basis for metaphor.

A final quote is instructive in shedding light on the metaphoric process. In this half-page excerpt, containing a dozen metaphors, one can almost feel the author (or editors) straining to match the metaphors to the actions of the immune system. Notice in the passage how the figurative element *follows* the descriptive statement. In other words, the descriptive statement ("The immune system helps you . . .") could have been followed by a non-metaphoric—or less metaphoric—element ("The immune system helps you . . . react to/deal with . . . bacteria").

> Let us conclude this chapter with a case study of how the immune system helps you survive **attack.** . . .
>
> All this time your body had been struggling against **an unseen enemy.** During a walk, one of your feet had picked up some soil bacteria. And when the tack broke through your skin, it carried several thousand bacteria cells inside it . . . their [the bacteria's] metabolic products were interfering with your own cell functions. If unchecked, **the invasion** would have threatened your life.
>
> If this had been your first exposure to the bacterial process, few B and T cells would have been around to respond to the call. . . . But when you were a child, your body did fight off **this invader** and still carries **the vestiges of the struggle**—memory cells.
>
> As inflammation progressed, B and T cells were also leaving the blood-stream. Most were specific for other antigens and did not **take part in the battle.** But memory cells **locked onto** the antigens and became activated. For the first two days the bacteria **appeared to be winning.** They were reproducing faster than the phagocytes . . . were **destroying** them. By the third day, antibody production peaked **and the tide of battle turned.** For two weeks more, antibody production will continue until **the invaders are wiped out.** After the response draws to a close, memory cells will go on circulating, prepared for some future **struggle.** (B402)

A third interpretation—and this would be my guess—is that once the metaphor is joined, there develops an intense *reciprocity* between metaphor and the actions described, each influencing the other. A danger of such an approach is that one comes to perceive the process through the metaphor. As science writer Joanne Silberner points out, the bulk of metaphors used in the popular press to describe immunology are military in nature (Silberner 1986, 254). According to immunologist Fred Karush of the University of Pennsylvania, "immunologists are more peacefully inclined" (Silberner 1986, 254).

FAMILY AND OTHER RELATIONSHIPS. The second-most-popular metaphoric theme is that of relationships, especially family relationships. These relationships are structured synchronically and diachronically—through time and space. On the one hand, we find ancestors and descendants, generations and lineages. On the other, an elaborate set of family relationships, including relatives, parents, sons and daughters, brothers and sisters, plus maternal and paternal relatives. A few examples:

> Suppose the shufflings [of chromosomes] were proceeding right now in one of your germ cells. We can call that cell's homologous chromosomes "**maternal**" and "**paternal**." (B109)

> The **daughter** cells are released after they produce and secrete enzymes that dissolve the jellylike secretions holding the **parent colony** together. (B213)

> Seeds [of fruits] can be dispersed to new locations, where they will not have to **compete with** the **parent plant** for soil . . . and sunlight. (B324)

Notice in sentence one the use of quotation marks that call attention to the figurative nature of the terms. Sentence two inserts a different kind of social relationship of a nonfamily nature *(colony)*. Sentence three adds the animating quality of competition to the family metaphor, while the idea of competition with one's parents draws us into the endlessly metaphoric realm of psychotherapy.

In addition to colonies, our biology text also displays other kinds of social relationships, such as hosts and guests, partners and companions, communities and kingdoms. Family and nonfamily social relations are sometimes mixed together:

> . . . at each gene locus along the chromosomes, one allele (variant gene) has come from the **male parent** and its **partner** has come from the **female parent.** (B119)

> Protistans are single-celled eukaryotes. . . . The **boundaries of the kingdom** are poorly defined, with some **lineages** extending into **kingdoms** of multicelled eukaryotes: plants, fungi, and animals. (B237)

HUNTING. The third chief metaphoric theme of the biology corpus is hunting, which overlaps slightly the theme of war and may partly derive from it. So we read of predators and prey, of traps and capturing, as in the following:

> Millions of cells of Myxococcus form **"predatory"** colonies that trap cyanobacteria and other microbes. Their enzyme secretions degrade the **"prey"** that becomes stuck to the **colony**. (B229)

> Among the members of this group are the foraminiferans and amoebas. Adult forms move or **capture prey** by sending out pseudopods. (B235)

> While the bacterial species showed up again, it encountered an **immune trap ready to spring**. (B402)

Notice the quotation marks as metaphor markers in sentence one and the collocations, in sentences two and three, of capturing one's prey and the trap ready to spring.

Personification, Animation, and Reification

The second-most-common trope, in both biology and chemistry texts, is personification and animation. We have defined personification as attributing a human quality to an inanimate object or abstract concept; animation as a subset, attributing an animal (nonhuman) quality to a concept or inanimate object. It is surprising to find both of them so prevalent in our corpus, since one does not normally think of them as major figures of speech in expository writing in general, and in scientific writing in particular. Nonetheless, here they are. Reification, as we recall, gives a physical quality to a nonphysical subject. I have included it here, as well, as a minor figure of speech. While personification and animation are quite common throughout both texts, they are more prevalent in our biology sample. Let us examine all three in greater detail.

Personification/Animation

As with metaphors, personifications appear in single-sentence and extended form. There are no leitmotifs in our corpus, although the themes of capture, escape, and liberation—especially the last—occur several times in both texts, as in the following animation:

> For the products [of heat exchange] to attain this more stable state, energy must be **liberated** and given off to the surroundings as heat. . . . When a solution of a base is neutralized by the addition of an acid, the **liberation** of heat energy is signaled by an immediate rise in the temperature of the solution. When an automobile engine burns gasoline, heat is certainly **liberated**; at the same time, part of the **liberated** energy does the work of moving the automobile. (C162)

We also find a thematic cluster related to the idea of passports and journeys; in this example, we observe an interplay of metaphor, reification, and animation:

> Spores, seeds, roots, and shoots containing internal **pipelines** for water and nutrients—these were some of the **passports** to life on higher and drier land. Be glad ancient plants made **the journey**. (B239)

> The oak **embarked on a journey** of continued growth. Cells divided repeatedly, grew longer, and increased in diameter. (B331)

The following extended personification is instructive. Notice, in its first appearance, how the personifying word *proofread* is marked as figurative by the use of quotation marks. In its second appearance, the personification is accepted as given, and by the third occurrence, it itself forms the basis of a further trope—the reification *net:*

> DNA polymerases are major replication enzymes. They govern nucleotide assembly on a **parent** strand. They also **"proofread"** the growing strands for mismatched base pairs, which are replaced with correct bases. The **proofreading** function is one reason why DNA is replicated with such accuracy. On the average, for every 100 million nucleotides added to a growing strand, only one mistake slips through the **proofreading net**. (B147)

Our next observation on the subject involves another extended personification. In the influence of its dominating metaphor, it calls to mind the earlier passage on the activities of the immune system. Here again, it is almost as if, once the insight of the figurative connection is made, it provides the writer a common thread—an image, or theme—for developing the rest of the topic. Notice the collocations and semantic associations that spring from the primary metaphor of investment:

> Most animals live under changing, unpredictable conditions. They rely mainly on sexual reproduction . . . Complete separation into male and female sexes is biologically **costly**. Getting sperm and egg together depends on large energy **investments** in specialized reproductive structures. . . . Even so, the **cost** is offset by the variation among the resulting offspring . . . males and females of the same species must be able to recognize each other, so **energy is invested** in chemical signals . . . and often courtship routines.
>
> Fertilization also comes **at a cost** with separate sexes. Most bony fishes simply release eggs and motile sperm into the water, and the chance of external fertilization would not be good if they produced only sperm or one egg each season. They **invest energy** in producing very, very large numbers of gametes. . . . They **invest energy** in elaborate reproductive organs. . . .

Finally energy is set aside for nourishing some numbers of offspring. . . . Sea urchin eggs are released in large numbers, and the **biochemical investment** in yolk for each one is limited. (B464)

In both texts, animation occurs chiefly in verbs rather than nouns. While verbs of animation in the biology text have no common semantic themes, a considerable number of those in chemistry relate to physical movement. Thus, we encounter words like *approach* and *attract, draw close* and *break free, climb, leap, run into,* and *escape:*

Eventually, the molecules will **break free** from the crystal. (C303)

The ten remaining electrons are now **attracted** by twelve protons and are thus **drawn closer** to the nucleus. (C231)

If the forces between the liquid and the container are greater than those within the liquid itself, the liquid **will climb** the walls of the container. (C300)

Another theme in our chemistry corpus—somewhat related to the first—is that of conscious choice, or volition, as shown in words like *seek* and *accept, share* and *maneuver, tendency,* and *being responsible for:*

Electron pairs will **repel** each other and will **seek** to minimize this **repulsion.** (C248)

The **tendency** for hydrogen atoms to form a molecule is very strong. In the molecule, each electron **is attracted** by two positive nuclei. (C237)

Water molecules can easily **maneuver** around smaller compounds like butyric acid, which is infinitely soluble in water. However, these same water molecules **run into** a huge barrier when they **encounter** the 18-carbon chain of stearic acid. (C767)

Reification

We have defined reification as attributing a physical quality to a nonphysical object. We can easily appreciate the use of reification when trying to explain phenomena—objects or processes—that are hard or impossible to visualize. While the figure of speech is fairly common in our biology text, it is practically nonexistent in the chemistry corpus (only one incidence). So in our biology text a ribosome is reified as a workbench (B152), messenger DNA (B152) as a blueprint. But these examples are really more microscopic than nonphysical. As in our other figures of speech, reification also appears in extended form:

Complex interactions between the atmosphere, the oceans, and the land are the **engines** of the biosphere . . . the human population has been straining the **global engines** without fully comprehending that **engines can crack.** (B569)

Analogy

Analogies, as we have seen, compare two different things that contain overtly similar forms or processes, in contrast to metaphors or similes, which suggest that two very different things are similar in some subtle way. Theoretically, analogies take the form A is to B as C is to D; this is not always the case in our corpus.

As we have noted, a lot has been written on the role of analogy in science. But while analogical thinking may be important in scientific speculation and discovery, it is far less common in our texts than several other figurative types. Moreover, analogy in scientific speculation and discovery is more of a "one-liner": a hidden similarity between X and Y—a single, sudden insight rather than the elaborated figures of speech that we tend, more commonly, to find in the texts. Let us examine the structure of analogies in our corpus.

Analogies, like some of our other figurative modes, may be (1) marked or unmarked. Interestingly, most of the analogies in the texts are marked. We also find examples of (2) incomplete, or tacit, analogies (e.g., item C may be implied or absent). In addition, our texts reveal numerous examples of (3) "extended analogies," in which the relationship contains not two, but three or more, similarities. Likewise, analogies often include (4) different figures of speech that interact with each other. The following examples have been chosen for the sake of brevity, as they illustrate two or more of the features mentioned above:

> Only mRNA [messenger RNA] carries protein-building **instructions** out of the nucleus. And it does not get **shipped out** without **alterations. Just as** a **dressmaker might snip off some threads or bows on a dress** before it leaves the shop, so does a cell **tailor** its mRNA. (B152)

The formal analogy gives us four correspondences:

cells =	tailors =	mRNA =	instructions out of the nucleus =
dressmaker	snips	threads or bows on a dress	dress leaving the shop

The analogy also contains an analogy marker: *just as* (just as X might happen, so Y happens), plus examples of reification *(instructions)* and personification (a cell *tailors* its mRNA).

The next excerpt contains an interesting double analogy comparing skin to a garment and to a Ferrari. It is also an incomplete analogy, inasmuch as it lists the many qualities of skin but none of the attributes of garments or Ferraris. The first analogy is unmarked, while the second is indicated by the phrase *just as*. We also find quotation marks indicating the figurative use of the word *covering*:

> No garment ever made approaches the qualities of the one covering your body—your skin. What besides skin maintains its shape in spite of repeated stretchings and washings, kills many bacteria on contact, screens out harmful rays from the sun, is waterproof, repairs small cuts and burns on its own, and with little care, will last as long as you do?
>
> Together the skin and structures derived from it . . . are called the integumentary system. Keep in mind that skin is much more than a **"covering,"** just as a Ferrari is much more than a hunk of metal. (B346)

The following, apart from its lexical and analogy markers (*so to speak, Imagine what would happen if . . .*), is interesting because of its historical affinities, for it brings to mind the passage from the ancient Greek anatomist Galen (second century B.C.), who, as we have seen, compares the city and its routes to the portal system:

> **Imagine what would happen if** an earthquake or flood closed off the highways around your neighborhood. Grocery trucks couldn't enter and waste-disposal trucks couldn't leave—so food supplies would dwindle and garbage would pile up. Every living cell in your body would face a similar predicament if your body's highways were disrupted. These highways are part of the circulatory system, which functions in the rapid internal transport of substances to and from cells. Together with the other organ systems . . . , the circulatory system helps maintain favorable neighborhood conditions, **so to speak.** (B374)

The next passage (also cited earlier) contains a four-part analogy:

> DNA is **like** a book of instructions in each cell. The alphabet used to create the book is simple enough: A, T, G, and C. But how is the alphabet arranged into the sentences **(genes)** that become expressed as proteins? How does a cell **skip through** a book, **reading** only those genes that will provide specific proteins at specific times? (B150)

DNA =	each DNA strand =	genes =	nucleotide sequences =
a book of instructions	letters	sentences	skipping through a book

We also find: (1) an analogy marker, *like,* (2) personification *(skipping through, reading)*, and (3) an explicit connection, *sentences (genes)*.

Our next example may provide some insight into how an analogy develops in the writer's mind. Notice how the initial comparison is stated in the first sentence (ATP as a form of currency). ATP is then described, but its resemblance to an economic system is not drawn for another five lines. Notice also the analogy marker *(analogous to)*; in addition, italics *(common energy currency)*, marking the phrase as analogous:

> ATP serves as the *common energy currency* for the cell. Energy from catabolism of many different kinds of molecules is stored in ATP. . . . To make direct use of this energy, the cell would need a separate series of reactions for each different energy source. Instead, the cell channels most of the energy derived from oxidation-reduction reactions into the high-energy bonds of ATP. This process **is analogous to** an economic system that values all goods and services in terms of a common currency, such as the dollar. Buying and selling within the system is thus greatly simplified. In the cell, utilization is greatly simplified by converting all stored energy to ATP, the common currency. (C907)

ANALOGY MARKERS. A final word is in order on the concept of analogy markers, which I would define as a verbal marker indicating the figurative use in general, and the analogical use in particular, of an upcoming word or phrase. Our excerpts have included such markers as *just as, Imagine what would happen if* (or some such phrases indicating an imaginary situation), *analogous to,* and *like.* In figurative language, the word *like* is also used to mark similes. Its use here, however, is with an extended comparison, while similes tend to be "one-liners." The corpus also includes items such as *by analogy, similarly, X outwardly resembles . . . , X can be likened to . . . , X acts somewhat like . . . , If you were to compare X to . . . ,* and *Think of X as . . .* As Latour and Woolgar point out, "logical connections of the form *A is B* are only one part of a family of analogical connections, such as *A is like B, A reminds me of B,* and *A might be B.* Such analogical links have proved particularly fruitful in science even though they're logically imprecise" (Latour and Woolgar 1986, 173).

Similes

Similes play a fairly small role in our corpus: about twenty in our biology text and four or five in chemistry. Interestingly, similes take the same highly restricted number of forms in the two parts of our corpus—essentially, one: *X-like* or *X-shaped,* most of which describe parts of the human body:

> In size and shape, human bones range from a **pea-like** wrist-bone to thighbones much longer than they are wide. Bones are classified as long, short (or

cubelike), flat, and irregular . . . Tiny, **needlelike** hard parts make up "spongy bone." (B349)

The *p* orbitals (p_x, p_y, p_z) are **dumbbell-shaped.** (B197)

Water is known to have the geometric structure . . . known as **"bent"** or **"V-shaped."** (B247)

Each **fist-sized** kidney has more than a million nephrons. (B420)

The fact that our biology text uses only one simile form suggests an idiosyncratic quality to the sample. But the fact the chemistry text chooses the same one suggests that the form *X-like* may be one of the more common forms that similes take, in science textbooks.

Clusters

A last feature of the corpus that I would like to touch on is what we might call *clusters:* passages that develop the same metaphoric theme over several sentences or paragraphs. We have seen examples of clusters as extended metaphors and extended analogies. They also appear as extended personifications and animations, and as a mixture of different figurative elements. Here are three examples, the first of which deals with the control agents of certain genes. It includes an implied analogy (These control agents are like a switch) that is developed by three personifications:

> Depending on the cell type and control agents acting on it, some genes might be **turned on** only at one particular stage of the life cycle. Others might be **left on all the time** or never activated at all. Still other genes might be **switched on and off** throughout an individual's life. (B159)

The next follows a similar pattern, in this case a marked *(like)* analogy developed by two reifications that are closely related to it:

> When [chlorophyll] P700 absorbs light energy, electrons are boosted even higher and passed to a second transport system. Transport systems, recall, are *like* **steps on an energy staircase**—and this boost places electrons **at the top of a higher staircase.** There is enough energy left **at the bottom of the staircase** to attach two electrons and a hydrogen ion . . . to NADP+. (B74)

The last example is from our chemistry corpus and describes the process of manufacturing micro- (miniaturized) machinery. It contains a marked analogy, "The plasma *acts as* a sandblaster . . . ," developed by three personifications, two of which *(sacrificial, excited)* have no logical collocation with the original analogy:

First a thin layer of silicon dioxide is applied (**sacrificial** material), then a layer of polysilicon is carefully applied (structural material). A **mask** is then applied and the whole structure is covered with plasma (**excited** gas). The plasma **acts as a sandblaster removing everything the mask doesn't protect.** . . . When the entire process is complete, the whole machine is placed in hydrofluoric acid, which dissolves all the **sacrificial** material and permits the various parts of the machine to move. (C186)

We can detect several processes occurring in these examples and in others quoted earlier (especially the extended metaphor of war and the immune system). For one thing, we find many examples of extended passages developed solely through one figurative form (extended metaphors, personification, reifications, etc.), almost as if the specific trope, once the association is made, then dominates the perception of the writer. In these, as in mixed forms, the metaphoric connection makes sense in some cases and not in others; in other words, some contain dubious collocations. Sacrifice and excitement do not go with sandblasters (C186). One does not *mount* an immune response (B267). Foreign agents are not engulfed and destroyed (B391ff.). As noted earlier, a danger of such an approach is that one comes to perceive the process through the metaphor. To what extent does the act of matching the metaphor to the physical process distort the accurate description of that process? Such questions must await other studies.

Markers

By far the most frequent figurative language markers in both texts are quotation marks. Lexical markers are the second most common, at least in the biology corpus, while there are none at all in the chemistry text—leading us to suspect a certain idiosyncratic quality here. The third type of marker is the use of italics, though it has a rare occurrence in both texts. In general, we find far greater use of figurative language markers in the biology text. This is to be expected, considering the fact that the biology text uses a lot more figurative language overall. Let us examine the various markers individually.

Quotation Marks

Taken together, the biology and chemistry texts in our corpus contain about forty words, used figuratively, that are signaled by quotation marks. There is no discernible pattern for this use of quotes as figurative language markers. Lexically, nominals predominate (nineteen instances), followed by verbals (thirteen instances) and adjectivals (eight). We find the occasional use of paraphrase, presumably to further elucidate the figurative nature of the term:

[Ribosomal DNA is] a type of molecule that combines with a certain protein to form the ribosome (the structural **"workbench"** on which a peptide chain is assembled). (B152)

[Messenger DNA] is the **"blueprint"** (a linear sequence of nucleotides) delivered to the ribosome for translation into a polypeptide chain. (B152)

Notice in our first example how the figurative term (a form of reification) is itself part of the paraphrasing definition.

We also find that quotes are used as markers for all of our various figures of speech: personification and analogy, animation and reification, simile and metaphor:

Water is known to have the geometric structure . . . known as **"bent"** or **"v-shaped."** (C247) (simile)

Vapor pressure may be thought of as an internal pressure, a measure of **"the escaping tendency"** of molecules to go from the liquid to the vapor state. (C298) (animation)

Bone tissue serves as a **"bank"** for calcium, phosphorous, and other mineral ions. (B348) (metaphor)

. . . any gene might come in several alternative forms, called alleles, that "say" slightly different things about how a trait will be expressed in an offspring. . . . One allele might **say "put a dimple in it"** and another might **say "no dimple."** (B105) (personification)

When a **daughter** cell inherits what looks merely like a blob of protoplasm, it really is getting **"start-up machinery"** for its operation. (B95) (reification)

Lexical Markers and Italics

It is interesting that only two figures of speech are marked—or rather sometimes marked—by specific words or phrases. These two figures are analogies and similes. Similes can be identified by *like* or *as*. But there are also fifteen or twenty other words or phrases—we might call them connectives—that mark a simile (Darian 1973). As for analogies, they often appear with such markers as: *equals, is equal to, is analogous to, just as, Imagine, In the same way, Similarly, X can be likened to,* and *Think of X as.* Notice the following:

Selective *agents* in the environment *sift through* the differences, **so to speak,** and tend to favor genotypes that make individuals well adapted to a given environment. (B131) (personification)

A tissue is a group of cells and intercellular substances that function together in one or more of the specialized tasks listed above. Tissues *split up the work,*

so to speak, in ways that contribute to the survival of the animal as a whole. (B337) (personification)

Together with the organ systems shown in Figure 26.1, the circulatory system helps maintain *favorable neighborhood conditions,* **so to speak.** (B374) (personification)

ITALICS. Italics appear infrequently in our texts as markers of figurative language, and are therefore probably idiosyncratic in nature. Notice in the first example the use of paraphrase to further explain the figurative term:

> Each person has a *genetic fingerprint,* a unique array of RFPLs inherited from each parent. (B166) (personification)

Notice in the next example that the first occurrence of the term is in italics. Later appearances occur without markers, suggesting that the term, in a subliminal way, is quickly on the road to literalness; which, as we have seen, is common practice:

> Vascular bundles called *veins* form a network through the leaf. The veins move water and solutes to the photosynthetic cells and carry products away from them. (B229) (personification/animation)

Some Applications

As we have seen, metaphoric thinking is a natural part of language. In school, when children are struggling to explain an idea, they may say *It's something like . . .* , and we sense, in Joan Solomon's words, that "another domain of experience is being used in an imaginary way" (1986, 45). Even more at the school level, suggests Solomon, similes and metaphors underlie the *mental modeling* that is crucial for learning and understanding science. In instruction, students are told to think of electricity as analogous to the flow of water, or of addition as analogous to piling up blocks (Gholson 1989, 296).

Our texts clearly illustrate this use of figurative language in explicating a wide range of scientific concepts. This being so, we can see the importance of teaching students to recognize, understand, and explain the major metaphoric themes of a discipline and the figurative forms that are used to present them. Such a component, urges Leatherdale, should play an "indispensable part in the structure of courses in science" (1974, 215).

Research shows that good metaphoric models are very effective in helping students develop their *qualitative,* conceptual knowledge of new topics, and that qualitative, conceptual knowledge is a key to science learning.

Accordingly, Mayer stresses that instruction should be aimed at the conceptual level first, *before* introducing the more quantitative elements of a topic (1993, 566).

In addition, studies on expertise in scientific problem-solving reveal that experts rely initially on models and qualitative reasoning, and "if the problem requires it, employ quantitative models *after* they analyzed the problem in conceptual, qualitative terms" (Mayer 1993, 567). All of which leads us in two different directions. The first deals with developing students' understanding of the material. The second deals with developing students' ability to think scientifically, which in essence means developing their ability to formulate theories, models, and hypotheses.

The name most closely associated with teaching metaphorics for science is, of course, W. J. J. Gordon, whose program in "Synectics" teaches students to "make the strange familiar" and "the familiar strange" (1973). Making the strange familiar, as he puts it, is most important in learning and understanding, as it requires placing a new concept in a familiar context (or as we have seen, going from the known to the unknown), while going from the unknown to the known (making the familiar strange) leads to new ways of looking at the world (or at a problem; in other words, formulating a hypothesis).

Gordon's work has evolved over many years and many volumes. Its importance is twofold. First, in its goal of developing *both* metaphoric functions: understanding and invention. Second, in its approach to helping students create their own, as opposed to text- or teacher-made, metaphors. Essentially, the methodology involves: (1) *direct analogy:* forming a simple comparison between two objects ("A crab walks sideways, like . . . a sneaky burglar"); (2) *personal analogy:* a description of how it *feels* to be a person or a concept, a plant or an animal, or a nonliving thing (Gordon 1973).

What are some lessons we have learned from our corpus? For one thing, we have observed the wide range of figurative types that are used in science texts. As we might have expected, metaphors are the dominant trope, followed, not by analogy, but, surprisingly, by personification and animation. After these, in frequency, come analogies and similes. The point here is that *all* of these figures should be included in the discourse of science, some for receptive, some for productive, purposes. The prevalent simile forms (X-like, or X-shaped, for example), are easy enough to understand. But they are important for productive purposes when a student is describing items in writing.

For non-native speakers, it is important to recognize metaphoric markers, since elements of figurative references are sometimes cultural. Some secondary connotations may differ, for example, so that parts of the metaphor, as Webber points out, may be lost on these students (1996, 42).

The trick to it all, as Lucretius once said, is to find a balanced tension between opposites (or was it Alcmaeon, I. A. Richards, or Mark Johnson?). This is the secret of metaphor, and, just perhaps, one of the secrets of life.

Chapter 5

Cause and Effect

Knowledge is the object of our inquiry, and men do not think they know
a thing until they have grasped the why of it.

ARISTOTLE

❋

The little boy was insatiable. Almost every word out of his mouth was:
Why? Why? Why? Why? Why? Finally his mother turned to him and said:
"Jimmy. Please stop asking me why!"

The boy paused for a moment, then looked at his mother and replied
somewhat dubiously: "Can I ask: 'How come?'"

Though it seldom appears as a major paragraph pattern in science texts,
cause and effect plays a central role in scientific thinking and writing. It is
a vital part of induction and deduction, probability and prediction, hypotheses and variables. According to philosopher Norman Rescher, it is probably "the most prominent of all modes of scientific thinking" (Rescher
1970, 121), perhaps, as physicist Percy Bridgman says, "as fundamental
as that of time and space" (1961 [1927], 80). And in some ways, just as
complex. There is a vast literature on causality—some of it written by scientists, most of it written by philosophers, including such luminaries as
Locke and Hume, Whitehead and Bertrand Russell.

Their discussions range from Hume's position that the very *concept* of
causality cannot be proven—that the only thing amenable to the senses is
a set of contiguous events—to the idea that causality was the most important single tool for the founders of modern science: "the touchstone in terms
of which they sought to test the truth or falsity of *any* explanation" (Wallace 1972, 210).

Though it seems like a reasonably straightforward idea, the concept
of cause and effect (let's call it *C&E* for short) presents many lexical, syntactic, and rhetorical problems for the reader of science textbooks. For this
reason, those who teach study skills in a first or second language, English
for science and technology, or individual sciences per se, and everyone involved in the teaching of thinking—need to understand the subtleties and
complexities in C&E thinking. There is no better example than its use in
science texts.

This chapter will first examine the major patterns of cause-and-effect thinking. Then we'll spend some time on problems caused by lexical and syntactic irregularities and ways of solving those problems. I'll also make some suggestions on items to include in teaching this thought pattern. To illustrate the workings of C&E thinking, I have chosen the text *Physical Geology* (Longwell 1969).

Patterns of Cause-and-Effect Thinking

There is a set of lexical items—words and phrases—that sometimes marks C&E relations. Regular markers for cause include: *because of, causes, due to, results from, as a result of*. These items, when they appear, always signal cause. Items like *when, since, by,* and *if* may show cause but may also indicate *different* rhetorical relations, and so may lead to potential misinterpretation. Regular markers for effect include items like: *accordingly, as a result, consequently, for this reason, hence, thus,* and *therefore*—and they always signal effect, or result. A word like *so* may indicate result but also a different relationship. There seem to be fewer ambiguous effect markers.

In the section "Problems in Cause-and-Effect Thinking," we will examine a variety of words used in C&E statements but *not* normally thought of as cause-and-effect markers, and which for that reason make it harder to discern the C&E relationship.

Major and Minor Cause-and-Effect Patterns

Here are the five major C&E patterns, as they appear in our text:

(1) X	transitive verb	→ Y.
(2) X	← be + noun/adjective	→ Y.
(3) Subordinate clause (If/When/As X happens, Y happens)		→ sentence OR
sentence		← subordinate clause
(4) X		← verb (mostly passive) Y.
(5) As a result of X,	→	Y happens.
Because of X,	→	Y happens.

In addition, we find the rare occurrence:

(6) The -er X,	→ the -er Y.
The more X,	→ the more Y.

There also exist *unmarked* C&E statements: those that have no lexical or syntactic features to mark them as a C&E relationship ("During the daytime [in deserts], air over hot places is heated and rises").

Each of the major patterns has its own features and peculiarities and deserves a few comments:

Pattern #1: X + transitive verb + Y.

Examples: 1. Seasonal distribution of rainfall **causes** → many streams to rise.

2. The trade winds **generate** → broad equatorial currents.

3. The Earth's rotation greatly **influences** → all movements of air.

This was the most widespread of all C&E patterns used in the text. While many cause-and-effect statements that take this pattern use what we might call regular C&E words *(cause, influence, result)*, many more do *not*. Our corpus contains words like the following to express C&E relationships: *account for, allow, confer, create, enable, generate, promote, raise.* Thus, apart from the regular markers, the lexical C&E clues of Pattern #1 are not especially strong.

Pattern #2: X + be + noun/adjective + Y.

Examples: 1. The Gulf Stream is responsible for → the warmth of the British Isles.

2. The arrangement of land masses and seas is **an influence** on → precipitation.

3. Most deserts have high winds, which are commonly ← **the result of** convection.

4. The vegetation in deserts is ← **a direct reflection of** dry climate.

The direction of influence in this pattern seems almost equally divided. On the one hand, X may be an influence on, a cause of, or responsible for Y (X → Y), as seen in examples one and two. On the other hand, it may also be a consequence of, an effect of, a reflection of, or a result of Y (X ← Y), as in examples three and four.

Pattern #3: Subordinate clause (When/As/If/Where), → sentence OR sentence ← subordinate clause.

Examples: 1. **When** the protective plant cover is weakened, → runoff is increased.

2. **As** the columns of air . . . are cooled, → the moisture they contain can condense.

3. Precipitation is heavy ← where air flows upward.

The key words in Pattern #3—*when, as,* and *if*—are what we might call *dual-function markers:* while they may indicate a C&E relationship, their major functions lie elsewhere (*when* for time; *if* for noncausal conditions; *where* for location; *as* for conditions and a range of other functions). As such, they are not reliable signals of C&E relationships. In addition, causal *if* statements may contain hypothetical conditions (contrary to fact)—which normally take a past tense verb in the *if* clause and a modal, *would,* in the main clause ("If the annual rainfall of a [desert] region *fell* in a single month, its effects on streams and vegetation *would* soon *be* lost")—a further syntactic twist. A final complexity is that the pattern operates in both directions, as seen in example three: Heavy precipitation (the effect) is caused by air flowing upward (the cause) (X ← Y).

> Pattern #4: X ← verb (mostly passive) Y.
>
> Examples: 1. Wind patterns ← **are caused by** heat from the Sun.
> 2. The strength of the solution ← **is increased by** the addition of carbon dioxide.
> 3. The patterns of rainfall ← **are governed by** movements of air.
> 4. Circulation of the atmosphere ← **results** chiefly **from** the distribution of solar energy.

The verbs used in this pattern fall into two categories. The first is *regular markers:* words whose meanings would normally indicate a C&E relationship: (X *is caused/created/influenced* by Y). At the same time, the pattern also contains a category of verbs that do *not* normally suggest C&E relationships: for example, X is *changed/controlled/governed/increased* by Y. As a result, the verb itself is not an especially reliable indicator of cause and effect. The outstanding feature of the pattern is that its verbs are almost always passive; thus effect comes before cause (X ← Y).

> Pattern #5: Sentence. + Sentence opener, + sentence.
> OR Adverbial phrase, + sentence.
>
> Examples: 1. With the 19th century came the steam engine. → **Accordingly,** at an almost incredible speed, a majority of the Earth's people substituted machinery for muscles.
> 2. Descending air . . . is able to retain moisture. → **As a result,** it absorbs moisture from the Earth by evaporation.
> 3. **Because of** the Coriolis Effect, → the trade winds in the Northern Hemisphere are deflected toward the right.

Pattern #5 contains most of our "traditional," or regular, cause-and-effect markers: lexical items such as *because of, accordingly, therefore, as a result.* Accordingly, it is probably the easiest C&E pattern to identify. We might arguably place this with Pattern #3, with the detached phrase functioning like the subordinate clause.

Pattern #6: The -er the X, the -er the Y.
The more X, the more Y.

Example: 1. The higher the temperature, → the greater the evaporation.

Pattern #6 may be hard to identify, as it is verbless. It was also quite rare in our corpus.

Multiple Causes and Effects

As we saw earlier—with Descartes and William of Ockham—a condition or event may have *several* causes or effects in scientific inquiry. This fact is not always clearly marked—a fact that can cause problems for the reader:

Multiple Causes: (1) Patterns of vegetation and (2) action of wind account for the movement of earth and sand in desert regions.

Multiple Effects: Convection is responsible for (1) high winds and (2) much of the rain in desert regions.

Notice the complexity of the following passage, in which both causes are responsible for each effect; in other words, causes one and two (C1 and C2) produce effect one (E1): C1 and C2 → E1. They also produce effect two (E2): C1 and C2 → E2:

Because of [C1] the effects of the Earth's curvature and [C2] the differences in thickness of atmosphere that solar radiation must pass through, [E1] the equatorial region receives much more heat than other parts of the earth [E2] while polar regions receive much less. (Longwell 1969, 31)

Without the drawing that accompanies the text (not reproduced here), the passage presents problems in understanding.

Partial Causes and Effects

Partial cause is related to the concept of multiple cause and effect. X may influence Y, but it may not be the *only* cause or even the most important one. X may be one of several causes of Y. In this case, the writer may simply state that X has an influence on Y:

The arrangement of land masses and seas *is an additional influence* on precipitation.

In cases like this, the other influences are often found elsewhere in the paragraph or in *other* paragraphs, thus making it harder for the reader to grasp the complete C&E relationship. At the same time, the other causes may not be relevant to the writer's discussion and so may be omitted. Partial cause is often indicated by phrases like these: *a partial cause, (X is) partially responsible for, A/One factor, One element, One cause/effect/result.*

Degrees of Influence

Sometimes a writer needs to note *how* important or influential a cause may be. This is indicated by a *degree word,* often—but not exclusively—an *-ly* adverb. In the following excerpt, from "Movements of Air," the two causes appear in sequence:

> Circulation of the atmosphere results *chiefly* from the distribution of solar energy. In addition, the Earth's rotation *greatly* influences all movements of air.

But this is not always the case. In the next sample, from "World Precipitation," the second sentence is separated from the first by three paragraphs:

> Movements of air *govern* the precipitation of moisture. . . . The arrangement of land masses is *an additional influence* on precipitation.

In situations like these, it is important to draw the connection among these several causes of the same effect. Degrees of influence are also marked by phrases like: *an important factor, a major influence, a minor cause, a crucial element.*

Tentativeness and Probability

An element in cause-and-effect thinking, especially in reports of scientific research, is its high degree of tentativeness. C&E statements are often the basis for hypotheses—which, as we'll observe in Chapter 6, are probabilistic by nature, a hypothesis in science being the possible reason why something happens or happened. When the reason is confirmed, it is no longer a hypothesis. Of course, some causal theories may never be completely confirmed:

> Meteorites *are thought to have* originated from the broken bits of former planets.

> Because we do not know precisely the volumes of the Antarctic and Greenland Ice Sheets, we can not calculate their influence on sea level very closely, but *it is likely* that the complete melting of those huge glaciers would add to the existing oceans a layer of water more than 70m thick. (Longwell 1969, 279; emphasis added)

Others have statistical validity:

> People who drink large amounts of alcohol *increase their risk* of having high blood pressure.

Oral contraceptives *can sometimes* cause high blood pressure, blood clots in veins or arteries, and *may damage* the artery walls. (American Heart Association booklet; emphasis added)

The topic of probability has received increasing attention in linguistics, under the rubric of *hedges*. The current view is that hedges are far more prevalent in research articles (where the author needs to defend against potentially critical peers) than in textbooks, which present information more as established facts and unmodified assertions. My analysis of geology and biology textbooks also reveals a high incidence of *epistemic* terms (words and phrases that express varying degrees of certainty) among the numerous hypotheses presented in the texts. Again, we'll examine this more closely in Chapter 6.

There are many ways to express probability in cause-and-effect statements, and in English in general. One analysis of several texts (Holmes 1988) reveals the relative frequency of epistemic words by parts of speech. In written language, the most common are modal verbs (36.8%) and lexical verbs (35.9%), followed by adverbials (12.8%). Kourilová, in her work on scientific discourse (1993), reports that modal auxiliaries form about 40% of all epistemic devices, adverbs and adverbials another 20%. In C&E statements from our geology text, probability is normally expressed in the following ways:

1. sentence opener, statement:

Quite likely, the shallow channel on the continental shelf, connecting the Hudson River with the Hudson submarine canyon, is the work of a lengthened Hudson River during a glacial time of lowered sea level. (Longwell 1969, 280; emphasis added)

2. sentence (of probability) + that + statement:

It is likely that the richer iron ores of the Lake Superior district . . . originated in a somewhat similar way. (Longwell 1969, 588; emphasis added)

3. subject or object + probability word + subject or object:

The volcano's eruption *appears to have raised* the temperature of the earth by several degrees. [emphasis added]

4. subject (a filler) + probability word + (that) + statement:

Early hypotheses *proposed* that submarine canyons were made by tidal currents. (Longwell 1969, 369; emphasis added)

The important thing is that the reader learns to recognize the cause-and-effect nature of such statements and pay heed to their tentativeness.

It is equally important that students are able to express degree and probability in their own writing, for research writing in general and science writing in particular. Mastery of the concept, in speech and writing, is a true mark of the sophisticated language user. Notice this sentence in Longwell, which contains examples of both:

> *Almost all* [degree] meteors *are thought to have* [probability] originated within the solar system. [emphasis added]

Some Problems in C&E Thinking and Suggested Solutions

Our analysis of the five main C&E patterns points up two potential problems in comprehension. First is the matter of inverted constructions. The second is the lack of clear lexical C&E markers. Related to the second point is a lack of dedicated syntactic patterns that mark a statement as cause and effect. This section will discuss these two points, plus another consideration that adds to the complexity of cause-and-effect discourse: the matter of series of C&E relationships. It will also recommend some ways of dealing with these problems.

Special Cause-and-Effect Markers

Apart from Pattern #5, which contains many regular (traditional) C&E markers—*because of, for this reason, thus, therefore*—cause-and-effect statements often use *special markers:* words or phrases that establish a cause-and-effect relationship but are *not* considered usual C&E markers. As we saw in our earlier analysis, they are common in all five of our patterns. In Pattern #1 (X causes Y), special markers include words like: *account for, confer, generate, govern, influence, promote, raise.* In Pattern #2 (X is an influence on Y), they include: *consequence, influence, product, reflection.* The only lexical clues in Pattern #3 (when X happens, Y happens) are the adverbials *if, as, when,* and *where.* Special markers in Pattern #4 (X is caused by Y) include: *were changed/controlled/governed/increased* by.

SOLUTIONS. One way of dealing with this uncertainty in lexical C&E markers is to teach those regular markers (1) that have the highest frequency, and (2) that occur in different parts of speech. The most common include: *cause, (effect), influence, product,* and *result.* The Roman numerals refer to the C&E patterns:

CAUSE: "Seasonal distribution *causes* many streams to rise and flood." (I) "Convection is a major *cause* of rain in desert regions." (II) "Wind patterns *are caused* by heat from the sun." (IV)

EFFECT: "*The effects* of uneven distribution of solar heat over the Earth . . . extend as well to deeper zones. Surface water that flows poleward is cooled and becomes denser." (II) X *affects* Y. (I)

INFLUENCE: "The Earth's rotation greatly *influences* all movements of air." (I) "The location of land masses is *an influence* on rainfall." (II) "Wind patterns *are influenced* by the rotation of the Earth." (IV)

PRODUCT: "Regolith, much of it *a product* of mechanical weathering, is thinner and has a coarser texture." (II) X *produces* Y. (I) X *is produced* by Y. (IV)

RESULT: "The circulation of the atmosphere *results* chiefly *from* the distribution of solar energy." (I) "Most deserts have high winds, commonly *the result of* convection." (II) "A majority of the Earth's people substituted machinery for muscle, *with the result that* between 1800 and 1960 . . ." (V)

Series of Cause-and-Effect Relationships

Scientific writing often uses cause-and-effect relationships in series. A C&E series can be clear or confusing, depending on the kinds of relationships between the items. We find several kinds of series, or patterns:

1. A creates B. B creates C. C creates D, and so forth. This can be fairly easy, depending on the kinds of markers. Special markers can make the relationship harder to understand than regular ones.
2. Sometimes, series B starts before series A finishes. In the following example, we have two series: (a) At higher altitudes, air becomes cooler, and (b) Air becomes cooler and loses its moisture:

At higher altitudes, **air becomes cooler** and loses its moisture.

Higher altitude causes cooler air. And the cooling air causes a loss of moisture.

The complexity becomes far more apparent in context. Notice the following passage, on world precipitation patterns, which contains two extended series of cause-and-effect relationships:

[A] Movements of air *govern* [B] the precipitation of moisture as rain, snow, and sleet. In general, [C] precipitation is heavy where [D] air flows upwards. [E] At higher altitudes, [F] air becomes cooler and [G] loses its ability to retain moisture—[H] which is then precipitated.

[I] Descending air, on the other hand, is [J] compressed, [K] heated, and is *thus* [L] able to retain more moisture. *As a result,* descending air [M] absorbs moisture from the Earth by [N] evaporation. These principles lead us to expect that [O] the greatest precipitation should fall [P] where air rises, near the equator and around latitude 60° N and S. [Q] The arrangement of land masses and seas is *an additional influence* on [B] precipitation. (Longwell 1969, 37; emphasis added)

The passage would be almost impossible without the accompanying illustration (Figure 5.1), which I've reproduced from the text.

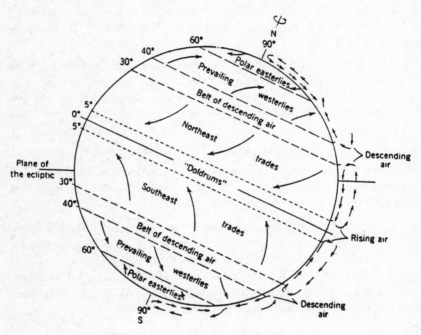

Figure 5.1. Movements of Air (Longwell 1969)

In the first series:

- (A) Movements of air govern (B) the precipitation of moisture . . .
- (C) heavy precipitation is caused by ← (D) air flowing upward (to higher altitudes)
- (E) higher altitude causes (F) cooler air
- (F) cooler air causes (G) inability to retain moisture
- (G) inability to retain moisture causes (H) moisture to be dropped.

In the second series:

- (I) descending air causes (J) compression
- (J) compressed air causes (K) heated air, which causes (L) retention of moisture
- (L) moisture-absorbing air causes (M) absorption of moisture from the Earth
- (M) absorption of moisture from Earth is further caused by ← (N) evaporation.

The selection invites a few further comments.

1. Note the regular C&E markers: *thus, as a result.*
2. Note the degree of influence: *govern,* which is also a special marker. Notice also the last line in the passage (Q), which is, as it says, an additional influence.

- (C) heavy precipitation is caused by ← (D) air flowing upward
- (L) greater retention of moisture → (M) absorption ← (N) evaporation.

In other words, one cause of M precedes it, another follows it, adding to the complexity of the phrase.

As for explaining some of this complexity, it is good to keep in mind that students of science and engineering are used to working with notation: numbers, letters (Greek and Roman), and other symbols. They respond well to the use of notation symbols, which—for non-native speakers—are often easier for them to grasp than the comparable English vocabulary. Here is a sequence for teaching the passage on world precipitation:

1. In the text or handout, mark each statement of cause *and* of effect with a different capital letter.
2. Demonstrate the relationships on the board or an overhead. For example:

- Heavy precipitation is caused by air flowing upward:

C	(is caused by) ←	A	
E	←	F	
F	→	G	
G	→	H	
I	→	J	
J&K	→	L	
L	→	M	← N
probO	←	O	(P is a probable cause of O)

This approach is especially effective when dealing with inverted patterns, which we'll examine now.

Inverted Patterns

In an inverted pattern, B causes A; the effect appears in the sentence *before* the cause. This, needless to say, can add further complications to what we may have originally thought of as a fairly straightforward pattern of thinking. For example:

> The vegetation in deserts is a *direct reflection of* dry climate.

In other words, dry climate causes the type of vegetation found in deserts. B causes A. Adding to the difficulty is the special C&E marker, *a direct reflection of,* which offers little help in identifying the pattern.

A further complication occurs in patterns like the following:

cause → effect ← cause OR cause → effect ← cause ← cause, where, as we saw in example three above, causes both precede and follow the effect. In context, the chain of thought can be even more daunting. Notice the next passage, which deals with the weathering processes of disintegration and decomposition:

> [A] disintegration, the mechanical breakup of rocks, *exposes* [B] additional fresh surfaces (of rock) to air and water. *Therefore,* [A] disintegration *aids* [C] decomposition, the chemical alteration of rock material. On the other hand, [D] some chemical changes are *directly responsible for* [E] mechanical disruption on a large scale.
>
> The active agents of decomposition consist of chemically active liquid solutions and water vapor. Rainwater brings to the ground with it, small amounts of carbon dioxide present in the air. This [F] gas combines with [G] water to make [H] carbonic acid. [I] As the water percolates down through the soil, [J] *the strength of the acid solution is increased many times* [K] *by addition of carbon dioxide* [J] *created by the decay of vegetation.* (Longwell 1969, 141; emphasis added)

The last sentence in the passage illustrates the pattern: effect ← cause ← cause:

> The strength of the solution is increased many times ← by addition of carbon dioxide ← created by the decay of vegetation.

Problems like this are best dealt with in four ways:

1. As we have seen, present the relationship in notation form.
2. Provide a diagram of the process.
3. Have *students* draw a diagram of the process.

4. Develop activities that require students to rewrite the sentences in inverted form (effect ← cause/cause → effect).

This does not necessarily result in a simple conversion exercise. In the following sentences, for example, the student must make other changes that require comprehension. For example:

A1. The Gulf Stream *is responsible for* → the mild weather of England.
A2. The mild weather of England ← *is caused by/is due to* the Gulf Stream.
B1. The uneven distribution of heat over the earth is the *chief* cause of the → major ocean currents.
B2. The major ocean currents *are caused chiefly by* . . . ←

For many complex cause-and-effect relationships, a visual can make the difference between comprehension and gibberish. Notice Figure 5.2, which illustrates the process of disintegration and decomposition.

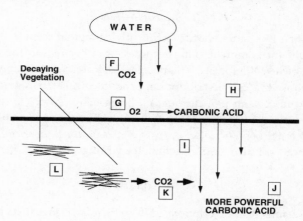

Figure 5.2. Disintegration and Decomposition

Here are some other observations from the passage:

- Regular markers: *therefore.*
- Special markers: *exposes, directly responsible for, is increased by, created by.*
- Partial cause: *aids.*
- Multiple causes: (F) gas + (G) water produces (causes) (H) carbonic acid.

Some of these various features are best illustrated by pointing them out on a transparency of the text.

As we have seen throughout the chapter, inverted forms appear in several patterns and may be indicated by regular or special markers. For example:

Regular Markers:

A is caused by B.

A is a result of B.

A results from B.

A is influenced/affected by B.

A happens as a result of B.

Special Markers:

A is a direct reflection of B.

A is increased/controlled/governed/produced/changed by B.

A originated from B.

Which Patterns To Teach?

All of the first five patterns occur frequently enough in science textbooks to be taught for comprehension purposes. Another reason for teaching Pattern #3 (when X happens, Y happens) is that it is very common in science textbooks in C&E descriptions of experiments. Patterns #1 and 2 (X causes Y, and X is an influence on Y), being major patterns, should be taught for writing purposes. At the same time, because of its rich vocabulary of C&E markers (because of, for this reason, thus, therefore, as a result), Pattern #5 is also worth teaching for writing.

Conclusion

Some cause-and-effect descriptions in introductory science texts have regular lexical markers and syntactic patterns. However, these regular features do not appear often enough to provide major help in identifying or understanding C&E statements. In addition, C&E explanations may contain special markers—words or phrases that *express* the C&E relationship in the particular sentence but do not *signal* it to the reader. Other cause-and-effect descriptions contain complex series, or syntactic irregularities such as inverted construction.

This chapter has suggested ways of dealing with the various comprehension problems found in cause-and-effect descriptions in scientific writing. Our conclusion is that C&E statements in science texts can be quite difficult to understand and should be given special attention—especially for non-native students—in classes dealing with study skills, and by all those concerned with the teaching of thinking in general.

Let's turn now to another crucial element—one that we glimpsed as early as Anaximander and his speculations on the origins of the Nile floods, one without which science as we know it would not exist: the language of hypotheses.

Chapter 6

The Language of Hypotheses

Perhaps the greatest danger in the teaching of science is to present students with a *fait accompli* universe.

W. J. J. GORDON

✻

Hypotheses are one of the most important tools in scientific thinking; perhaps, as physiologist William Beveridge suggests, "the principal instrument in [scientific] research" (1950, 71). Hypotheses come in many shapes and sizes, from a one-sentence statement to a series of tentative suppositions extending over several paragraphs. They can be introduced by a seemingly infinite number of verbs—although a short list predominates. They are expressed in a limited number of patterns. A hypothesis can be *marked* (by a word or phrase indicating its tentativeness). Or it can be unmarked (a simple assertion that one might easily take for fact). Hypotheses can appear in question form. In some texts and, especially, in spoken discourse, the word *theory* is sometimes erroneously used for *hypothesis*.

For these and other reasons, it is crucial for anyone interested in the language of science, the teaching of science, and the scientific enterprise in general to understand hypotheses—their forms and functions. I would like to begin by *defining* the term, and examining its essential elements. From there, we will look at the several *kinds* of hypotheses—theoretical, heuristic, and statistical. After that, we will analyze the *language* of hypotheses: their specific patterns and subpatterns, the verbs and other collocations that they take, and the myriad hedges they appear with. We will end with a few words on the teaching of hypotheses, including vocabulary selection, pattern selection, and problems caused by the sometimes elaborate use of tenses.

Definitions and Sources of Hypotheses

Definitions

As philosopher of science Max Wartofsky observes: "No term in science suffers a greater ambiguity than does hypothesis" (1968, 183). For this reason, it is worth pinning it to the wall as best we can. A hypothesis is a *possible* cause or reason for something, a possible solution to a problem.

We can consider it an *assumption* based on the best available information. At a deeper level, it is a tentative explanation of why something *happens* or *happened*. The key word is *tentative*. The essence of a hypothesis is its tentativeness, its provisionality, its *suspension of certainty*.

Linguistically, the various strategies used to express that tentativeness, or probability, are subsumed chiefly under the label of *hedges*—words and phrases such as: *probably, likely, As far as we know . . . , X seems to be . . .* The role of hedges in scholarly writing has received a great deal of attention in the last decade. The current view is that hedges are far more prevalent in research articles (where the writer needs to defend himself or herself against potentially critical peers) than in textbooks, which present information more as established facts and unmodified assertions.

While this may be true for science texts in general, there seems to be a considerable variation between fields. Of the four textbooks I examined for this chapter (Longwell 1969; Starr 1984; Hein 1993; Ohanian 1989), the physics text (1,200 pages) contained about 20 hypotheses, the chemistry text (900 pages) about 35, the geology text (600 pages) over 150, and biology (700 pages) over 130. In addition, the geology and biology texts contain far more *grouped* hypotheses (multiple assertions appearing close together, each one usually based on a previous statement). This would make the disparity even greater. There are reasons for these differences that I won't go into here.

Sources of Hypotheses

A hypothesis may or may not be grounded in facts. As John Stuart Mill cautioned: "A hypothesis being a mere supposition, there are no limits to hypotheses other than those of the human imagination" (Mill 1950, 261). If we accept Mill's opinion, as people tend to do, it follows that hypotheses can come from a wide variety of sources. In philosopher of science Edward Madden's words, they may derive "from intuition, trial and error, past experience, accident, imagination, even a dream" (1960, 7). Hypotheses may spring from subconscious analogies or metaphors, or recall of archetypal patterns. They drive the eureka syndrome: Newton's apple, Archimedes' leap from the tub!

A hypothesis may pop up at almost any stage in scientific inquiry: before or after observation, before or after experiments. Let's step back a moment and view this in a wider frame. As we have seen, scientific thinking is *recursive* more than sequential. We may have observation-hypothesis-experiment-observation, or observation–hypothesis–information gathering–hypothesis–observation. "An alert scientist," says philosopher of science George Schlesinger, "is likely to spot the hypothesis . . . before completing the data-gathering process; adopt it, and as a rule make use of it in predicting further experimental results" (1991, 126).

Elements of Hypotheses

There are several elements normally associated with hypotheses, though not all of them are always available. They include:

- assumptions
- generalization and prediction
- observation
- experiment
- inference and induction
- probability

Let's look at them individually.

Assumptions

Every hypothesis is based on several assumptions, assumptions that we may or may *not* be aware of. Different assumptions, can, of course, lead to very different hypotheses. Every experiment tests not just an isolated hypothesis, but a whole body of knowledge that lies behind it. If an experiment claims to refute a single hypothesis, it is because the assumptions underlying it are believed to be well founded. But as philosophers of science Morris Cohen and Ernest Nagel remind us, some of these beliefs may be mistaken (1934, 220).

In teaching people to read and *use* the language of science, it is important to make them aware of the assumptions underlying both writers' and readers' hypotheses—to state them and examine them. Progress in science, says Irving Copi, "is often achieved by formulating explicitly an assumption which had been previously hidden, and then scrutinizing and rejecting it" (in Madden 1960, 33).

Generalization and Prediction

Hypotheses can be general or specific. There is normally only one solution to a murder mystery or a mechanical problem. That solution may be A, B, C, or D. Until the answer is found, all of these options are no more than *possible* answers, or hypotheses. Scientists and philosophers of science speak of *predictability* as a key element of hypotheses: "Under X conditions, Y will happen." Yet in the specific examples above, there *is* no predictability, except in the unreal sense that if party X is killed, the murderer will always be party D. But where the topic allows for it, predictive power is a major factor in promoting a hypothesis to a theory, a principle, or a law (defining a theory as a hypothesis that has been around for a while and has acquired considerable evidence to support it).

There are basically two kinds of supporting evidence for a hypothesis: (1) the evidence collected earlier, which the hypothesis is supposed to account for, and (2) novel evidence predicted on the basis of the hypothesis. Students of scientific method feel that verifying a prediction based on a hypothesis provides much more support for it than using it to explain what is already known.

Some hypotheses come from a sample population based on observation, experiment, or statistical information, which is then generalized to the entire population. Such hypotheses must remain tentative; they can never be completely proven. In truth, one of the defining features of hypotheses is their unprovability. Once they are proven, they are no longer hypotheses. "Every generalization is a hypothesis," suggests the great French mathematician Henri Poincaré (1952, 150).

Observation

As we have seen, hypotheses are not necessarily based on observation. But where they are, the *reciprocity* between the two is very strong. A hypothesis *guides* observation. Wartofsky puts it nicely: "It is only within . . . the narrower framework of a particular hypothesis that observation attains to that focus and selectivity which makes it germane for science" (1968, 190). In more specific terms, the hypothesis helps determine which factors are noted and which are not. What is seen through observation may acquire meaning only when it is connected with what is *not* seen (Cohen and Nagel 1934, 216). At the same time, observation leads to hypotheses. The scientist observes, infers, interprets, classifies, and formulates. It is worth recalling the role of hypotheses in the observations of Darwin and physiologist Claude Bernard.

Experiment

Not all hypotheses are based on experiments or can be tested by them. But where experimentation *is* possible, it is often governed by a hypothesis. Physiologist William Beveridge suggests that the main function of hypotheses "is to suggest new experiments and new observations." He asserts that "most experiments and many observations are carried out with the deliberate object of testing a hypothesis" (1950). This, of course, is the main thesis of Karl Popper, the guru of hypothesis-testing. According to Popper, the main tool of scientific investigation is: creating hypotheses, then subjecting them to experiment and observation, with the aim of *disproving* them.

Mill captures very nicely the *reciprocal, interlocking* nature of the hypothesis and its elements:

> The hypothesis, by suggesting observations and experiments, puts us on the road to independent evidence. . . . This function . . . is one which must be reckoned absolutely indispensable in science. . . . *Nearly everything that is now theory was once hypothesis.* (1950, 265; emphasis mine)

Inference and Induction

Inductive reasoning assumes that facts similar to observed facts are true in cases that have not been observed. It involves going from many particulars to the universal. It is a generalization about all members of a class. But while it shares with the hypothesis this feature of generalizability, it is not one. Induction reasons from the particular to the general, hypothesis (inference) from effect to cause; induction classifies, hypothesis explains. A hypothesis is a conclusion that is different from the facts observed, and is often something impossible for us to observe directly. "When we stretch an induction quite beyond the limits of our observation," says philosopher C. S. Pierce, "the inference partakes of the nature of hypothesis" (Pierce 1957, 140).

John Stuart Mill, in a brilliant passage from his *Philosophy of Scientific Method,* describes the inseparable relationship between fact and inference. In this case, he is referring to Kepler's discovery that Mars traces an elliptical orbit around the Sun. I have included it here because of its keen insights:

> The ellipse was *in the facts* before Kepler recognized it [the orbit of Mars]. . . . Kepler did not *put* what he conceived into facts, but *saw* it in them. A conception implies and corresponds to something conceived; and though the conception itself is not in the facts but in our mind, yet if it is to convey any knowledge relating to them, it must be a concept *of* something which really is in the facts, some property which they actually possess, and which they would manifest to our senses if our senses were able to take cognizance of it. . . . If the facts are rightly classed under the conception [SD: the hypothesis?], it is because there is in the facts themselves something of which the conception is itself a copy. (Mill 1950, 180)

Probability

While observation, experiment, and predictability are normally considered the most important operational features of a hypothesis, these features—as we have seen—are not always available to the scientific investigator. The one constant in hypotheses is their provisionality—the crucial awareness that they may or may *not* be true. Indeed, some of the greatest effort of science is spent in establishing the truth or untruth of hypotheses. Accordingly, almost all hypotheses contain *epistemic* terms (words or phrases that express varying degrees of certainty). This "hedging of claims," says linguist Greg Myers, "is so common that a sentence that looks like a claim but has no hedge is probably not a statement of new knowledge" (1989, 13).

Just as epistemic terms are central to hypotheses, so the *degree* of probability is crucial for expressing and establishing their validity. With the seemingly infinite variety of epistemic terms available, it is important to differentiate shades of meaning, since the nuances can be incredibly fine. What is the difference, for example, between: *The results suggest . . . , The results appear to be . . . ,* and *The results clearly suggest . . . ?* The vocabulary of probability is huge and requires a painstaking match of words and ideas. For the non-native speaker who is studying science, it demands considerable training.

Types of Hypotheses

There are basically three types of hypotheses: theoretical, statistical, and heuristic. Let's examine each one briefly.

Theoretical Hypotheses

A theoretical hypothesis can be based on a single item or event. If so, it is not generalizable or predictable. With additional confirming evidence, theoretical hypotheses have a greater probability of being correct, but not in a quantifiable way. There is a difference between something being possibly or probably true (ultimately, it either *is* or *isn't*) and a .05, .10, or .50 correlation.

Theoretical hypotheses predominate in the geology and biology texts, especially in sections dealing with the origins of things—whether rock formations or organisms. Most living things have behind them millions of years of development, and a major part of biology is tracing that development, in order to understand how they function today. In fact, the majority of hypotheses—in all four of our texts—are theoretical, as indicated by the epistemic words they contain. Statistical findings, based on samples and experiments, are more common in research articles. This fact has implications for teaching the language of science to non-native speakers, implications we will explore throughout the chapter and specifically in the final section on pedagogy.

Statistical Hypotheses

Statistical hypotheses are based on a sample of more than one. In general, the larger the sample, the more reliable the evidence. Accordingly, statistical hypotheses are generalizable and have predictive value. For this reason, they form the basis of actuarial and epidemiological studies. Statistical hypotheses inhabit their own subuniverse of discourse and belong to the languages of statistics and of experiments. They are therefore the subject of an important area of research, but one that falls just outside the limits of our study.

It is interesting to see that in the introductory biology text, written for the nonspecialist or specialist-to-be, correlations of smoking and cancer are translated into the language of epistemic probability:

> The [mucous] membranes [of the respiratory tract] are extremely sensitive to cigarette smoke, *probably* because of the chemical nature of the concentrated particles. . . .
> Cigarette smoke is also known to contain compounds that *can* lead to lung cancer. These compounds . . . are found in coal tar and cigarette smoke. *It appears that* they become chemically modified in the body . . . into highly reactive intermediaries that are the real carcinogens. (Starr 1984, 407; emphasis added)

Heuristic Hypotheses

A heuristic hypothesis is one that makes no necessary claim to truth. It makes no pretense to observation or experiment. Instead, it invents a "hypothetical" question or situation, as a means of exploring the topic. We find it in the classroom technique "Let's imagine that two masses in space are connected by a spring." Or "Let's suppose that space is filled with a perfectly elastic fluid" (Barker 1957, 95). As we will see in the next section, it is characterized by Patterns #5 and #6, with phrases such as: *If . . . , then . . . , Suppose . . . , Imagine . . . , What if . . . ?*

The Language of Hypothesis

In this section, I would like to discuss the various *patterns* that hypotheses take and some of the problems that go with them. We will then examine some of the *lexical* considerations that accompany them, specifically, the matters of collocations, synonyms, and hedges.

Patterns of Hypotheses

One reason hypotheses seem less frequent in science texts than in research articles is that they appear in such diverse forms. Apart from Pattern #8 (unmarked) and Pattern #9 (which is a combination of other patterns), there are basically seven different patterns. Let's explore these patterns and some of the comprehension problems they engender. I have labeled Patterns #1 through #4 epistemic, since they contain words or phrases normally used to express varying degrees of certainty.

Pattern #1 (Epistemic 1): Subject of hypothesis + epistemic verb/adverb + rest of hypothesis.

The mantle and core of the earth . . . *are believed* to consist of metallic iron and nickel. (Hein 1993, 51; emphasis added)

Mutations *probably* led to alterations in metabolic machinery. (Starr 1984, 133; emphasis added)

The tentativeness of this pattern may be in a verb or an adverb. In teaching the pattern, it is important to establish that the subject of the hypothesis is connected to the "postepistemic" phrase, since in the other epistemic patterns, the entire hypothesis appears in the sentence in one piece.

Pattern #2 (Epistemic 2): Subject (filler) + probability statement (epistemic verb) + (that) + hypothesis.

In 1913, Niels Bohr *made the radical proposal* that, at the atomic level, the laws of classical mechanics and classical electromechanics must be replaced or supplemented by another law. (Ohanian 1989, 1058; emphasis added)

The results *indicated* a metabolic pathway for fatty acids in which the carbon chain is shortened by two carbon atoms at each stage. (Hein 1993, 939; emphasis added)

One fairly common device in Pattern #2 is the use of double hedges in the verb slot, which enables the writer to fine-tune his assertion. Some examples:

We *infer with little doubt* that together they represent continuous, unbroken sedimentation on the ocean floor. (Longwell 1969, 391; emphasis added)

Darwin *inferred correctly* that the fossils could not have been distributed in this way if the sediment had been deposited in water as thick as the strata. (Longwell 1969, 404; emphasis added)

We have *every reason to believe* that local contraction may occur within the [Earth's] mantle and be responsible for local compression within the lithosphere. (Longwell 1969, 553; emphasis added)

Pattern #3 (Epistemic 3): Word or phrase containing probability statement + that + hypothesis.

It appears that when life originated, the environment contained simple molecules that contained mostly carbon, hydrogen, nitrogen, and oxygen. (Starr 1984, 133; emphasis added)

We can view the first unit of the pattern as a slot that includes a probability (epistemic) word or phrase. Structurally, we have several subpatterns here. These include:

A. It	may be/had to be/is likely/is possible/is assumed/is widely held/appears/was thought (that the environment contained simple molecules).
B. There is/are	a possibility/a probability/reason to believe/every indication/ [strong] evidence (that in southern Arizona a cycle of erosion has been in progress . . . for millions of years).
C. One	explanation/idea/proposal/hypothesis is (that [viruses] are the noncellular remnants of ancient parasitic forms of bacteria).

D. There is also a miscellaneous group containing phrases like:

- *The only reasonable explanation* of this topography is that a wide landscape was eroded by streams . . . and was later submerged by crustal deformation. (Longwell 1969, 404; emphasis added)
- *The only hypothesis consistent with the seismic observation* . . . is that an inner spherical mass below a depth of 2000 km constitutes the core of the Earth. (Longwell 1969, 441; emphasis added)

For purposes of analysis, it is useful to be aware of these permutations of the general pattern. For pedagogical purposes, such distinctions are too fine to be included in a syllabus.

Pattern #4 (Epistemic 4): Probability word or phrase as sentence opener, + sentence including hypothesis.

Example:

As far as anyone can foresee, the universal rise in entropy will reach a maximum some billions of years hence. Then the universe will be everywhere identical and at the same temperature, and nothing will ever change again. (Starr 1984, 100; emphasis added)

While the sentence opener position takes single-word adverbials like *probably* and *perhaps*, I would like to call attention to phrases of degree or extent that do not necessarily appear in discussions of epistemic terms. They include such items as: *As far as we know . . . , As far as we can tell . . . , For all we know . . . , In almost all cases . . . , As far as anyone can foresee . . . , According to one scenario . . .*

Pattern #5. Counters: Hypotheses containing a disaffirming word or phrase. Let's call them *counters,* in the sense of countering the hypothesis. The hypothesis is also followed by an explicit *refutation* in the next or a soon-to-follow sentence. However, these markers are not epistemic terms or hedges in the traditional sense—words or phrases like *unlikely, not very probable, little chance*—which indicate the writer's degree of certainty about her statement (since hedges are such an important part of hypotheses, we will say more about them later). Instead, the refutation is conveyed more subtly, in various ways such as:

A. phrases with simple *past* tense markers *(popular belief held, the prevailing view was, one explanation was, the scientific community was adhering to a notion that . . .).* Here is an example:

Early geologists thought that the sea had become saltier with time and that the annual increments of sodium would serve as a basis for calculating the age of the oceans. . . . *The modern view is* that the salinity of the world's oceans reached its present level at least 500 million years ago. (Longwell 1969, 110; emphasis added)

B. complex past tense constructions in the passive *(was seen to extend, were thought to originate, were supposed to have been).* An example:

Tiny grains [chromosomes] *were thought to become* joined together to form chromosomes when the nucleus was about to divide. . . . Refinements in microscopy *have since changed the picture.* (Starr 1984, 69; emphasis added)

C. time phrases *(During the nineteenth century, For a time, At that time, Traditionally).* An example:

Traditionally, the ancestors of these [early] plants are thought to have evolved from aquatic cells that also gave rise to the green algae. *Yet,* there is recent speculation that their ancestors were already multicellular, of entirely separate lineages. (Starr 1984, 546; emphasis added)

There are several things to note with these patterns:

1. The complex tense construction of subpattern B would be very difficult for the non-native speaker and should be explained and practiced.
2. Since the refutation occurs in a subsequent sentence, it is necessary to include discourse-level excerpts for illustration and exercises.
3. The examples in A, B, and C above are similar to Patterns #1, #2, and #4. The difference is that these Pattern #5 varieties all have a refutation in a subsequent sentence, and that they are always negative.

Pattern #6. IF . . . , (THEN) . . . *If . . . , then . . .* sentences may be either hypotheses or simple statements of fact. Here is an *if . . . , then . . .* statement as hypothesis:

[re: zoologist Georges-Louis de Buffon's attempt to explain the existence of vestigial structures in animals] *If* there had been only a single center of creation . . . , *then* species spreading out from it would have been stopped sooner or later by mountain barriers or oceans. *What if* there had been several centers of creation? (Starr 1984, 28; emphasis added)

Students must be able to distinguish the hypothesis from the nonhypothesis IF . . . , THEN . . . form. It should also be noted that the pattern sometimes appears without the word *then*.

Pattern #7. Questions and questionlike forms as hypotheses. These appear in three subpatterns:

7.1 WHAT IF . . . ? An uncommon form; there were only two examples in the corpus of four texts, and both occur together with *if . . . , then . . .* statements. Notice the *what if* hypothesis in the sample above. Here is the second below. It deals with genetic experiments in breeding red and white flies, and an anomaly that contradicts one of Mendel's theories.

What if there were no eye-color gene on the Y chromosome? *If* only X chromosomes carried the gene being studied, *then* it would be expressed in males regardless of whether it were dominant or recessive. (Starr 1974, 181; emphasis added)

7.2 SUPPOSE/IMAGINE . . . This is a more common question-hypothesis (nine instances). All of the *suppose/imagine* sentences appear in series of hypotheses, and have a heuristic value. The example on the rearing of infants among early primates:

Suppose that the Miocene hominids began to develop a kind of home base strategy. With the evolution of mosaic environments, more time would be required to search for food. . . .

Lovejoy [a professor of anatomy] carries this line of thought one step further. *Suppose* that males began provisioning for their female mates and offspring by collecting and carrying back food to the home base. (Starr 1984, 596; emphasis added)

7.3 COULD/DO/WAS . . . ? There are only four examples in all of the four texts. Here are three of them:

What about more complex behavioral traits [in animals and humans]—sexual jealousy, for example? This behavior is prevalent among human societies, although its expressed forms are remarkably diverse. *Could* sexual jealousy *be* a more embroidered version of the mate-guarding behavior described earlier in the chapter? (Starr 1984, 696; emphasis added)

Taken as a whole, the fossil record shows immense periods of stability in form—and periods of rapid change in form. How can such a record be interpreted? *Do* species *evolve* most rapidly when they are first branching from ancestral lineage? Or *does* most of the evolution *occur* gradually . . . ? (Starr 1984, 497; emphasis added)

Why do the coals of the two districts [bituminous around Pittsburgh, anthracite near Scranton, Pennsylvania] differ so conspicuously? *Was* the coal everywhere the same initially but converted by deformation into anthracite in northeast Pennsylvania . . . ? (Longwell 1969, 503; emphasis added)

Pattern #8. Unmarked: A simple affirmative declarative statement with no indication of tentativeness. For this reason, we might call this an *unmarked* hypothesis. The example refers to the theory (hypothesis?) of continental drift:

Toward the end of the Ordovician [period], storms of mountain building were brewing as plate movements put Laurentia on a collision course with a smaller land mass to the east. Volcanic outpourings along the eastern edge of Laurentia created immense ancestral mountains as the plates closed in. (Starr 1984, 512; emphasis added)

The problem with this pattern is clear: with no hypothesis marker the reader is not sure whether the statement is fact or hypothesis.

Pattern #9. Grouped Hypotheses. What I have called Pattern #9 is really a collection of hypotheses from all of the previous patterns—grouped together in the same or ensuing paragraphs. They follow one of three subpatterns: (1) *sequential:* one hypothesis is built on another; (2) *multiple:* different, perhaps competing, hypotheses; and (3) *mixed:* a passage containing both sequential and multiple hypotheses. Here are some examples of each. *S* indicates members of a sequential series.

Sequential Hypotheses

The first passage speculates on why the various organs of the endocrine system are located in such diverse parts of the body:

What possibly could link the system's components together? [S1] The answer *may lie* in their ancient origins. [S2] *It is possible* that many endocrine elements evolved as specialized regions of nervous systems in animals not much more complex than flatworms.

[S3] *Suppose* that long ago, mutations in a . . . neuron led to . . . [S4] Molecules of the substance *might have started* to diffuse throughout the surrounding tissues. [S5] They *might even have begun* slipping in and out of the bloodstream.

[S6] *Suppose* their surface configuration enabled them to . . . [S7] *If* the alterations somehow enhanced cell function, *then* the mutation *would have conferred* advantages on the individual. Over time, [S8] the mutant cells *might have become* modified . . . ; [S9] they *would have been* forerunners of endocrine cells and tissues. (Starr 1984, 347; emphasis added)

One feature of sequential hypotheses is that they often contain *sequence markers,* anaphoric words (double underlined below) referring back to the original hypothesis. We have space here for only a short excerpt:

We can *speculate* that for as long as the general circulation of the atmosphere has been approximately like that of today, [S1] *there must have existed* wide regions with descending drying air. [S2] *Probably, therefore,* arid climates have persisted wherever those latitudes have coincided with continental mass.

[S3] *Probably, too,* the interiors of large continents have contained at least some desert throughout much of geologic history. (Longwell 1969, 290; emphasis added)

In teaching scientific writing, it is important to point out the need for these markers in sequential hypotheses.

Multiple Hypotheses

Paragraphs with multiple hypotheses are pretty straightforward, especially since they tend to be shorter than those with sequential or mixed hypotheses. Here is a brief example, dealing with the origins of underwater canyons. M1, M2, and M3 simply designate the different hypotheses:

> [M1] *Hypotheses* invoking processes operating on land *assert* that canyons were made by streams. . . . [M2] Early *hypotheses* involving submarine processes *proposed* that canyons were made by tidal currents, tsunami, or submarine artesian springs. [M3] Later the *hypothesis* of turbidity currents became popular. (Longwell 1969, 369; emphasis added)

Mixed Hypotheses

Passages with mixed hypotheses may contain several independent, or alternative, hypotheses, each with several sequential hypotheses flowing from it. For this reason, they are harder to process. In the example below, I have used the following notation: M1 indicates hypothesis #1, while M1A indicates a speculation (sequential hypothesis) flowing from it; similarly with M2 and M2A. The passage deals with ways to explain clam-shell borings as high as 6 meters above the waterline, in columns of a Roman building west of Naples:

> We can formulate several hypotheses to explain these observations. [M1] One of them *states* that throughout the world, sea level rose and later fell and that land did not move. [M1A] The most important *deduction* from this hypothesis is that a record of such sea-level changes would be present in coastal belts everywhere. . . .
>
> Our second hypothesis *states* [M2] that a local part of the Italian coastal belt sank and was reelevated within very recent times. Because this accords with all the known evidence, we can *adopt* it *with confidence.* . . . We *infer* [M2A] that the building was constructed with its floor lying some distance above sea level and that it later sank to a depth at which the water could reach 6m above its former floor. (Longwell 1969, 402; emphasis added)

Really long strings of grouped hypotheses occur in the geology and biology texts, especially regarding topics dealing with prehistoric reconstructions, which are not usually possible to verify through observation or experiment.

Lexical Considerations

A tremendous vocabulary is involved in the language of hypotheses. I would like to touch on several aspects of that vocabulary, specifically the areas of synonyms, collocations, and hedges.

Synonyms

There are a great number of words—formal and informal, oral and written—that may contain the meaning *hypothesis*. Some may be considered synonyms, others near-synonyms. Some have other major connotations as well. These are reasons that it is hard to isolate hypotheses in a text.

The minimum requirement of synonymy is the presence of tentativeness. This we find in words like: *assumption, conjecture, generalization, guess, hunch, inference, speculation, supposition.* There are several near-synonyms, which need a qualifying word to add the required element of tentativeness: *(a preliminary) conclusion, (a possible) explanation, (one) reason.* Then there are those that have other major connotations: *interpretation, model, prediction, proposal.*

Collocations

Several things happen to hypotheses. Basically, they are stated, examined, and either confirmed or rejected:

Negative	Neutral		Positive
	To state	To examine	
disprove	devise	examine	prove
disconfirm	form	test	confirm
reject	formulate		accept
	frame		
	postulate		

Hedges

Since they are chiefly a mark of tentativeness, hedges are probably the clearest indicators of hypotheses. As we have seen, four of our eight hypothesis patterns are marked by overt hedges. Pattern #8 is unmarked and Pattern #9 contains a variety of the others. Like hypotheses, hedges come in a diversity of forms—syntactic and semantic. They are found in every part of speech: nouns (the *view* that . . .), verbs (We *infer*), modals (It *may* contribute to . . .), adverbs *(presumably)*, adjectives *(Current* opinion favors . . .), articles *(One* solution is . . .), and function nouns *(Some* feel that . . .). They can serve as—

- intensifiers: *definitely, rather, indeed*
- approximators: *roughly, some, virtually, approximately*
- impersonalizations: *the modern view* is . . . , *A contrasting view* is . . . , *According to this view* . . .
- indicators of personal involvement: *We wish to suggest* . . . , *As best we can tell* . . .

—and serve other functions. The topic has been treated extensively in the scholarly literature.

Holmes's analysis of several corpora (1988)—reveals the relative frequency of epistemic words by parts of speech. In written language, the most common are modal verbs (36.8%) and lexical verbs (35.9%), followed by adverbials (12.8%). Holmes also identifies the most frequent words in different categories. Her findings have implications for teaching the language of hypotheses, which we will focus on in the next section.

MULTIPLE HEDGES. One of the complications of hedgery in our corpus is the use of multiple hedges, which deserves a word or two. Our four epistemic patterns (#1, 2, 3, and 4), by definition, all contain hedges. Pattern #5 (Counters) also contains hedges. In this case, multiple hedging is a defining feature of the pattern, though its special feature is that the second hedge, or refutation, as I have called it, appears in a subsequent sentence.

One subtype of Pattern #2 (filler subject + epistemic verb + that + hypothesis) is also characterized by multiple hedging—there are three in this example:

> *Indirect evidence suggests* that differentiation of other kinds also takes place.

Multiple hedges of hypotheses are fairly frequent in our corpus, and come in twos ("The glacial ages *are thought to represent perhaps* . . ."), with a few in threes and fours ("We have *every reason to believe* that . . ."). The longest multiple hedge, admittedly rare, runs to six:

> [Although the steps in the creation of oil are still very poorly known,] the following simplified [1] *theory* is [2] *rather* [3] *widely held* and is supported by enough facts to be [4] *at least* [5] *somewhat* [6] *near the truth*. (Longwell 1969, 575; emphasis added)

Some Considerations in Teaching Hypotheses

Following is a list of considerations for teaching about hypotheses. It focuses on pattern selection and vocabulary selection. The list is too long to discuss each item individually. However, I have included a few suggestions and frameworks that should be useful for pedagogical purposes.

Vocabulary Selection

1. Epistemics
   A. Students need to understand varying degrees of certainty (negative, mild, strong, very strong), and which words belong in each category.
   B. Students need active mastery of several terms for each category—to cover the full range of meaning.
   C. Students need to recognize that epistemic meaning can be found in all parts of speech (N, V, Adj, Adv, etc.).
   D. Students need to understand shades of meaning: in single words and double hedges.

2. Criteria for vocabulary selection
   A. Words that appear in more than one pattern.
   B. Words that appear in more than one part of speech *(possible, possibly, possibility)*.
   C. High frequency words.
   D. Useful collocations.
   E. Synonyms—as a way of recognizing the presence of hypotheses.

Specific Suggestions

The vast array of epistemic words in English can be arranged by varying degrees of probability. This fourfold division should cover almost every need:

	Conjecture		Certainty
Negative (N)	Mild (M)	Strong (S)	Very Strong (VS)
• supposed to have	• may have	• reasonably	• must have
• little evidence	• For all we know	• confident	• the modern view
• unlikely	• hazard a guess	• probably	• it is viewed as
• was thought to be	• it could be that	• is believed to be	• it is viewed as
			• Without a doubt
			• every indication

Given the unruly number of epistemic words, it is necessary to choose several of the most frequent in *each* of the probability categories (N, M, S, VS). This selection can be guided partly by Holmes's excellent analysis of several corpora, which, however, include samples of more general spoken and written English, rather than science texts. My lexical candidates in this section derive from Holmes's work, but also from the corpus supplied by my four science texts. Kourilová—in her work on scientific discourse—reports that modal auxiliaries form about 40% of all epistemic devices, adverbs and adverbial phrases another 20% (1993, 14). While introductory science texts may differ in certain respects from scientific discourse in general (we have seen that their hypotheses show differences from research articles), these approximations are worth keeping in mind.

MULTIPLE HEDGES. Especially for the non-native speaker, multiple hedges are bound to cause problems. One way to treat such a problem is to work with the probability table (N, M, S, VS) and help students equate a multiple hedge with one of the four degrees.

WORDS THAT APPEAR IN MORE THAN ONE PART OF SPEECH. The most common and *productive* are: *possible, likely,* and *probable.* With their various intensifiers, these words cover the entire probability range, apart from absolute *yes,* which, as we have seen, is no longer a hypothesis. For example:

> It is impossible. It is not impossible. It is unlikely. It is possible. More than likely. In all likelihood. It is probable. In all probability.

Pattern Selection

Before addressing the matter of pattern selection for teaching, this seems an appropriate place for a compact list of patterns, considering their sometimes complex features and the nature of the discussion to follow:

(1) The species	*probably*	has been the same for a million years.
(2) Studies	*indicate*	that the species has been the same for a million years.
(3) *It appears*		that the species has been the same for a million years.
(4) *As far as we know,*		the species has been the same for a million years.
(5) *Early biologists thought*		that the species had been the same for a million years. *The modern view is . . .*

(6) *If* the species had been the same for a million years,	*(then)* how can we account for the numerous variations existing today?
(7) *Has*	the species been the same for a million years?
Suppose	the species has been the same for a million years. In that case, . . .
(8) Unmarked	
(9) Sequential Patterns	

From analysis of my corpus, by far the most common patterns of hypotheses are #1 ("The core of the earth *is believed to* consist of metallic iron nickel") and #2 (Calculations *suggest* that the comet will return in 60 years"), with #3 ("*It is assumed* that early environments already contained simple molecules") a distant third. Further analysis, however, reveals that the various patterns of hypotheses fall into two groups. In Group A (Patterns #1, 2, 3, and 4), the hypothesis is clearly stated; and the epistemic, or probability word, appears in different places in the sentence. Thus, the same idea may be expressed equally well using *any* of the four patterns.

The patterns in Group B (#5 and 6) seem to function differently. They contain the element of *contrast*. In #5, for example, the contrast is between *earlier* and *later* beliefs. In #6, the contrast is between X and Y: "If X had happened, then how can we account for Y?" Pattern #7 contains specimens of both groups. For Group A: "Has the species remained the same for a million years? (There is reason to think so.)" For Group B: "Suppose the species has remained the same for a million years. (In that case . . .)"

The results of this analysis and of the earlier examination of hypothesis patterns suggest the following:

1. Teach the most frequent patterns (#1, 2, and 3).
2. Teach theoretical hypotheses for reading introductory science texts.
3. Include work in both theoretical and heuristic hypotheses (#6 and 7).
4. Include statistical hypotheses for (a) writing and (b) reading research articles.

Depending on how much time is available for teaching hypotheses, the instructor might want to deal with some of these pattern problems:

A. Pattern #1: Establishing the connection between the subject of the hypothesis and the rest of it, since this is the only pattern in which they are separated.

B. Pattern #5 (Counters): Establishing the connection between past tense and (invalid) hypotheses. The complexity of some of these verb forms is discussed in more detail under Tense Problems (below). In addition, you should point out the connection between the counter in one sentence and the refutation in the next.

C. Pattern #4: Recognizing the epistemic nature of idiomatic phrases ("For all we know . . . ," "As best we can tell . . .").

D. Pattern #8 (Unmarked): With no marker, it is hard to distinguish hypothesis from fact. One way of doing this is by presenting a passage containing both factual statements and unmarked hypotheses and having students distinguish between them.

E. Pattern #9 (Grouped Hypotheses). Teaching students to recognize the difference between sequential and mixed hypotheses.

TENSE PROBLEMS. Compound tenses in hypotheses are a further signal of their truth and untruth. Compound verb forms in the past (active or passive) are untrue, those in the present, almost always true. For example:

Many igneous rocks *are thought to have originated* by partial melting of the upper mantle.

Such sediments *are believed to have been deposited* during glacial ages.

A Great Chain of Being *was seen to extend* from the lowest forms, to humans, to spiritual beings. Each kind of being, or species as it was called, *was seen to have* a separate fixed place in the divine order of things. The tiny grains *were thought to have become joined together* to form chromosomes.

Traditionally, the ancestors of these [early] plants *are thought to have evolved* from aquatic cells that also gave rise to green algae.

Notice that the last example *is* in the present. Yet, the statement is untrue. This is indicated by the counter word *(traditionally)* as sentence opener (Pattern #5). Interestingly, hypotheses with compound past tense verbs often appear with counter words, almost as if the writer feels the need for additional negative emphasis to supplement the tortuous verb construction. Whatever the reason, the construction is so daunting for the nonnative speaker that it demands special attention.

Conclusion

Hypotheses play an important role in introductory science texts and in the practice of science in general. Accordingly, whether one is a working scientist or is teaching children, adult native speakers, or foreign science students, it is necessary to develop a command of this vital tool of scientific method—for purposes of both reading comprehension and writing. That command includes an understanding of the diverse elements that go into hypotheses—elements such as: observations and assumptions, generalization and prediction, experiment and induction.

The variety of patterns that hypotheses appear in can pose problems for the second-language learner. For writing, it is probably best to concentrate on the three most common patterns, while exposing students to a wider range for reading purposes. Even for native speakers, especially younger students, it is helpful for them to command a selection of patterns.

There are also important lexical considerations involved in mastering the forms and functions of hypotheses. These considerations include an appreciation of synonyms and near-synonyms that mark ideas as hypotheses. They include an awareness of the verbal things that are done with hypotheses: Hypotheses are formulated, tested, and either accepted or rejected. Finally, there is the problem of hedges and the bewildering range of lexical and syntactic forms they appear in.

Ultimately, the whole enterprise turns on the concept of *tentativeness*. It is really mastering the idea of tentativeness—in reading, in writing, and in our own thought process—that helps us develop hypotheses as a fine tool for solving problems of scientific inquiry . . . and of life in general.

Chapter 7

The Language of Experiments

❋

Ever since Galileo, experiment has been the hallmark of modern science. Research in the history and philosophy of science features many studies of classical experiments and the development of experimental method. To date, however, little has been written on the language of experiments per se. Though commonalities exist, there are, in truth, *several* languages of experiments, depending on the genre one is dealing with. These genres include: school- and university-level textbooks, lab manuals, lectures and research presentations, scientists' research notes, and research articles (both review and experimental articles).

As genres, the science research article in general and the experimental article in particular have received a lot of attention through the works of Swales (1990) and Bazerman (1989). Swales's volume (117–176) examines the structure of the research article at the discourse level of Introduction-Method-Results-Discussion. He also summarizes a range of studies at the syntactic and lexical levels, none of them dealing specifically with experiments. Bazerman's 1989 study dealt with the evolution of the experimental report and the social, psychological, and, to a slightly lesser extent, the rhetorical considerations that help shape it.

For several reasons, this chapter will focus on the language of experiments in university-level science texts and laboratory manuals. For one thing, university texts (and lab manuals) serve a wider variety of functions than school texts: as Halliday and Martin (1993) point out, the main purpose of reporting experiments in school texts is exemplifying selected facts. In addition, university-level texts are more likely to be encountered by non-native speakers studying science in English-medium institutions. And finally, unless the student becomes a professional scientist, there is less chance of his or her reading research articles in scientific journals.

Introduction

This chapter will begin with a definition of the term *experiment,* followed by a brief discussion of various kinds and functions of experiments. We will then examine the parts, or elements, of an experiment, including the place of observation, hypotheses, experimental design, measurement, and evaluation.

From there, we will explore the language of experiments. Our corpus is drawn from three introductory science texts: one each in biology (Starr 1984), chemistry (Hein et al. 1993), and physics (Ohanian 1989), plus laboratory manuals in physics and chemistry (Wilson 1981 and Hein 1992, respectively). We will analyze the treatment of experiments in these texts, at the levels of discourse, syntax, and vocabulary, in order to discover patterns, peculiarities, and potential problems in understanding.

Finally, I'd like to offer a few comments and suggestions on teaching the language of experiments, including some problem areas and selection of materials.

Definition, Functions, and Kinds of Experiments

Among the many definitions of experiments, the most recurring elements mentioned are *observation, hypothesis,* and the *artificial* quality of experimental *control and manipulation.* Wartofsky, for example, defines an experiment as "observation controlled by the framework of scientific hypothesis" (Wartofsky 1968, 190), while philosopher L. S. Stebbings's definition is "deliberate observation in the light of a definite expectation as to what will be observed" (1933, 302). The term *expectation* can be read *hypothesis.* Tweney, Wartofsky, and Ziman all emphasize the artificial nature of experiments, which Tweney considers "an essential feature of the experimental method, one that provides both its power and weakness" (1981, 409), while Ziman asserts that "modern science is largely founded on the results of experiments, where the natural world is deliberately interfered with in order to observe the consequences" (1984, 22). Psychologist William Ray considers the experimenter "an interventionist, one who deliberately and systematically introduces change into natural processes and then observes the consequences of those changes" (1960, 6). These and other features of experiments, as well as their relation to our corpus, will be explored more fully in the next main section.

Functions and Kinds of Experiments

Experiments serve essentially three functions. We can characterize these functions as (1) *inductive,* (2) *deductive,* and (3) *illustrative.*

1. INDUCTIVE. In the inductive function, the hypothesis, result, or conclusion grows from the experiment: experiment → hypothesis. This is often the case with chemistry, in which various compounds are

brought together under controlled conditions and their reactions carefully observed.

2. DEDUCTIVE. Hypothesis → experiment. The deductive function of experiments is to test a hypothesis. As we will see later, this is a major function of experiments in physics and physics texts. It is especially true in the areas of quantum and subatomic physics, where the objects of investigation are too small for direct observation. For this reason, the researcher often starts with a theoretical or mathematical model, which is then examined in the experiment.

3. ILLUSTRATIVE. The purpose of this function is to illustrate or demonstrate a theory that has been worked out mathematically or in some other theoretical way to the satisfaction of the investigator. A classic example—as we have seen—is Galileo's inclined plane experiment demonstrating the Law of Descent, which states that heavy bodies start to fall slowly and gradually accelerate. Galileo had proven this mathematically, but there was need to demonstrate this to a less sophisticated audience. This he did by constructing a diagonally sloping plane containing a groove for the gradual descent of a ball, with equal sections marked out along the path (Galilei 1974 [1638], 84–90). From the works in our corpus, this illustrative function is by far the most common in the physics text, which is more concerned with laws and theories than with detailed descriptions of experiments. Such lack of details seems characteristic of physics texts in general (Trigg 1975, vii).

Just as there are different functions of experiments, so we find several different *kinds* of experiments. Those in our corpus include *controlled experiments,* and, to a far lesser extent, *imaginary,* or *thought, experiments.*

CONTROLLED EXPERIMENTS. The most common kind of real-world experiment is the *controlled experiment,* in which one or more hypotheses or samples are subjected to varying conditions, and the results carefully observed and recorded. This is especially common in biology texts (Beveridge 1957, 35), including ours, and less so in the physics textbook, with chemistry somewhere between the two.

IMAGINARY, OR THOUGHT, EXPERIMENTS. A thought experiment, as the name implies, is conducted in the mind instead of the laboratory, using words and logic for its only tools. It is based on an imagined experimental situation and governed totally by theoretical principles. Such thought experiments were important for Galileo's work and are central to the changing world of modern physics, specifically in the areas of relativity and quantum mechanics.

Thought experiments per se are rare in our corpus, occurring only twice in the physics text (Ohanian 1989, 4, 507). We do, however, find the same conceptual approach in the framing of hypotheses, notably in the developmental sections of our biology text (Starr 1984, 28, 181, 503, 507, 515, 596, 696). In both cases, the speculations are introduced by words like *suppose* or *imagine,* or by questions starting with *What if . . . ? Could . . . ? Was . . . ?* An example from the physics text involves the potential collision rate of gas molecules. The theoretical apparatus is a cylinder with a diameter twice the width of the molecules, in which the particles are traveling back and forth:

> Since the molecules must come to within a distance of 2R [radii] of another molecule to suffer a collision, we must *imagine* that the molecule sweeps out of a tube of radius 2R and engages in a collision whenever the center or another molecule lies within this tube. (Ohanian 1989, 507)

Elements of an Experiment

The elements of an experiment are partly sequential, partly *recursive.* The stimulus for an experiment may come from an hypothesis *or* an observation; either may come first. Once the need for experiment is felt, however, the next step is to set up an experimental design, which may include: establishing controls, variables, and apparatus. Provision is then made for measuring and recording one's information. The final step involves evaluation, through probability, prediction, or replication. Thus we have:

- observation or
- hypothesis
- experimental design: controls, variables, apparatus
- measurement and recording
- evaluation: probability, prediction, replication

This section will briefly examine each of these elements, their interrelationships, and their occurrence in our corpus.

Observation and Experiment

Let us take observation to mean apprehension of the external world by any of our senses. Observation is a necessary part of experiments, although the opposite is not necessarily true: many observational discoveries are made without experiment. Distinction is sometimes made between experimental sciences (physics, chemistry, "functional" biology) and nonexperimental sciences (evolutionary biology, paleontology, comparative anatomy, anthropology, and, to a great extent, astronomy). Probably the greatest work based almost wholly on observation was Darwin's *Origin of Species*.

Observation may be both a reason for designing an experiment and an integral part of conducting it. One reason for designing an experiment is eliminating as many extraneous conditions (controlled variables) as possible, so that relationships between phenomena are revealed through careful observation. It has been argued, however, that even the most experimental sciences, such as physics, contain an unavoidable element of observation. As Philip Goldstein points out, the first test of Newton's Laws came from astronomical observation, though those Laws were later elaborated in laboratory experiments.

OBSERVATION AND HYPOTHESES. Many scientists and philosophers of science have commented on the relationship between observation and hypothesis. Observation is *governed* by hypothesis, *before, during,* and *after* an experiment. At the start of an inquiry, before an experiment begins, it is necessary to limit one's range of observation. The element that delimits that frame of inquiry is the theory or hypothesis. As the nineteenth-century American geologist T. C. Chamberlin remarked:

> No one who goes into the field with a mind merely receptive, or merely alert to see what presents itself, however nerved to a high effort, will return laden with all that might be seen. Only a part of the elements and aspects of complex phenomena present themselves at once to even the best observational minds. . . . To make a reasonably complete set of observations, the mind must not only see what spontaneously arrests its attention, but it must immediately draw out from what it observes, inferences, interpretations, and hypotheses, to promote further observation. (Chamberlin, in Tweney 1981, 101)

There is widespread agreement in scientific literature on the constant need to interpret one's observations in light of hypothesis. The hypothesis helps *organize* observation at all stages of the experiment. Sometimes a hypothesis (or mental model) so dominates an experiment that the investigator ignores items that do not fit into the image. Physicist Martin Deutsch was struck by the degree to which colleagues' mental models in a nuclear physics lab often determined the outcome of their experiments (Deutsch, in Lerner 1959, 96).

OBSERVATION AND MEASUREMENT. With the increasing sophistication of instruments and the growth of microphysics, direct sense observation is replaced more and more by a reading and adjusting of measuring apparatus. Philosopher of science Max Wartofsky goes as far as to suggest that all measurement and observation have become relatively indirect. This tendency is especially strong in the field of subatomic physics, in which direct observation is no longer possible, and the chief guide to investigation becomes a hypothesis, or more specifically a theoretical model. We have here, in Martin Deutsch's words, "a situation in which the experiment is carried out under conditions in which almost all sense impressions concerning its operation are irrelevant to the question investigated" (Deutsch, in Lerner 1959, 99).

Hypothesis and Experiment

Like observation, hypotheses are intimately linked to experiments. As we saw earlier, a hypothesis may lead to an experiment, an experiment may suggest a hypothesis, or both. Thus we have: hypothesis → experiment → hypothesis. In fact, a major function of experiments is hypothesis testing (deductive), a viewpoint strongly argued by Karl Popper and others.

At the same time, it is common for experiments to suggest new hypotheses. Newton was especially forceful on the priority of experiment over hypothesis. One need only recall the often-quoted line from his *Opticks:* "We are certainly not to relinquish the evidence of experiments for the sake of dreams and vain fictions of our own devising [i.e., hypotheses]" (Newton 1952 [1730]).

A further role of hypotheses is that of helping design and interpret an experiment. In actual laboratory studies, hypotheses are usually tested in pairs, with one the rival of the other. This in turn leads to the need for experimental and control groups and the number or types of variables. The hypothesis can further help the investigator interpret an otherwise confusing mass of data resulting from the experiment.

Experimental Design

The key elements in designing an experiment are: *control* and *test groups,* and *controlled, dependent,* and *independent variables.* In the life sciences, one encounters *placebos* and *blind* and *double blind* experiments. Little if any of this vocabulary shows up in the regular prose of the textbooks or manuals. The concept of control groups appears five times in the texts (Starr 1984, 23, 193, 295, 297, 299), but two instances are in picture text (the paragraph following a caption, which describes a picture) and one in a nontext insert discussing the process of scientific inquiry itself. That same insert contains the only reference to the different kinds of variables (Starr 1984, 23). None of the other concepts is labeled as such, though of course there appear many instances of control and experimental groups with different classes of variables. As for apparatus and instruments, the next main section will outline the pattern normally used for describing them. In general, however, it is fair to conclude that the language of experimental design is given rather slight treatment in both textbooks and manuals.

Measurement and Recording

As we will also see in the next main section, the measurement language for experiments, in the laboratory manuals, is contained almost exclusively in verbs *(calibrate, compare, compute)* and adverbials ("Measure the distance *to the nearest 0.1 cm"*), plus a limited range of verbs for recording *(note, describe, record)*. Commonly measured quantities in the chemistry manual include mass, length, volume, pressure, temperature, and time (Hein 1993, 15).

One of the more common forms of measurement in our corpus involves *comparison,* in which the investigator compares usually two, occasionally more, items. Professor Lee Kok Cheong suggests that "for every comparative sentence, there is an implied measurement" (1978, 241). While this is not completely supported in our analysis of the chemistry text, the role of measurement is often significant in experiments involving comparisons. All of the introductory textbooks, however, tend to use nonmathematical quantities in describing experiments of comparisons, rather than exact numbers. The biology text uses phrases like the following:

> elongation proceeds *about as fast as it does* in an intact coleoptile (Starr 1984, 293; emphasis added)

> . . . cells often elongate *faster* after application of [the hormone] gibberellin (Starr 1984, 293; emphasis added)

> They [the leaves] had *longer* stems, *smaller* leaves, and *smaller* root systems. . . . When the surface of a mature leaf is painted with a cytokinins solution, the leaf often remains green *longer*. (Starr 1984, 295, 299; emphasis added)

Presumably, exact numbers were used (where applicable) in the original research articles, and the authors felt that such a high degree of specificity was not needed in a textbook.

Evaluation

Another important element of experiments is *evaluation:* the way or ways of verifying their results. Evaluation can be done through *replication, probability* (statistical and otherwise), and *prediction.* The most frequent reference in our corpus is to replication—a statement that the experiment has been repeated several times with like results. Here are several examples, including Galileo's experiment testing whether rates of free fall for different kinds of bodies are exactly the same. Long after Galileo's original experiment:

a series of much more precise . . . experiments were performed early in this century by Lorand Eötvös . . . *The most recent* . . . *experiments have verified* that the rates . . . are equal to within 1 part in 10^{12}. (Ohanian 1989, 233; emphasis added)

Many generations of the progeny of these cells *have continued to* express the foreign allele (alternate gene) and produce normal hemoglobin. (Starr 1984, 244; emphasis added)

Such experiments have been repeated many times . . . *The results invariably* show that all building blocks in living systems . . . can form under abiotic conditions. (Starr 1984, 502; emphasis added)

He [Becquerel] *repeated the experiment many times* in total darkness and obtained the same results, *proving that* . . . (Hein 1993, 456; emphasis added)

However, like the language of experimental design, the element of evaluation is not stressed in our corpus.

The Language of Experiments

The language of experiments differs somewhat between introductory textbooks and laboratory manuals. In general, we can identify three levels for both genres:

1. the discourse or section level
2. the sentence level
3. the lexical level

In Textbooks

Discourse-Level Pattern

At the discourse level, textbook descriptions of experiments include some or all of the following features:

1. A FRAMEWORK. This may be the broader topic or inquiry that the experiment fits into. The framework may be a heading or subhead, a few sentences, or the better part of a paragraph. It is normally in the present tense.

2. A FOCUS. The focus concentrates the reader more narrowly on the upcoming experiment. It may be in the form of a hypothesis or some other kind of statement that explains the purpose of the experiment. Statements of purpose are often written as a noun phrase *(Effect of daylight on plant growth . . .)*. If it is historical, it often includes the name of the scientist involved.

3. A Description of the Experiment. The description contains the procedure followed, including the instruments or apparatus. It is interesting that about 60% of the experiments in the chemistry text were descriptions of historical investigations, and were thus chiefly in the past tense.

4. Conclusion. The conclusion describes the immediate results of the experiment. If it is historical, the conclusion is normally in the past tense.

5. Generalization. Sometimes the experiment provides the basis for a more general statement, which usually appears in the present tense.

6. A Visual. The visual and its subtext play a special part in the overall pattern. Sometimes the subtext will describe the experiment *and* state the results. In the following example (illustration omitted), a picture contains three flower pots, the one at the left containing a very short plant, the remaining two, plants that are progressively taller:

> Figure 19.16. [Focus] Effect of the relative length of day and night on Douglas fir plant growth. [Description] The plant at the left was exposed to twelve-hour light and twelve-hour darkness for a year: [result/conclusion] its buds became dormant because daylength was too short. (Starr 1984, 300)

More commonly, the subtext provides a description of the experiment, and the results are presented by the visual. In the following example, the *only* place where the results are presented is in the visual. The caption is often unmarked; that is, it is stated in plain type and not set off from the subtext. It normally serves as the focus. The illustration (omitted) contains photographs of three pairs of plants:

> Figure 19.13. [Focus] Effect of daylength on flowering of short-day plants and long-day plants. [Description] In each photograph, the plant on the left was grown under short-day conditions, the plant on the right was grown under long-day conditions. (Starr 1984, 298)

While some experiments appear in "canonical form," with all six elements (framework, focus, description, conclusions, generalization, visual), most do not. In addition, the sequence is not always fixed. While the discourse of experiments normally follows the pattern of framework, focus, description, conclusion, generalization, there are instances in which a generalization appears after the framework and before the introduction and description, as in the following example:

> [Framework] Thigmorphogenesis [in plants] is a response to mechanical stress, [generalization] the result generally being an inhibition of overall plant

growth. [Focus] Contact with rain, grazing animals, farm machinery . . . causes this plant response. . . . [Description] Shaking a plant daily for a brief period can do the same thing. (Starr 1984, 297)

Here is a good example of the sequence. Notice how the focus narrows progressively from framework to focus to description:

[Framework] Nutritionists face the difficult problem of deciding the kinds of nutrients that should be in a diet. They often establish dietary needs by correlating physical well-being with nutrient consumption. [Focus] James Lind, a physician in the British Navy during the middle of the 18th century, was one of the first to use this approach. [Description] In a study of scurvy, a disease that affected sailors on long voyages, he placed seamen who suffered from scurvy, on various diets, some of which contained citrus fruits. By observing changes in the conditions of the seamen, Lind was able to conclude that [conclusion/generalization] citrus fruits provide a nutrient that prevents scurvy. (Hein 1993, 872)

INSTRUMENTS AND APPARATUS. In textbooks, the discourse-level description of instruments and apparatus takes the following pattern:

1. the name of the instrument or apparatus
2. its function
3. a physical description of it
4. a description of its operation
5. a visual

The following passage, along with a picture of the instrument, illustrates the pattern:

Radiation from radioactive sources is so energetic that it is called ionizing radiation. When it strikes an atom or a molecule, one or more electrons are knocked off, and an ion is created. [Function] One of the common instruments used to detect and measure radioactivity, [name] the Geiger counter, depends on this fact. [Description] It consists of a Geiger-Müller detecting tube and a counting device. The detector tube is a pair of oppositely charged electrodes in an argon gas–filled chamber fitted with a window. [Operation] When radiation, such as a beta particle, passes through the window into the tube, some argon is ionized . . . (Hein 1993, 467)

Syntactic Patterns

Each of the textbooks uses three syntactic patterns for describing or talking about experiments. Each pattern expresses a different aspect of the experiment, specifically, *its purpose, procedure (description),* and *result (conclusion):*

Pattern #1. Pattern #1 presents the *reason,* or *purpose,* for the experiment:

	A	B	C	
One may	design	conduct	replicate	an experiment
	devise	run, do	repeat	
	create	perform	confirm	

The words in groups A and B need additional information to complete their meaning (the reason for the experiment). That information appears in the preceding sentence or at the end of the pattern:

> [Ernest] Rutherford used alpha particles [purpose] to establish the nuclear nature of the atom. In experiments *performed* in 1911, he directed a stream of positively charged helium ions [alpha particles] at a very thin sheet of gold foil. (Hein 1993, 94; emphasis added)

Sometimes a B word will anticipate the result:

> The classical experiment proving that alpha and beta particles are oppositely charged *was performed* by Marie Curie. (Hein 1993, 460; emphasis added)

The referent of the words in group C is tacit: the experiment is repeated in order to test its original results:

> Such experiments have been *repeated* many times. . . . The results invariably show that all the building blocks in living systems . . . can form under abiotic conditions. (Starr 1984, 502; emphasis added)

Pattern #2. Pattern #2 expresses both *procedure* (description) and *result:*

If/When/After you do X,	Y happens.
Y happens	when you do X:

When extra hydrogen ions are added to the water, the excess quickly combines with the bicarbonate. (Starr 1984, 47; emphasis added)

Crystals of table salt (NaCl) separate into N+ and Cl− *when* they are placed in water. (Starr 1984, 88; emphasis added)

Pattern #3. Pattern #3 emphasizes the *results* (conclusion) of an experiment:

Physicists	found that . . .	(altitude does not affect them).
Smith	discovered	
Experiments	indicate	

Experiments	prove	(altitude does not affect them).
	show	
	suggest	
	verify	

Experiments with beta rays *show* that negative beta particles are nothing but high-speed anti-electrons. (Ohanian 1989, 2; emphasis added)

Brenner *discovered* that one or two extra nucleotides inserted in the middle of a gene made the protein it specified completely defective. (Starr 1984, 214; emphasis added)

Pattern #3 is especially common in the physics text, which tends to focus more on results (conclusions) than on detailed descriptions of experiments. This follows from our earlier observation that experiments in physics are often designed to prove or illustrate theories rather than discover new information. Here is another example of Pattern #3:

The failure of absolute time was explicitly *verified* in delicate experiments with very accurate atomic and nuclear clocks. Physicists *found* that even when these clocks are moved with high speeds or lifted to high altitude above the Earth, they lose or gain time relative to clocks at rest on the surface of the Earth. (Ohanian 1989, 4; emphasis added)

Lexical Items

We have already examined some of the various collocations that appear with the word *experiment*. The corpus also reveals several synonyms or near-synonyms, such as: *experimental demonstration, experimental investigation,* and *experimental test*. We also find collocations that appear in more than one part of speech, the most common being: *investigate, demonstrate,* and *observe*:

- investigate, investigating, investigation
- demonstrate, demonstrating, demonstration
- observe, observing, observation

Others include *control* (to control for variables, a control group, a controlled experiment) and *replicate* (replicate, replication, replicable).

In Laboratory Manuals

Discourse-Level Patterns

There is only one prominent discourse-level pattern in the laboratory manuals, and that appears in the physics manual. In addition to a reference to a visual, that pattern involves the use of alphabetic symbols, presented in the following rhetorical sequence:

A. reference to a *visual:*

As shown in *Figure 14.4* . . . (Wilson 1981, 133; emphasis added)

B. a *definition* of symbols:

As shown in Figure 14.4, a force F applied tangentially to the wheel with a radius R can lift a load w by means of a string or rope wrapped around the axle. (Wilson 1981, 133; emphasis added)

C. an *equation* containing those symbols:

Considering the magnitude of the force of friction f to be proportional to the magnitude of the load or normal force N, we may write

$$f \propto N$$

or

$$f = \mu N \text{ (Wilson 1981, 103; emphasis added)}$$

D. followed by *definitions* of other symbols used in the equation:

The actual mechanical advantage (AMA) of a machine is defined as

$$AMA = \backslash FF_o/F_i$$

where F_o and F_i are the actual output and input forces, respectively. (Wilson 1981, 131; emphasis added)

At times some of the symbols used in an equation may not have been mentioned for at least a page. This lack of an immediate referent could conceivably cause comprehension problems.

Syntactic Patterns

Syntactically, the language of experiments in the chemistry manual is dominated by six major patterns, five of them containing *imperatives*. The sixth includes imperatives and other forms as well. Semantically, we have one major set and a subset. All five express the imperative. Patterns #4 and #5, additionally, express the *manner* and *degree* of the procedure:

1. Subordinate clause, imperative sentence.

- While the tube is cooling *dry* a piece of cobalt chloride test paper. (Hein 1992, 40; emphasis added)
- After the filtration is completed *take* the filter cone . . . (Hein 1992, 8; emphasis added)

2. Imperative sentence, -ING verbal _____.
   -ING verbal ____, imperative sentence.
   - Proceed as in the above paragraph *using* enough tubing to handle it from both ends. (Hein 1992, 4; emphasis added)
   - Fit the open filter cone into a funnel, *placing* the torn edge next to the glass. (Hein 1992, 7; emphasis added)
   - *Leaving* the cover plate on the mouth of the lower bottle, raise the top bottle straight up. (Hein 1992, 34; emphasis added)
3. A series of imperatives. Groups of sequenced imperatives take two forms. The first is a triplet separated by commas:

   Remove the tubing from the flame, *bend* to the desired shape, and *set aside* to cool on the Ceram-fab pad. (Hein 1992, 4; emphasis added)

Since laboratory procedures often involve a lengthy sequence of steps, the first group may serve as preface to a longer set, which appears in the form of separate sentences:

   Mix them together, *transfer* to the ignition tube, and *spread* the mixture out so that it covers about one-third of the tube. *Insert* the stopper . . . *Insert* the end of the delivery tube . . . *Adjust* the burner . . . (Hein 1992, 24; emphasis added)

Extended sequences employ all of the other patterns, in order to achieve a degree of stylistic variety.

4. Sentence-initial adverbial (mostly -ly adverbs) + imperative sentence.
   - *Completely* fill five wide-mouth bottles with water. (Hein 1992, 24; emphasis added)
   - *Accurately* weigh a clean, dry crucible and cover. (Hein 1992, 41; emphasis added)
5. Imperative sentence + by + verb+ing (adverbial of manner).
   - Remove it from the flame and bend *by grasping* with tongs or by inserting the tang of a file . . . (Hein 1992, 4; emphasis added)
   - Dry a piece of cobalt chloride test paper *by holding* it about 20 cm above a burner flame. (Hein 1992, 40; emphasis added)
6. Deleted/Elliptical Forms. Though not a syntactic pattern as such, there are a *great* number of sentences containing *deleted,* or *elliptical,* forms. Deleted sentences are used to express sequences and other functions. Nearly all the deletions occur in direct objects and articles:
   - Insert [the] stopper and shake [it] gently for about 20 seconds. (Hein 1992, 55)

- Wet [the filter] with distilled water. . . . Fold [it] in half. . . . Crease [the] paper slightly. . . . Fold [it] in quarters. (Hein 1992, 7)
- Transfer the crystals to a watch glass, cover [them] with filter paper and finish drying [them] by storing [them] in your locker. . . . Then reweigh [them] and determine the weight of [the] aspirin. (Hein 1992, 241)

Lexical Level

The chemistry and physics manuals are structured somewhat differently. The thrust of the physics manual is to illustrate various physical theories. Accordingly, it contains a lot more description and explanation and far fewer instructions. Compared to the chemistry manual, which exhibits several additional areas of heavy lexical clustering, the physics manual primarily employs verbs of *measuring* and *recording (calculate, compute, determine, mark, measure, plot, record),* and to a lesser extent verbs of *placing (add, attach, hang, suspend, tighten)* and of *fine adjustment (adjust, pivot, rotate).*

The chemistry manual contains several areas of lexical interest, some normative, some unique to the genre, and some problematic. For one thing, we find a large number of -ly adverbs of *manner,* in sentence-initial position *(accurately, carefully, continuously, immediately).* These supply the lexical material for the opening position in Pattern #4 (sentence-initial adverb + imperative sentence):

> *Accurately* weigh a clean, dry crucible and cover. (Hein 1992, 41; emphasis added)

In addition, the corpus contains many adverbials of manner in the form *by + verb+ing* (by adding/comparing/grasping/holding/inserting/placing/ pressing/storing/treating). These supply the lexical material for the final element of Pattern #5 (imperative sentence + by + verb+ing):

> Remove excess moisture from the casein *by pressing the precipitate* between absorbent paper. (Hein 1992, 273; emphasis added)

Another adverbial cluster in the manual is that of *time,* an essential element in many chemistry experiments. (Warm the tube for a minute or two. Take accurate temperature readings at 30-second intervals. Shake vigorously for about 40 seconds.)

WARNINGS. One of the most characteristic features in the chemistry manual is that of *warnings,* which appear in various forms. For one thing, they occur as different parts of speech. They can be verbs *(avoid, be care-*

ful, do not, don't use, note, take care) or nouns *(caution, danger, precaution)*. They can be adjectives *(hazardous, important, protective)* or adverbials *(carefully, never)*. We also find the frequent use of *boldface* to indicate warnings. In addition, the manual employs an exclamation mark at the end of a sentence (!), or an exclamation point inside a triangle, to indicate danger. One may also find multiple signals to indicate procedures especially susceptible to accident. The following example contains a total of five warnings and emphasizers: (1) an exclamation point in a triangle, (2) the word *caution*, (3) in capitals, (4) the imperative *do not*, and (5) boldfaced text:

⚠ CAUTION: **Do not put your head over the tube while the sodium is reacting.** (Hein 1992, 32; emphasis added)

WORDS IN DUAL FORM. The chemistry manual reveals a high incidence of words that appear in both noun and verb form. Many of these words, while somewhat common in their noun form, are *rare* as verbs, and thus pose potential comprehension problems, particularly for the non-native speaker. The corpus includes verbs such as: *bubble* (as a passive), *catalyze, centrifuge, decant, denature, ester, pipet, stopper* (again, as a verb), *titrate*, and *zero*. Here are a few examples in context:

- The oxygen produced from the hydrogen peroxide *is bubbled* into the cylinder.
- *Centrifuge* the plasma sample . . . for about five minutes.
- *Decant* the . . . liquid through filter paper in a funnel.
- *Pipet* 3.0 mL of 3 % hydrogen peroxide . . . and quickly *stopper*.
- This solution is used to *zero* the instrument.

Most of these verbs may also be considered *verbs of handling*, that is, verbs that tell the student what action to perform. In addition to these more obscure terms, there are better-known verbs of handling: *adjust, attach, dissolve, fasten, insert, place, pour, shake*.

MEASUREMENT LANGUAGE. Clearly, a major element in the language of experiments is *measurement*. In the manuals we have examined, measurement is expressed chiefly as verbs and adverbials. Among the verbs of measurement are: *add, adjust, calculate, calibrate, compare, determine, make calculations, take a reading, weigh*. Adverbials normally occur in phrases:

- Roll the sheet of paper into a cylinder *small enough to pass through the mouth of the flask*. (Hein 1992, 281; emphasis added)

- Mix a quantity of casein *about the size of a pea* with the appropriate amount of water (3-5mL). (Hein 1992, 273; emphasis added)
- Measure the distance *to the nearest o.1 cm*. (Hein 1992, 282; emphasis added)

Statements of measurements appear in different places in a sentence:

- The results of the last two weighings *should agree within o.05 g*. (Hein 1992, 42; emphasis added)
- Take *accurate* temperature readings at 30-second intervals. (Hein 1992, 42; emphasis added)

As we can see from the above examples, measurement language can be specific or general, mathematical (to the nearest o.1 cm, within o.05 g,) or nonmathematical *(small enough to pass through the mouth of the flask, about the size of a pea)*.

Apart from these more significant categories, we find smaller semantic groups that are integral to experimental activities. These include words for *reactions (converted, disappear, indicate, produces, react, reacts to form, substrate)* and a short list of verbs for observing, describing, and recording *(describe, note, observe, plot, record)*.

Teaching the Language of Experiments

In teaching the language of experiments, a major factor to keep in mind is that of audience. That audience may be: mainstream elementary, secondary, or university students; the disadvantaged; or non-native speakers. Clearly, there are some different linguistic and conceptual presuppositions when dealing with a Chinese university student and a disadvantaged secondary school native speaker of English. Apart from the fact that our corpus consists exclusively of university-level material, the study up to this point has been chiefly text-based, not reader-based.

For reasons mentioned at the beginning of the chapter, I have argued that introductory university-level texts represent the fullest development of the language of experiments, that they contain the broadest range of linguistic and rhetorical forms used to express that language. For that reason, I hope the foregoing analysis will be helpful to all those involved in the teaching of science at any level, or language specialists in study skills, content-area teaching, or English as a Second Language.

In analyzing the language of experiments, I have followed what seems to be an intuitively satisfying procedure of going from discourse to syntactic to lexical level, where possible. Teaching the language of experiments involves the inevitable mixing of different levels. Still, let us hold to the original structure where we can.

At the Discourse Level

As we have seen, the major discourse pattern in our textbooks involves the sequence: *framework-focus-description-conclusion-generalization-visual*. To improve students' comprehension, one would do well to include various reading passages containing these features, in descriptions of experiments, and give students practice in identifying them. Awareness of these features, and their normal sequence, should be of help for writing purposes as well.

As for visuals, subtext, and body text, we often find a special reciprocity among them. While the different discourse features may be presented in the body text, the subtext may also describe the experiment and state the results. Sometimes the visual is the *only* place where the results are presented (Starr 1984, 298). For these reasons, and especially the last, it is worth calling attention to these reciprocal and sometimes redundant features. This can be done by an *explication de texte;* also by including reading samples containing the three items (visual, subtext, and body text) and having students locate different elements in the different sources.

As for descriptions of instruments and apparatus, it is probably worth including a few sample descriptions containing the pattern (name of instrument–function–physical description–description of operation–visual) (Hein 1993, 467) and having students identify the parts:

1. name: _____
2. function: _____
3. physical description: _____
4. operation: _____

The last discourse-level item in our corpus derives from the laboratory manuals and follows the pattern: (a) reference to visual, (b) definition of symbols, (c) equation containing symbols, and (d) further reference to symbols in equation. One potential problem is that some of the symbols in the equation (c) are not always defined in parts *b* or *d,* but earlier on, sometimes as far as a page previously. It is worth checking to see that students understand those undefined symbols and pointing out their most recent occurrence in the text.

At the Syntactic Level

At the syntactic level, we have observed two sets of patterns and the vocabulary needed to produce them. The first set, essentially three patterns, is found in the textbooks and expresses some of the basic semantic elements in the language of experiments: the reason (or purpose) for the experiment, description of the experimental procedure, and the results (conclusion) of the experiment. They are reproduced here for easy reference:

Pattern #1. Reason (or purpose) of the experiment: One may design conduct replicate an experiment.

Pattern #2. Procedure (description) and result:
If/When/After you do X, Y happens.
Y happens after you do X.

Pattern #3. Result (conclusion) of the experiment:

Physicists	found	that	(altitude does not affect them).
Experiments	show		
	discovered		

Since we have here only three patterns and a limited number of words connected with them, it is worth teaching both syntax and lexis, at the very least for receptive (reading) purposes.

The second set (five patterns) appears in the laboratory manuals, and all express imperatives:

1. After the filtration is completed, *take* the filter cone . . .
2. Fit the open filter cone into a funnel, *placing* the torn edge next to the glass.
3. A sequence: *Mix* them together, *transfer* to the ignition tube, and *spread* the mixture.

Patterns #4 and #5, additionally, express the *degree* and *manner* of the procedure:

4. *Completely* fill five wide-mouth bottles with water.
5. Remove it from the flame and bend by *grasping* with tongs.

Syntactically, Patterns #1, #2, and #3 seem pretty straightforward and should pose no serious comprehension problems. Pattern #4 deserves a bit of attention, partly because it is not commonly found in speech. The irregularity lies in the sentence-opener adverb, but fortunately, there are a limited number of words found in that slot *(accurately, carefully, completely, continuously, very gently, immediately, slowly)*. The only potential difficulty in Pattern #5 is the form and position of the adverbial of manner. Again, we find a limited number of words, no more than a dozen, the most common being *by adding* and *by placing,* and including others such as *grasping, holding, inserting, pressing.*

At the Lexical Level

An item that we treated earlier under syntax, but which would fit just as well under lexis, is the matter of deleted, or elliptical, forms. As we have seen, they are extremely common in the lab manuals (especially chemistry) and occur almost wholly in the deletion of articles and direct objects. There are a few potential problems with these elliptical forms. For one thing, they provide an erroneous model for the reader, for writing purposes. For another, deletion of the direct object may conceivably create ambiguity in the referent:

- Transfer the crystals to a watch glass, cover (   ) with filter paper. (Hein 1992, 241)
- Casein is released from its salts and precipitated from nonfat milk by treating (   ) with dilute acetic . . . acid. (Hein 1992, 271)

And finally, they may sometimes cause confusion in identifying a part of speech:

- Cover open just enough to let gas escape. (Hein 1992, 41) [Comment: Does this mean "Leave the cover open just enough . . ." or "The cover is open just enough . . ."? Fortunately, the accompanying drawing helps establish the meaning *in this case*.]
- Insert a thermometer in the cork and *position* in the test tube. (Hein 1992, 46; emphasis added) [Comment: Is *position* a noun or verb?]

DUAL FORMS. Another potential lexical problem is what we referred to earlier as words in dual form. This is the widespread practice, in the chemistry manual, of using, in noun and verb form, words that are fairly common as nouns but rare as verbs:

- If the liberation of gas is slow, *stopper* the tube loosely. (Hein 1992, 83; emphasis added)
- This solution is used to *zero* the instrument. (Hein 1992, 265; emphasis added)
- The oxygen produced from the hydrogen peroxide decomposition *is bubbled* into the cylinder. (Hein 1992, 306; emphasis added) [rare in passive voice]

Or words that are rare in both forms:

- Since cholesterol is an alcohol, it can be *esterified*. A major portion of blood cholesterol exists as *esters* of fatty acid. (Hein 1992, 306; emphasis added)

- Rinse *pipet* and *pipet* 2.0 mL of the solution . . . into the cooled hydrogen peroxide and mix quickly. . . . Using a *pipet*, add 2.0 mL of barium hydroxide. (Hein 1992, 264; emphasis added)

One way of dealing with these potential ambiguities is to have students rephrase difficult verb forms as nouns, and rewrite the sentences in the following manner:

- *Pipet* 3.0 mL of . . . hydrogen peroxide into Tube A and quickly *stopper*. **Rewrite:** Fill a pipet with 3.0 mL of hydrogen peroxide, pour it into Tube A, and put a stopper on the tube.
- *Centrifuge* the plasma sample . . . for about five minutes. **Rewrite:** Stir the plasma sample in a centrifuge for about five minutes.

At the Operational Level

Over and above the levels of discourse, syntax, and lexis, there is the matter of going through the actual process: being confronted with a question or problem, observing, formulating one or more hypotheses, setting up an experimental design (with its controls and variables), taking measurements, and evaluating the results. In order to understand the language of experiments, students need to experience the process, in real and simulated ways. Accordingly, it is important to design activities that allow practice in developing these skills. This can be done by setting up verbal situations that require students to go through the processes mentioned above.

The following example requires students to (1) formulate hypotheses and (2) design an experiment to test them:

The silver salmon has good vision and well-developed olfactory sacs for smell. It is born in the freshwater streams of the U.S. Pacific Northwest. The young fish swim downstream into the ocean, where they spend five years growing to maturity. Then, in response to some unknown stimulus, they return to freshwater streams to lay their eggs. By tagging the fish, it was discovered that they returned to the precise streams where they were born. How are they able to do this? (adapted from Baker and Allen 1968, 18)

Here are two possible hypotheses:

1. They may find their way home by recognizing certain objects they passed earlier, on their way to the ocean.
2. Perhaps there are distinctive chemicals in different streams, which they can detect with their sense of smell.

How can you test these hypotheses experimentally?

1. For hypothesis #1: Blindfold the tagged salmon, and see how many of them return to their original streams.
2. For hypothesis #2: Block the fish's olfactory sacs and see how many of them return to their original streams.

A key element in experimental design is handling the three kinds of variables:

- *independent variables:* the problem being studied;
- *dependent variables:* those that can change as a result of the independent variable;
- *controlled variables:* conditions that could affect the result of the experiment, but that do not because they are held constant.

An example like the following requires students to decide what those variables would be (adapted from Starr 1984, 23):

Suppose you want to determine the relationship between the amount of water in the soil and the rate of growth for a particular plant. You would use several genetically identical specimens of the plant, each in a container of soil of different moisture. What would be the:

1. independent variable (the amount of water in each container)?
2. dependent variable (plant height measured over a specific time)?
3. controlled variables (light, temperature, soil composition)?

There are numerous sources for such activities. The important thing is that they oblige students to analyze the problems and go through the steps required to design and carry out the experiment in what may be, literally or figuratively, a foreign language.

Let's turn now to one of the more appealing, misunderstood, and crucial elements in the enterprise of science—the role of visuals.

Chapter 8

More Than Meets the Eye:
The Role of Visuals

Visualization is the way we think. Before words, there were images.
Visualization is not just an idea; it is one half of consciousness.

DON GERARD

❋

In this chapter we will examine the role, or functions, of visuals in our introductory science texts. These functions are surprisingly varied and numerous—as many as ten or fifteen, depending on what you might consider primary or secondary functions. But more of this in a moment. My point is that visuals do a lot more than meets the eye, far more than the traditional role we attribute to them—that of creating or heightening the reader's interest.

We will begin with a look at the iconic nature of language as it emerges from its pictorial origins. We will then examine the significance of visuals, including a few words on scientists' use of visuals, a topic that has received a great deal of attention by scholars and scientists alike; this section also treats the reader's use of visuals. The next section addresses the problem of understanding visuals, including the degrees of reality, or *similitude,* of various visuals, and deals with various problems specific to different genres. The third section will explore the many functions of visuals that appear in our corpus and other genres of scientific writing.

Part Four will analyze the corpus, which is drawn from a biology and a chemistry text (Audesirk and Audesirk 1993; Ebbing and Wrighton 1990, respectively), with quotes from the biology text designated as B, those from the chemistry text as C. This section will examine such verbal-visual relationships as captions and figure references, complementarity and redundancy, linearity and branching, and the interaction between graphics. It will also discuss the reciprocity between genres and functions. Let's begin with a few remarks on the iconic nature of written language.

The Iconic Nature of Written Language

The evolution of language started with pictures, progressed to picto-graphs . . . to phonetic units, and then to the alphabet.

The symbol systems we call language are inventions and refinements of what was once the object perceptions in picture-strip mentality.

DONIS DONDIS

＊

The use of visuals in human communication has been with us since the start of recorded time. Twenty thousand years ago, before alphabets and written language, there were cave paintings, with iconic meanings behind them, that reported the world as people understood it at the time.

As philologist I. J. Gelb emphasizes, all writing is basically pictorial, rep-resentational, in origin. "Thinking in concepts," suggests Arthur Koestler, "emerged from thinking in images through the slow development of the powers of abstraction and symbolization, just as phonetic script emerged by a similar process out of pictorial symbols and hieroglyphics" (1964a, 322). Egyptian hieroglyphics, for example, blended iconic and phonetic signs into what C. E. Hodge calls a superb semiotic system.

Indeed, graphic devices, as information designer Macdonald-Ross re-minds us, have been invented "to help *represent, explain,* and *control* the world in which we live" (Macdonald-Ross 1977, 48; emphasis added). We find, for example, a clay map from Mesopotamia dated as early as 2500 B.C.

The *iconic* nature of written language comes down to us today, in Chi-nese and Arabic. We find iconic elements, as well, in languages that use the Roman alphabet; for instance, in certain typographic marks: the amper-sand (&), percent sign (%), and parentheses, or the exclamation point for emphasis (!), plus various prosodic markers like the interrogative (?) and others that indicate different degrees of pause. Typographic marks, in short, are nonalphabetic and thus represent an additional semiotic system that is integrated with what we think of as writing.

Other elements of typography provide emphasizers, signaling the im-portance of certain information—items like boldface, italics, and under-lining, as well as different type size in quotes and headings.

We find further remnants of the iconic in our use of Arabic numbers, in which one mark may signify a series of letters that spell out the word (7 and seven, for example), or two marks representing a single word (19 and nineteen). In fact, the entire symbol system of mathematics has a strong iconic bias.

The Significance of Visuals

It is impossible to think, analyze, or create without mental imagery.

ARISTOTLE,

De Anima

❋

Our first learning comes through tactile awareness, quickly integrated with the senses of taste, smell, and hearing. These senses are soon over-shadowed by iconic forces—the perception of the world by visual means. "From nearly our first experience of the world," urges designer Donis Dondis, "we organize our needs and pleasures, preferences, and fears, with great dependence on what we see" (Dondis 1973, 1). Art historian Rudolph Arnheim argues for the perceptual basis of thought itself, especially for such operations as *comparisons* and *problem-solving* (functions we will examine below). He states that "Concepts are perceptual images, and . . . thought operations are the handling of those images," a strong claim modified by the caution that "images come at any level of abstraction" (Arnheim 1969, 13, 227).

Estimates are that about 85% of all the messages we receive are visual, 10% auditory, and the rest taken in through other channels (Doblin 1980, 89). We can divide visual messages into two classes: *orthographic* (words) and *iconographic*, including elements like pictures and diagrams. In this chapter, I will use the term visuals to refer to iconographic elements. Similarly, we may distinguish graphic from typographic, using graphic to refer to visuals.

The role and significance of visuals vary with the genres they appear in. About 30% of scientific and technical prose in general is illustrative in nature (Rubens 1986, 80). This would include a range of types, from textbooks to research articles and technical manuals. Similarly, visuals (figures, tables, etc.) occupy one-third to one-half the space in typical research articles, as shown in an analysis of *Science* and *Nature* (Miller 1998, 29). Within that genre, experimental reports tend to display more graphics, theoretical analyses more equations (with their strong iconic element).

Scientists' Use of Visuals

The words or the language, as they are spoken and written, do not seem to play any role in my mechanism of thought. The psychical entities which seem to serve as elements in thought are certain signs and more or less clear images which can be "voluntarily" reproduced and combined.

ALBERT EINSTEIN

❋

Many scholars—historians, philosophers of science, and scientists themselves—have commented on the role of visualizing among practitioners, both for *discovering* and *explaining* their work. Einstein, for one, always claimed to think in terms of nonverbal imagery. Indeed, nuclear physicists in general rely heavily on *models,* especially those that can be drawn on paper (Giere 1979, 137). As we will see, models—specifically three-dimensional models—represent the closest thing to "reality," even more than do photographs. Many studies have shown a strong correlation between physics and spatial visualization (for references, see Lord 1983, 5).

One study revealed that spatial ability was very important in conceptualizing chemical reactions (Baker and Tally 1972). And, of course, we have Kekulé's well-known narrative describing his discovery of the benzene ring. (For an excellent list of citations in different sciences, see Lord 1983, 3ff.) Indeed, an investigation of sixty-four eminent scientists found that all of them possessed an extremely high degree of spatial conceptualization (Roe 1952).

What explains this strong correlation between scientific inquiry and visualization? As philosopher of science Steven Toulmin explains: "The heart of all major discoveries in the physical sciences is the discovery of *novel methods of representation* and so of fresh techniques by which inferences can be drawn" (Toulmin 1953, 103; emphasis added). Macdonald-Ross cites, as examples of these, the use of the calculus in Newtonian dynamics and the role of chemical equations in the periodic table. The visual element also provides "the material form of scientific phenomena"; in other words, a form in which the object of one's inquiry may be examined and manipulated (Lynch 1985, 43). Linguist Jay Lemke offers a further insight, suggesting: "The concepts of science are not solely verbal. . . . They are *semantic hybrids,* simultaneously . . . verbal, mathematical, and visual" (1998, 87).

EXPLANATION. As anthropologists Lynch and Woolgar point out, "engineering, botany, architecture, mathematics, none of these sciences can describe what they talk about with texts alone" (1990, 34). When scientists communicate in print, they combine these verbal, mathematical, and iconographic elements "and a host of specialized visual genres seen nowhere else" (Lemke 1998, 87). Many scientists actually write their articles in order to highlight the visual (Miller 1998, 30; for a deeper analysis, see Miller 1981, 383–395).

The Reader's Use of Visuals

Scientists and nonscientists sometimes read things differently. An expert reader may actually study the visual before reading the rest of the article.

In the field of biology, Lord has described how the entire discipline has shifted from a taxonomic to a "conceptual" approach, with greater stress on lab work and a deemphasis on lecture. Likewise, a movement from rote recall to inquiry. And finally, the movement from dull two-dimensional graphs to color-filled multidimensional displays and the manipulation of models. All this has brought with it the development of iconic processes. At this point, competence in visual literacy "became an important aspect of achievement" (Lord 1983, 16–17).

Understanding Visuals

Before we proceed to the functions of visuals and the analysis of our corpus, I would like to say a few words on the matter of understanding visuals. We will then use this information in the inquiries that follow.

Degrees of Similitude

A central concept for our study is the *degree of similitude* of a visual, or graphic. In other words, how close does the graphic come to "the real thing," to the actual phenomenon? For this analysis, I would like to draw on the work of industrial designer Jay Doblin, who presents an excellent typology of messages in print media (Doblin 1980, 89–111). Doblin divides messages into three classes, or forms, which we can call verbal (lexical), numeric, and visual. Every message, suggests Doblin, has an independent form and content, citing, as example, the phrase "It is three o'clock," which can also be represented as 3:00 or ⊕.

He then offers three subsets under the category of visuals. Let us call them *ideographic, diagrammatic,* and isogrammatic, or *realistic. Ideographs* include such things as Chinese characters, road signs, and flags. He also uses the term *marks* for geometricized symbols with ascribed arbitrary meanings; in other words, letters. *Diagrammatic* visuals include charts and graphs "used for visualizing processes that are otherwise difficult to comprehend." *Realistic* techniques are visual representations of reality, and include items such as drawings, photographs, and models. Maps would be somewhere between the last two categories, since their contours have similitude but their contents may not. We can arrange degrees of similitude along the following scale:

abstract							realistic
marks	tables	charts & graphs	diagrams	maps	drawings	photographs	models

The segment including charts, graphs, and diagrams forms a bridge between the abstract (words) and the most realistic representations. This makes them better suited to describe processes than pictures. Winn cites as an example a simplified diagram of the digestive system, which, he suggests, illustrates more effectively how it works than a realistic picture of organs and tissues (Winn 1987, 153).

Doblin notes that "the most realistic form of drawing—illustration—is nearly as realistic as color photographs, but not nearly as realistic as prototype models" (1980, 95). He goes on to say that an object can be represented in any of the forms listed above, a claim open to some dispute (Lemke 1998, 110; Gombrich 1972, 87).

Representations and Reality

Our biology text itself discusses some of the problems in representing simple molecules (B33). The authors describe *six different ways* of visualizing a water molecule (H_2O), each with its own benefits and drawbacks. Notice the visual from the textbook (Figure 8.1).

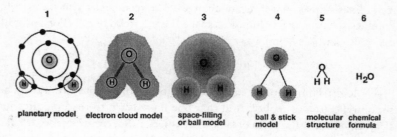

Figure 8.1. Ways of Representing a Water Molecule

The most familiar is (1) the planetary model, depicted as a miniature solar system, with the electrons revolving around the nucleus. Despite the fact that the planetary model is inaccurate, it best illustrates how atoms bond together to make a molecule. The (2) electron cloud model (in which the three atoms form a triangle, with the entire surrounding area shaded in) is the most accurate representation, since it captures the idea of electrons roaming over a relatively large area. But it is hard to draw.

This roaming nature of electrons is best captured by a (3) space-filling, or ball, model, which shows two small balls marked H (hydrogen) in front of a large ball marked O (oxygen). This contrasts with (4), the ball-and-stick model, which shows three small balls connected by sticks (single, double, or triple sticks, depending on the number of bonds). Ball-and-stick models are easier to draw and best represent the bonding feature of molecules. The simplest and easiest geometric representation (5) shows the three atoms in triangular relationship, with simple lines connecting the two hydrogen atoms to the one oxygen atom. Finally, if the structure doesn't need to be shown at all, one can use (6) the simple chemical formula.

Thus we have trade-offs: *different criteria* as a basis for the various forms of representation. These criteria include: accuracy #1, methods of bonding; accuracy #2, number of bonds; and ease of drawing—to which we may add the saving of space (with the chemical formula).

Problems Related to Specific Genres

Individual graphics have their own problems: in design, function, and comprehension. Design considerations fall outside of our inquiry. The relation of graphic to function will be discussed in Part Four. Here, I would like to examine some of the comprehension problems posed by several visual forms. But first, I would have a word about definitions. There is some confusion about the words *chart* and *graph*. The two words are often used interchangeably, even by experts. Graphs are sometimes considered a type of chart. In this chapter, I will use the term *graphs* for those items that have trend lines—lines that indicate changes. The term *chart* will be used for graphics that enclose volumes of space (bars, circles, etc.). (For a slightly different view, see Winn 1987, 153.)

Photographs

Psychologist Philip Kolers suggests that few photographs are a truly accurate reflection of reality. And that one must learn to read pictures just as much as any other form of symbols (Kolers 1980, 257; Gombrich 1972, 89). The greater the realism in a photograph, the more information. But realism does not necessarily correlate with learning. As one scholar points out, the important factor is whether or not that realism adds information that the viewer needs (Perkins 1980, 269). We may even find "too great a degree of realism." In its effort at achieving the highest fidelity, a photograph or realistic drawing may include *too much* irrelevant information that detracts from the function of the visual.

Another consideration is the problem of multiple photographs. As soon as the reader is confronted with a series of pictures, she must decide on the relationship among them. In our corpus, these relationships are ones of: (1) comparison, (2) sequence, or (3) details (e.g., a large picture and several small inserts).

Tables

A problem with tables is the difficulty of deciding what is important, since all items receive equal emphasis. They do not specify relationships and so are easy to misinterpret. A significant trend is much harder to identify in a table than in a chart or a graph. There are many people who cannot interpret the simplest table. This may be due in part to its unfamiliar perspective, resulting in the need to process information vertically and horizontally at the same time—which, of course, is so different from the way we read. Another weakness, as Macdonald-Ross suggests (1977, 63), is its abstract nature, composed as it is solely of words and numbers. In this way, it is one of the least iconic of all graphical forms.

Graphs

After tables, graphs seem to pose the greatest problem to understanding. One reason is that they are hard to interpolate because of their continuous nature. In order to get even an approximate value, one has to interpolate, or mentally connect the point on the graph line to its corresponding points of the vertical and horizontal axes. In addition, some graphs contain more than one trend line, which adds the function of comparison to the other correlations. In short, graphs are good for presenting data but not especially good for teaching. As Winn says: "Their function is mainly descriptive and not really instructional" (Winn 1987, 192). We find an acknowledgment of this complexity in our biology text (B366), where the text goes into considerable detail explicating the graph in general and the four individual trend lines in particular.

In a study of seventh graders, Roller found that graphs actually increased the difficulty of reading despite the adequate literacy and math skills of the students. Vernon (1951) came to a similar conclusion in her study with an older population. Roller suggests that "text and graph information are not commonly merged in the mind of the reader" (1980, 307).

Functions of Visuals

Thought needs shape.

RUDOLPH ARNHEIM

✲

Visuals serve far more functions than meet the eye. Our corpus reveals at least a dozen. We can examine them along several dimensions. One is to think in terms of primary and secondary functions of visuals. Primary visuals are those that are an end in themselves, aiding understanding or remembering. Secondary functions are those that ultimately serve a primary function. One such is summarizing, which can serve the primary functions of understanding, remembering, and so forth. Secondary functions are no less important than primary ones.

I would like to begin this section by noting the various functions of visuals and offering a few comments on each:

1. Interest-Motivation

A chief function of visuals in most genres of science writing, apart from research articles, is that of interesting or motivating the reader. From the creator's point of view, it may also be seen as an instance of artistic expression. One study by Mayer found that 85% of the illustrations in sixth-grade science textbooks were "decorational," which the author defines as having no useful information; or they were "representational," such as an unlabeled photo of a rocket ship in test flight (Mayer et al. 1995, 31). We find comparable graphics in our corpus—usually photographs. I would suggest, however, that such visuals serve a very important function, namely, that of enhancing interest.

As for artistic expression, Gelb points out that historically, there was no sharp division between artistic and communicative graphics. "The aims of communication and expression are so closely intertwined in all forms of human behavior that normally it is impossible to discuss one without being forced to consider the other" (Gelb 1980, 8; Gombrich 1972, 94).

2. Understanding

Another main function of visuals in our texts is that of understanding. There are many items that are hard to grasp through words alone: various concepts and physical relationships, processes and temporal occurrences. Some simultaneous events are hard to understand through the linear constraints of text. In Arnheim's words: "Intellectual thinking dismantles the *simultaneity* of spatial structure" (1969, 246; emphasis added). Even sequentiality—especially if complex—may also be hard to follow in words. Visuals such as diagrams are particularly well suited to express temporal events, both simultaneous and sequential. Similarly, a long stretch of text may be quite inadequate for describing the parts—say, of an organ or bodily system—and the relative position of those parts. Visuals serve the following major subfunctions in our corpus. Understanding of (1) abstract processes (B338), (2) parts and spatial relationships (B33, 196, 247, 248; C202), and (3) movement and sequence (B244, 404; C192).

In general, according to Lemke, "our visual discrimination is far better than our linguistic system at dealing with . . . continuous variations in space, line, shape, and color" (Miller 1998, 31, quoting Lemke 1995).

Visuals also eliminate the lexical and grammatical complexity often found in text. They have no *ifs, althoughs, howevers,* or *instead ofs* that can make the verbal message extremely confusing. There is one less symbol system the reader must decode. This, of course, depends on the visual's degree of similitude. Graphs, as we have seen, require a great deal of interpretation, especially for the uninitiated, while photos require far less.

Dondis suggests that people actually *prefer* visual representations to written explanations, noting: "In the modern media . . . the visual dominates; the verbal augments. Print media is not dead yet, nor will it ever be, but, nevertheless, our language-dominated culture has moved perceptibly toward the iconic" (Dondis 1973, 7). The dominance of the iconic is apparent in the ever-increasing influence of television and computers. As we have seen, it is also reflected in the changed approach in the teaching of biology, which emphasizes visual, object-oriented, hands-on phenomena.

FOR QUICK UNDERSTANDING. Speed of processing is an additional factor in our discussion of understanding. Certain visuals in our corpus allow the reader to grasp information much faster than does printed text. This realization is the basis for those semiotic systems in which rapid understanding and reaction are crucial, systems such as road signs and warnings (on labels and otherwise). We respond to these stimuli quickly once they are learned. As a result, "they diminish the amount of decoding time needed" (Goodman and Groddol 1997, 42). "Sight," in the words of one scholar, "is swift, comprehensive, simultaneously analytic and synthetic" (Gattegno 1969).

3. Remembering

Sight . . . requires so little energy to function—as it does—at the speed of light, that it permits our minds to receive and hold an infinite number of items of information in a fraction of a second.

CALEB GATTEGNO

❋

Psychologists have conducted a great many experiments on the relationship between visuality and memory. The general consensus is that information entered visually is more easily remembered than information taken in verbally. Fleming emphasizes that "objects and pictures are remembered better than their names, and concrete words . . . better than abstract words" (Macdonald-Ross 1977, 56, citing Fleming 1970). And Pressley, in a study with eight-year-olds, found that having the children form a picture in their heads after reading each paragraph of a story improved their recall of the information, compared to a control group that did not form images (Pressley 1976).

Gombrich speaks of the *mnemonic* power of the image (1972, 91), as does Levie (1987, 16). And Yates, in his classic study, describes how Roman orators would remember their topics by placing them in imaginary rooms in an imaginary house, and stroll from one room to another, retrieving them.

Shepherd and Chipman (1970) describe the relationship of the mental image to the real event or object as a second-order isomorphism. In other words, people tend to form a one-to-one relationship between the mental representation and the thing itself. As for the range of graphics found in our corpus, most do *not* have a high degree of similitude. Only photographs, three-dimensional models, and some drawings "pretend" to an approximation of reality. We will examine the idea of degrees of realism later in the chapter.

Samuels and Samuels suggest what we might call a certain "haptic" or "synesthetic" function of visuals—I'm not sure there is a word for it—when they say: "Visualization enables a person to incorporate into his body or being, in a concrete way, that which must otherwise be an abstract idea" (Samuels and Samuels 1975, 28). We might think of this as a process of *reification:* making real—in this case, with a visual—a concept that does not have a natural physical form. We can infer that the more tangible a concept or phenomenon, the easier it is to understand and remember it.

4. Elaboration

As we will see in Part Four, a major function of visuals in our corpus is elaborating on statements in the text. Graphics can show physical relationships, size, shapes, etc., without having to describe them in detail. They can provide additional information, sometimes in the form of details, sometimes in the form of *examples*. Examples thus become a secondary function of visuals.

5. Economy

One of the factors which makes graphic organization so powerful is that it can draw simultaneously on a number of different codes and so achieve great economy of expression.

M. MACDONALD-ROSS

✳

Conversely, visuals provide a source of economy; specifically, lexical economy. A visual requires fewer words to be processed than does text. As Lord points out, this saves space in a textbook (Lord 1983, 94; Miller 1998, 30). In this context, let us examine one or two graphics from our corpus and see how they would be rewritten as text.

The first is a photograph from our chemistry book, in which the text states: "Figure 11.38 shows a demonstration of the electrical conductivity of graphite" (C440). The photo then shows an eight-volt battery, a meter, and a graphite pencil, all connected to each other by alligator clips. The visual-to-verbal rewrite might look something like this: "The conductivity of graphite can be easily demonstrated by an eight-volt battery, connected to a meter and a pencil by wire. The six-volt reading on the meter indicates that the graphite pencil conducts electricity."

That was a short one—what designer Edward Tufte calls a visual with low *information density*. However, visuals often contain a lot more information, requiring a lot more words to compensate for their absence. Take another example, in this case, a drawing of the regions of the brain, labeling the functions of the various regions (B799). The lead-in from the textbook reads: "The functions of the cerebral cortex are localized in discrete regions." My rewrite:

> The human cerebral cortex is divided into four regions: the frontal, parietal, occipital, and temporal lobes. The frontal lobe deals with the higher intellectual functions such as speech. It is also the premotor and primary motor area, governing the movement of legs, trunk, arms, torso, hands, face, and tongue. The parietal lobe is the primary sensory area and governs sensory associations. The occipital lobe is the area of visual association, while the temporal lobe governs language formation and comprehension.

The drawing presents the information in a far more *holistic* way.

6. Summarizing

A major function of visuals, in our corpus and universally, is their ability to summarize—to pull together in one focused space—a considerable amount of previously given information. At the same time, we must consider summarizing as a secondary function. What are the reasons for summarizing? They include: remembering, understanding, and quick reference.

When placed at the beginning of a section, such visuals can serve as *advance organizers,* providing an organizational framework for the material (Winn 1987, 159; Levin et al. 1987, 56).

7. Reasoning/Analysis/Exploration/Discovery

> We envision information in order to reason about, communicate, document, and preserve . . . knowledge.
>
> EDWARD TUFTE

※

The chief function of statistical graphics, according to visual designer Tufte, is helping people *reason* about quantitative information (1983, 91).

One way of accomplishing this is enabling people to perceive new relationships. This a visual can do by providing comparisons and bringing out cause-and-effect relationships. "Such displays," urges Tufte, "are often used to reach conclusions and make decisions" (1997, 10).

MAKING COMPARISONS. Several writers on the subject stress the importance of graphics for making comparisons. Otto Neurath, father of the isotype chart, states that comparison is the major function of visuals (in Macdonald-Ross 1977, 55). Likewise, Howard Paine, art director of *National Geographic,* mentions comparison as an important function of visuals (Paine 1980, 143). Similarly, Tufte (1983, 13) notes that graphics "encourage the eye to compare different pieces of data." Macdonald-Ross (1977, 403) notes that "many of the formats [such as bar charts and isotypes] are naturally adapted for visual comparison, and would hardly be chosen if rote recall of exact numbers was the intention." In research articles, according to Miller (1998, 37), the most important use of visuals is highlighting relationships of comparison, in order to imply cause-and-effect relationships. In our texts, comparison is presented chiefly by tables, drawings, and multiple photos.

8. Problem-Solving

Studies of cognition suggest that humans have two types of cognitive processes: a linguistic-analytical type and a holistic image-based model (Loftus and Bell, 1975). French (1965) found that most cognitive tasks can be solved by using one or a combination of both strategies.

As we have seen, visuals can represent a simplified or codified form of information that is more easily analyzed and manipulated than text, thus making them suitable for solving problems (Szlichcinski 1979, 254). Herbert Simon suggests that one of the key steps in solving a problem is to represent it "so as to make the solution transparent" (Simon 1969). For certain types of problems, graphics provide an ideal format. Some of the more useful graphic formats for solving problems include: tables, algorithms, and diagrams. "Even diagrams in anatomy texts," suggests Macdonald-Ross, "could be considered as problem-solving tools for dissection and surgery" (1977, 60).

It is instructive to recall certain idioms in the English language that reveal the visual nature of analysis, understanding, and problem-solving. These include words and phrases like: *insight* and *imagination.* Or the terms *visionary* and *farsighted,* referring to someone who is able to "see" beyond the ordinary and thus achieve a creative solution to a problem. Similarly, the words *seer* and *enlightening;* or the word *illumination,* meaning a sudden understanding. Likewise, the act of *reflecting,* a synonym for thinking itself. We have, in addition, words like *viewpoint* and *perspective,* meaning a different way of examining a problem, which, as we have seen, is often a key to solving it. Even words like *uncover* and *research* have a visual substratum. And the phrase "I see what you mean" has come to have the connotation "I understand." Arnheim goes as far as to suggest that "words that do not now refer to direct perceptual experience did so originally" (1969, 232).

Design scholar Donis Dondis describes the process from the visual thinker's point of view: "In some mysterious way, we form the sight of something we never saw before. Vision—previsualization—is intricately linked to the creative leap . . . *as a primary means of problem-solving.* And it is this very process of moving around in mental images in the mind that frequently takes us to the point of breakthrough and solution" (Dondis 1973, 8; emphasis added).

Significant treatments of the topic include Bobrow and Collins (1975), Kleinmutz (1966), Newell and Simon (1972), and McKim (1980).

9. Argument-Persuasion

> There is no such thing as "facts displayed" pure and simple. All facts presented in papers and textbooks are selected from a huge pool of possibilities.
>
> M. MACDONALD-ROSS

❋

The persuasive function of graphics is far more prominent in research articles than in textbooks. And logically so. The main purpose of textbooks is to instruct. The chief function of research articles is to prove a point— to persuade the reader of one's argument. In doing this, the author tries to make the facts "speak for themselves" (Miller 1998, 30; also Bazerman 1989; Myers 1990). Those facts, in the forms of graphs, photos, and tables, "give the illusion of direct access to the data" (Miller 1998, 30). Thus, while persuasion is a major function of visuals in research articles, it does not play a prominent part in our texts.

Analysis of the Texts

I would like to approach the texts from two points of view. The first examines the reciprocity among major elements, specifically: (a) book text, (b) visuals, and (c) caption text. We will explore such questions as: How do the three elements interact? How do different kinds of visuals interact with each other? We will also look at the use of figure references in the text, plus the issues of complementarity and redundancy, linearity and branching. The second section will examine the relationship between functions and genres: What are the main functions of different genres (of tables, for example)? And conversely: Which genres are used for different functions (which genres are most used for comparisons, for instance)?

Verbal-Visual Relationships

The concepts of science . . . are semiotic hybrids, simultaneously verbal, mathematical, visual.

JAY LEMKE

❖

This being the case, it is natural to find these modalities used in science textbooks. In our corpus, they include *prose* (text), *visuals,* and *caption text,* and, of course, formulas and equations. Captions are less common than one might think, at least in the biology text, which uses them only for tables and occasionally for graphs, reflecting, perhaps, the realization that these two genres need support for interpretation. Other visuals in the biology text have no captions. In contrast, the chemistry volume uses captions for all visuals except cartoons and beginning-of-chapter photos, which are repeated on the following page, in reduced form and with captions. The chemistry volume makes additional use of formulas and equations.

Interaction of Different Modalities

Our corpus shows great variation in the relationship among text, visual, and caption text. At one extreme, we find a case in which the text contains no verbal reference to the photo (a cesium clock) (C14), only a figure reference. At the other extreme, we find two pages of text describing the first appearance of land plants and animals. The accompanying artist's rendering of a Carboniferous swamp forest adds no new information whatsoever, but does provide a visual *summary* of the information (B412).

Where the Information Lies

In different instances, the bulk of the information may be found in one modality or another. In the case I just mentioned—of the cesium clock (C14)—the bulk of information is found in the caption text, which contains information on the visual, and which also adds information to the general discussion. Here are some ways that text, visual, and caption text relate to each other:

1. A short statement in the text, plus information in the visual (B243, B402, B403).

2. A short statement in the text, plus information in the caption text (C14).
3. A short statement in the text, plus information in visual and caption text (B340, B341, B346).
4. Main discussion in the text, plus information in the visual. That information often takes the form of example, comparison, summary, or illustrating a process or sequence (function: understanding).
5. Text gives detailed extended description of the visual (C144).

Caption Text

Caption text is an unacknowledged part of the package. It serves a variety of functions, some of them crucial. These functions include:

1. explaining the visual (B347);
2. adding information to the general discussion (B346);
3. a combination of both functions, as in the cesium clock example (C14).

In one interesting case, the text sentence is a general statement ("To maintain homeostasis and to grow, organisms need materials and energy") (B5). The visual is a photograph of a cape buffalo grazing in the tall grass. Nothing in the text relates it explicitly to the visual. This is done in the caption text, without which there would be no connection between text and visual.

The "success" of a visual depends greatly on its relationship to text, caption, and caption text. The more iconic visuals (photos, models, realistic drawings) may be described in the text by a particular sentence. But there are a hundred other statements one could also make about the visual (Gombrich 1972, 82). The viewer of a visual requires verbal guidance unless the purpose of that visual is strictly one of interest.

Complementarity and Redundancy

The relationship of the modalities may be one of *complementarity* (adding new information) or *redundancy* (restating old information). The choice of one or the other seems to depend on the complexity *or* importance of the concept. The greatest number of iterations—eight—occurs in the chemistry text, in the explanation of Boyle's Law (C146). This includes two separate discussions in the text, an equation, three graphics (table, graph, and drawing), and two caption texts. Though not strictly redundant—the second text discussion, table, and graph contain *elaboration* of details—this provides a canonical form of the interaction among the various modalities.

While information in some of our cases may be redundant, functions are not. For example, a passage from the biology text (B242) describes the steps in the life cycle of a certain bacterium. The accompanying drawing gives a visual depiction of the sequence, its function being *understanding* (understanding a sequence of events).

Complementarity in a visual often takes the form of details, examples, or comparisons. In a sample from our corpus (B347), on homologous (comparable) structures in animals, we find all three. The text states: "Despite the enormous diversity of functions, the internal anatomy of all bird and mammal forelimbs is remarkably similar." The visual (a drawing) then includes examples of various animals—nine in all—highlighting the homologous structures (in wings and feet).

Interaction among Graphics

In addition to the modalities discussed above, visuals also interact with each other. These interactions usually take the form of: (1) comparison (B795, B1015), (2) examples (B416), or (3) details (B778, C34–35). For instance, we find several instances of photographs as "main topic," with three or four small insets providing details (B945, 953, 1023, 1026, 1031, 1033, 1035). A typical display is a large photo of a tropical rain forest, with four insets of plants and animals that live in it. An explanation of their ecology appears in the caption text.

We also find reciprocities between different types of visuals. The biology text contains several cases of a graph paired with a photo (B1018–1019, B948). One (B952) shows the effects of introducing an animal population (reindeer, in this case) into an area that has no predators. The statement in the text is brief and general ("Other dramatic cases of overgrazing have occurred when herbivores such as reindeer have been introduced onto *islands* without large predators"). The photo shows a herd of reindeer, while the graph plots the introduction, the sharp rise, and dramatic decline of the population. Interpretation is left to the caption text, which describes the event in words. This grouping reveals an added function of caption text: keeping text in the main body of the book from becoming "clogged," that is, from becoming too detailed, which runs the risk of drowning the reader in a sea of information.

Figure References

Figure references—references in the text, to an accompanying visual—fall into two classes: (1) as part of a sentence, and (2) subordinated in parentheses. We may refer to them as the strong form and weak form:

As Part of the Sentence (strong form):

1. "The interrelationship of experiment and explanation is displayed in Figure 1.5." (C7)
2. "In Figure 1.6, a steel rod has been placed next to a ruler." (C8)
3. Full sentence in parentheses: ("Figures 1.11 and 1.12 dramatically show the relative densities of substances"). (C17)
4. "Table 2-1 lists the most common elements in the universe, the Earth, and the human body." (B24)
5. "Figure 17-3a illustrates two important points about genetic drift: (1) . . ." (B366)

Subordinated in Parentheses (weak form):

1. "Balances measure mass . . . the quantity of matter in a material (Figure 1.2)." (C4)
2. "The flash from a [flash] bulb accompanies a chemical reaction triggered by the heat of an electrical current (see Figure 1.3)." (C5)
3. "Most laboratory glassware (Figure 1.10) is calibrated in liters or milliliters." (C17)
4. "A crystal of table salt (Fig. 1-1a), for example, consists of just two elements . . ." (B1). *Note:* The sentence mentions the function of the visual.
5. "The phylum name means 'spiny skin,' which is *especially obvious* in sea urchins (Fig. E1-13)." (B11)
6. "Because the water molecules at the surface of a pond cohere to one another, the surface film acts almost as a solid—supporting relatively dense objects such as fallen leaves [and] *water striders* (Fig. 2-13a)." (B38)

A COMPARISON. In the strong form, the actual reference may appear in initial, medial, or final position. In the weak form, it appears only in medial or final. Sentences in the strong form normally explain what the visual contains or does; that is, they often state or infer the function of the visual. In this way, the strong form provides greater cohesion between text and visual. The strong form is also closer to natural language.

Sentences with the weak form do not refer to the visual, except obliquely, as we can observe in the sea urchin example above (#5), where the phrase "especially obvious" points the reader toward the photo located directly below it. Similarly, in sentence #6. Here the sentence *does* mention the topic of the visual (an insect called the water strider). Thus, we can discern, even in the weak form, different *degrees of reference,* with sentence #6 exhibiting a high degree of reference (also B23, B65, B66, B67, B68), sentences #5 and #4 a medium degree, and sentences #1–3 a low degree of reference. Weak forms are far more frequent in our corpus.

Linearity and Branching

Lemke notes that "scientific text is not primarily linear" (Lemke 1998, 96) and is not meant to be read sequentially. In this light, it is interesting to observe the placement and operation of figure references; and also of chapter references—those little notations that say: "See Chapter 12" or "We will discuss the matter in Chapter 27."

Figure references point in various directions. They may refer to a figure on the same page or an adjoining one. They may also refer to a graphic that appeared several pages earlier. We also find examples of double branching, in which the text points in two directions; in one case, to the same page and also to a later chapter (B5). As for chapter references, they are overwhelmingly forward-branching (for examples of backward branching, B69 and B361).

Several questions come to mind: How does the reader respond to the author's suggestion? And how does the author *want* her to respond? If the reader indeed follows the author's invitation and skips to the visual, what effect does it have on her comprehension? For verifiable answers, these questions are best answered by empirical studies. We may, however, offer a few comments on the matter.

Presumably, chapter references in the form of "See Chapter 24," if the reader is currently on Chapter 7, serve as a type of forecasting statement, or advance organizer. However, the actual referent usually appears so much later in the book that this function probably has little effect. More likely, the purpose of the reference is the equivalent of saying: "This is a preliminary discussion. We will discuss it in more detail in Chapter 24" (B4, B5, B6). It is not even likely that the author *wants* the reader to interrupt what she is reading and turn to the distant chapter. My guess is that—almost invariably—the reader rejects the invitation. What about figure references? Here the situation is less certain. Most figure references direct the reader to nearby graphics, in which case, it is more likely she will accept the invitation. There's even a good chance she will encounter the visual before actually reading the text. Either way, we are forced back to the question of reciprocity.

VISUALS AND BRANCHING. A visual may relate to the end of a topic (say, an item mentioned at the end of a paragraph), in which case, it does not interrupt the passage, but provides instead a transition from the end of one topic to the beginning of the next. This is much less disruptive, and may even have a beneficial effect for the reader, somewhat akin to white space or a paragraph ending (e.g., B23).

It is also much easier to skip from text to photo and back to text than from text to a graphic that needs considerable analysis, and back to text again, which is often the case with nonpictorial graphics. In this way, photos are less disruptive than most other visuals and are thus a preferable way—for the reader—of receiving details and examples (B51, B367). For visuals that require a great deal of interpretation, the figure reference, if followed, can make comprehension more difficult.

Genres and Functions

Several problems arise in our effort to understand the relationship between genres and functions. These include, among other things, issues of interest, multiple functions, and demonstrability.

INTEREST. While the function of interest may be seen to hide behind most visuals, some seem more challenging and repelling than inviting. Some seem to say: "Figure me out if you can." This, as we have seen from our earlier analysis, includes graphs and tables. It also includes certain types of drawings.

With drawings, we can distinguish between drawings of the familiar and those of the unfamiliar. Drawings of the familiar are more pictorial, depicting things that we have seen and that we know. Drawings of the unfamiliar—of the microscopic or submicroscopic, or internal bodily systems—have a less pictorial "feel" to them and thus are closer to the abstract.

DEMONSTRABILITY. It is easier to determine when a visual increases interest, adds detail, provides an example, or summarizes. Apart from empirical studies, it is harder to decide how much it increases understanding, persuades the reader, or aids in remembering. For this reason, I have omitted the function of remembering, analysis, and persuasion from the tabulation. Earlier on, we reviewed several laboratory studies that *did* evaluate some of these functions. And that is as far as we can go in terms of efficacy. However, our study focuses more on function than on efficacy.

This said, let's look at the various functions and visuals and see which—in our texts—are used to express others. I've presented the information in the form of a table (Table 8.1), after which, I will offer a few comments. A capital *M* in the cell means that it is a major function of the visual—a function that has appeared a dozen or more times in the corpus. A small *m* indicates a minor function; one that appears a half dozen times or less.

THE PICTORIAL. The more pictorial a graphic, the greater the *interest* it arouses. Similarly, it is things pictorial that create emotions; the farther from the pictorial, the less emotional. In this way, the more pictorial graphics tend to be more *persuasive,* since ultimately we are persuaded more by emotions than by numbers and logic. Pictorial genres give us tangible ob-

	Photo	Table	Drawing	Diagram	Chart	Graph	Ma
Interest	M						
Understanding	M		M	m			m
Elaboration by details	M	M	M			m	m
Comparison	M	M	M			m	
Example	M		M				
Summary		M					
Handy reference							

Table 8.1. Interaction of Genres and Functions

jects, things closer to the real world as we know it. For this reason, the best *examples* are also things closest to real-world phenomena, in contrast to numbers, which are one step further removed from reality.

PHOTOGRAPHS. As we can see from the matrix, the major functions of photos are interest, understanding, adding details, comparison, and examples. In short, even photos—the most pictorial of graphics—serve vital functions apart from simply heightening interest. In fact, several studies showed that subjects who viewed a picture after reading a passage improved their understanding of the material (Bradford and Bradford 1983, 264). With the prominence of computer graphics, the line between drawings and photographs grows thinner, as does the difference between artifice and reality.

MAPS. Maps have their own uniqueness. They are not pictorial in the literal sense. Still, the average adult has seen enough globes and maps of the world to have a strong visual image of them. In that sense, maps do have a pictorial feel to them, a feeling of the known, the familiar. There are actually very few maps in our corpus: seven in the biology text and none in the chemistry. For this reason, though I have had to enter a small *m* next to their functions for understanding and details, these are their two major functions in the corpus.

TABLES. Tables, as we might have guessed, serve the three major functions of summarizing, adding details, and comparing, and a minor function as a handy reference. It is important to realize that tables *are* implicit comparisons.

DRAWINGS. Drawings, as we might expect, also serve several major functions in the corpus. However, I would stress that many drawings in the corpus are very difficult to understand, and so fail to accomplish the purpose they were intended for. These include especially drawings of microscopic and submicroscopic processes, things most people have no internal representation of.

Viewing the matrix from the other direction, it is also interesting to see which genres the authors rely on most for presenting the major functions of understanding, details, comparisons, and examples. Here we find elaboration of details done chiefly by photos, tables, and drawings. Likewise, comparisons are also made chiefly by photos, tables, and drawings. Examples are expressed chiefly by photos and drawings. And understanding is achieved chiefly through photos, drawings, and diagrams. As we saw in Chapter 7, visuals are often used to show the results of experiments. In some cases, the results are presented *only* in the visual and not in the text.

Conclusion

We have touched on the ontology of language and its development from iconographic to more typographic forms. We have also noted that iconic elements are still quite prevalent in modern written language—as seen in typographic and punctuation marks and in the "alphabet" of numeracy.

We have also examined, in greater detail, the relationship between visuals and reality—what I have called degrees of similitude. We have seen that, in some cases, reality—as exemplified by photographs—is not the ultimate criterion for the creation of a visual. But that a picture does have certain specific benefits, such as speed of processing, which is important as the reader's eye flits from text to visual and back again.

We have explored the functions of visuals, from which come the following recommendations: When deciding to use a visual, or graphic, to illustrate a text, there are important things to be aware of, including: (1) the best form of representing the information; (2) whether the information in the graphic should be complementary or redundant; (3) the function of the visual; and (4) the reciprocity among text, visual, and caption text. There are, likewise, important considerations for the reader. These include items three and four, just mentioned, and the need, in some cases, for training in interpreting graphs and tables.

We come away with the thought that the relationship between visuals and text is extremely complex, subtle, and crucial—to the communication of ideas in science and to the communication of knowledge in general.

Chapter 9

The Language of Quantifying

All things which can be known have numbers; for it is not possible that
without numbers anything can be either conceived or known.

PHILOLAUS,

Pythagoras's chief disciple

*

While quantification . . . has the last word on verifying the correctness
of any scientific statement, it is a fundamental error to assume that
knowledge can progress on the basis of quantification alone. The current overrating of quantification as a source of knowledge has serious . . . consequences. The first and foremost is that it leads to
contempt of *observation* pure and simple, which . . . is the basis of all inductive science.

CONRAD LORENZ

[emphasis added]

*

Joys divided are increased.

JOSIAH HOLLAND

*

Like metaphor, quantifying seems to be an integral part of language,
sometimes almost as much as phonemes themselves. To quote philosopher
of science Max Wartofsky: "Measurement concepts become part of the
everyday language, built into its commonest terms and its most ordinary
usage, and into its structure itself" (1968).

The quantifying sense pervades all parts of speech, and attracts words
and phrases that originally had nothing remotely to do with the process of
quantifying. In fact, the problem in dealing with English quantifiers is their
very pervasiveness and irregularity.

A lot has been written about quantifying—more than half a dozen
books on the topic. Linguist Dwight Bolinger's 1972 monograph serves as
a benchmark, from which several other studies have developed, in different directions. These studies have dealt with the various *exclusive subsets*
of quantifiers, exclusive here meaning categories containing a limited number of items. They have also explored words and phrases that, as I've noted

above, were not originally designed to express quantity but were pressed into service for that reason. May's dissertation treats quantifiers from a transformational point of view; Kanazawa and Piñón treat them more from the standpoint of symbolic logic. And Nishigauchi's 1990 study examines quantifiers in their comparative setting (Japanese, English, German).

In this chapter, I would like to develop a number of broader frameworks for classifying quantifiers, at the same time, proposing several new categories for specific items. We will accept the major division of *partial* and *universal* quantifiers, suggested by Hogg and others, which will be discussed below. We will then look just beneath this at a host of subsets, such as *exclusive* (as defined above) and *inclusive* quantifiers: subsets into which all quantifiers can be divided.

Let's start by examining (1) the *concept* of quantity, a concept that is not always as easy to define as one might expect. The section will also touch on the functions of quantifiers, numerical and nonnumerical quantification, and what I have called "numerolatry." (2) Next, I will offer what I hope will be a provocative list of inclusive and exclusive subsets, plus a few observations on some of the more traditional ones. (3) Following this is a discussion of context and precision, two major forces influencing the creation and behavior of quantifiers. (4) I will also explore the topic of *scaling* (scales, scalarity), another major element of quantifiers. Finally, (5) I will close with an analysis of two sample passages from a biology text.

So far I have tried to build toward a general theory that helps explain why English contains hundreds of quantifiers, many of them redundant, to cover a limited range of quantities: essentially, from 0 to 100%. My thesis is that the reason for this diversity is chiefly rhetorical, not semantic. Given the pervasive use of quantitative statements—especially in scientific discourse—there is considerable need for redundant terms in order to avoid an unseemly repetition of words.

THE CHOICE OF CORPUS. There was specific reason to choose a biology text as our corpus (Starr and Taggart 1990). For while biology as a natural science demands a high degree of precision in its research, it also deals with approximations in several of its inquiries (evolution and ecology, for example). At the same time, it tends to have somewhat greater "quantitative tolerances" in its explanations. By contrast, physics and chemistry are a lot more numerical in their quantitativeness, and numerical expressions of quantity—such as 12 meters, or 14 cc—offer far less linguistic and semantic food for thought. For this reason, we'll spend a minimal amount of time on numerical quantifying. It would be interesting to compare the proportion of numerical to nonnumerical quantification in texts from the three sciences. But that would take us too far afield.

The Concept of Quantity

Let's at once broach the *concept* of quantity. Quantifiers, suggest psychologists Moxey and Sanford, are expressions that "make *assertions* about the number of things being talked about, or indicate a *subset* of some superset" [emphasis added]. These expressions, they emphasize, are concerned with numbers or *proportions* of things (1993, 4). So far, so good. Some quantifiers answer the questions "How much? How many?" But what about "How much time?" Is *this* a question of quantity? Take the term *half-life,* in the sentence "The half-life is the time it takes for half the nucleus in any given amount of radioactive element to decay into another element" (B21).

In this case, half-life equals the *amount* of time needed for something to occur. In fact, quantity deals with the amount of *anything* needed for a certain purpose, for some measure, for something to occur; for example: "How long? How far (distance)? How big? How often?" Does it then equal the formula HOW + ADVERB? Clearly not, considering the myriad environments and parts of speech in which quantifiers appear.

MASS AND COUNT NOUNS. As linguist Wallace Reid urges, "before counting can [even] *begin,* one must settle on what is being counted, and this makes the act of counting inextricably bound up with conceptual categories" (Reid 1991, 50). The results depend on how we categorize. Only when we subsume apples and oranges under the category of fruit can we say there are two units. In Frege's words: "We only think of things in terms of number after they have first been reduced to a common genus" (1950, 62). Grammatical distinctions of mass and count do not necessarily correspond to semantic ones, as we can see from the contrast of *oats* and *wheat,* one being mass, the other a count noun (Palmer 1978, 34ff.).

Given these—and a host of other subtleties, distinctions, and generalities—it is no wonder that the concept of quantification continues to elude any grand theory. Still, I would like to make a few observations pointing toward such a theory.

Functions of Quantifiers

Quantifying, measuring, and counting are things we do day and night, consciously and unconsciously. Wartofsky goes so far as to describe the human organism as "a system of activities preserved by an apparatus of measurement," an organism that "performs conscious measurement in that whole spectrum of actions which mark him as a thinking and speaking being" (1968, 153).

Historian of science Tobias Dantzig distinguishes between counting and what he calls the "number sense," a faculty that enables a person to recognize "that something has changed in a small collection when, without his direct knowledge, an object has been removed from or added to the collection" (1939, 1): a few sheep from the flock, a few members of the party. Counting, he asserts, is strictly human, while other species of animals seem to possess a rudimentary number sense akin to our own. As David Smith points out, spiders conform to regular polygons in spinning their webs, "and the laws of maxima and minima are followed by the bee in building up the hexagonal wax cells of the honeycomb" (1958, 5).

The earliest human efforts of noting quantities appear in the prehistoric caves of the Old World—in Europe, Asia, and Africa, while the earliest systematic written records for noting specific quantities are those of the ancient Egyptians and Sumerians, which date to around 3500 B.C. (Dantzig 1939, 22).

Numericals and Nonnumericals

We will never know which came first—the general quantifying sense or the practice of counting. If we assume an evolutionary perspective, we might conclude that the general perception was the first to appear. Both, of course, serve primary functions, depending on the purpose they are used for. As we will see in our corpus, *nonnumerical* quantifiers greatly outnumber numerical statements. This is all the more so in general communication—in print and broadcast media. Even in questionnaire research, it has been found that people prefer to answer questions with general quantifiers or frequency expressions (e.g., *rarely, seldom, sometimes, usually*) rather than those posed with specific numbers (Moxey and Sanford 1993, 61).

THE NEED FOR NUMBERS. In scientific research, we observe that "the planets move among fixed stars, that iron expands when heated . . . Similarly . . . we wish to know how *far* the planets are away from us, how *rapidly* they are moving, how *much* iron expands under known conditions of heating" (Cohen and Nagel 1934, 289). Numerically quantifying an observation or hypothesis helps us to confirm or refute it.

"In principle," urges geographer David Harvey, "it should be possible, in all spheres of our understanding, to improve the quality of our understanding by some form of quantification" (1969, 308), and whether or not we can measure it depends *not* on the thing itself but on our ability to conceptualize it.

Moxey and Sanford argue that for nonnumerical quantifiers, "listeners may not necessarily compute amounts at all . . . that speakers may not intend them to do so," and that an association between a general quantifier and a specific amount is really a secondary characteristic (1993, 17).

All of these considerations need to be taken into account in building toward a general theory of quantifiers. In addition to our general theory of quantifiers as being rhetorically conditioned, we should also recognize that: (1) for certain statements, *specific numbers are simply not known* (e.g., "Proteins have potentially *limitless* combinations of amino acids" [B204; emphasis added]), or (2) numerical values may be irrelevant (e.g., "By the beginning of the 20th century, the promise of understanding the basis of immunity *loomed large*" [B681; emphasis added]).

Numerolatry

Specificity in quantifying serves several functions, such as: *impressing* and *persuading, understanding* and *verifying.* People are impressed by our knowledge of specific data. In trying to persuade someone to our thesis or point of view, one of the more convincing arguments is citing "the facts." And finally, as we saw above, exact figures can aid us greatly in our understanding and verifying of phenomena. Yet, as Harvey reminds us: "Pretending to a level of precision that is not attainable has pernicious rather than illuminating results" (1969, 307).

Our enchantment with numbers can be traced back to Pythagoras, who—as we saw—discovered simple numerical musical intervals and applied them to distances in the planetary system. Ever since then, numbers have exerted a powerful influence on people's thinking, in virtually all realms of inquiry: religion (the Trinity, the Kabbala), philosophy (Marxian and Hegelian thought), psychiatry (the ego–the id–the superego), to name but a few. Visual historian Rudolph Arnheim cites the seventeenth-century Florentine astronomer Francesco Sizi, who rejected Galileo's discovery of the moons of Jupiter, insisting there were seven windows in the head and seven days of the week, named for the seven planets: "If we increase the number of planets, this whole system falls to the ground" (Arnheim 1969, 213).

In short, a strict—or *overly numerical*—quantification runs the risk of forcing one into the traditional deductive fallacy: trying to make the facts fit the theory.

Where hard data are not required or not known, general quantifiers—or *approximations*—are completely appropriate. Indeed, Arnheim suggests that numbers come rather late to human thinking, and that counting is preceded by a "perceptual grasp of groups." "There are," in Arnheim's words, "two quite different ways of ascertaining a quantity— by counting or measuring, and by the grasp of perceptual structure" (1969, 212).

Classes and Subsets of Quantifiers

Hogg (1977) has parsed the major divisions of quantifiers into *absolutes* and *relatives,* a set championed by scholars Lakoff, Carden, and, originally, Partee. Against this, he suggests the terms *universal* and *existential,* adopted from symbolic logic. The two pairs, while not synonymous, have a rough equivalence. Absolutes and universals refer to the entire set, the whole of an item, such as: *all, every,* or *none.* Relatives and existentials refer to a subset, such as: *some, much,* or *certain* (as in *certain* people). Hogg provides a further analysis of the two sets (1977, 44ff.). For the sake of descriptive simplicity, I have chosen the terms *universal* and *partial quantifiers* to represent the two categories.

SUBSETS. One of the challenges of our inquiry is to discern the various inclusive and exclusive subsets that quantifiers fall into. This has been done, to a certain extent, in studies we have cited. However, the potential range of classifications is vast, and new insights are always enlightening. In this section, I would like to add a few new categories to the list and also offer a few comments on several of the traditional ones.

Exclusive Subsets

Let's start with exclusive categories: those that accept a limited number of quantifying words and phrases. These can be further subdivided into *scalar* (words that can be placed on a scale) and *nonscalar* groups (those that cannot). Scalars include such items as: degree (How much? To what extent?), frequency (How often?), probability (What is the probability of x happening?), quantity-mass (How much?), quantity-count (How many?), size (How big?), and sufficiency (How much? Answer: We have enough/ too much.). Here are a few new categories we might add to the list of exclusive quantifiers:

1. *default words:* words indicating what is left over from the main topic of the discussion:

   The sclera . . . protects most of the eyeball, and the cornea covers *the rest.* (B610; emphasis added)

   Other enzymes convert *the remaining* strand of DNA to the double-stranded form. (B250; emphasis added)

   The *remaining* radiation warms the earth's surface. (B848; emphasis added)

2. *descriptors:* quantity words that provide a nonquantitative description of an item:

Phagocyte white blood cells . . . include . . . macrophages, the *big eaters.* (B682; emphasis added)

Some experiments with *large* domestic animals have not been successful. (B256; emphasis added)

In water, its [the platypus's] *oversized,* webbed feet become paddles. (B443; emphasis added)

3. *false quantifiers:* words that have a numerical element but are not quantifiers:

You may be reluctant to scratch *one* [a bat] behind the ears. (B598; emphasis added)

Such bats routinely *zero in* on vocal but unlucky male frogs. (B588; emphasis added)

In *deep*-water fishes, gulping air is something of a problem. (B449; emphasis added)

4. *infinites:* words that express a huge unspecified quantity. Infinites are the most dramatic class of quantifiers and, as such, add a strong rhetorical flavor to the exposition. They represent a number from huge to infinity. In that sense, they are *scalar* and *range words* (to be discussed below). On the other hand, they indicate a certain but unspecified quantity. Bolinger also notes the presence of nouns as intensifiers, that may "include almost any non-human noun referring to something of great size or abundance, especially large measures" (1972, 58) *(oceans/mountains/bucketfuls of love).*

Only rarely does the text combine an infinite with a numerical ("The plasma cells are weapons factories. They make *vast numbers* of copies of the particular antibody. . . . For the next few days they secrete *about 2,000 antibody molecules per second* into their surroundings" [B687; emphasis added]). Here are some sample sentences containing infinites:

Genetic messages have changed *countless* times; this is the source of life's diversity. (B245; emphasis added)

DNA technology has *staggering* potential for medicine. (B245; emphasis added)

Proteins have potentially *limitless* combinations of amino acids and subunits. (B204; emphasis added)

It took a *fantastic* amount of photosynthesis . . . to form each major seam of coal. (B34; emphasis added)

5. *normatives:* Words that indicate the normal or usual state or condition of a situation; e.g., *tend to, usually, typically, overall, generally, dominate,* as in the following examples:

> *Overall,* their distribution [that of major biomes] *tends to* correspond with climate, topography, and soil type. (B852; emphasis added)

> A layer of ice *typically* forms over a temperate lake in midwinter. (B862; emphasis added)

> [In grasslands] warm temperature *prevails* during summer in the temperate zones. (B856; emphasis added)

> Spruce and fir *dominate* the forests to the north. (B860; emphasis added)

6. *numericals:* nonnumber words that give an exact quantity: *double, pair, half, (semi-),* as in the following sentences:

> They [bacteria] *doubled* in number and were on their way to *doubling* again. (B694; emphasis added)

> Each new DNA molecule is really *half old, half new.* This is why the process is called *semiconservative* replication. (B210; emphasis added)

7. *sufficiency words:* words that indicate the level of sufficiency; e.g., *enough, too much/old/*etc., *excess, close enough.* Notice the sample sentences:

> PCR . . . is being used in studies of samples that are *too old* to contain intact DNA. (B249; emphasis added)

> Normally, the enzyme functions in a pathway by which *excess* adenosine monophosphate (AMP) is stripped of its phosphate group. (B24; emphasis added)

> The world's major forest biomes have tall trees growing *close enough* together to form a fairly continuous canopy. (B858; emphasis added)

8. *universals:* a well-known class that we have discussed earlier. Apart from the terms normally associated with this class (e.g., *each, all, every),* we find less typical words like *total, fully able,* and *lethal,* as in:

> Some groups [of salamanders] have sexually precocious larvae that are *fully able* to breed. (B454; emphasis added)

> Ultraviolet wavelengths can be *lethal* to most forms of life. (B848; emphasis added)

Nonscalars include the traditional *approximators (about, roughly, more or less, much)* as in:

> Each type of nucleotide in DNA has its component parts joined together in *much* the same way as the others. (B206; emphasis added)

Oceans, mountain ranges, deserts, and other barriers have often kept them [certain species] *more or less* isolated from one another. (B851; emphasis added)

Also, *intensifiers,* or *emphasizers:* words that stress a fact without changing its quantity; for example:

Each B cell . . . makes many copies of *just* one kind of antibody. (B686; emphasis added)

Protein-degrading enzymes had no effect *at all* on the transforming activity. (B207; emphasis added)

To these we might add:

9. *partition words:* words that indicate part of a whole *(part, portion, section, segment),* as in:

Sensory neurons, nerve pathways, and brain regions are required for these tasks. Together, they represent the *portions* of the nervous system that are called sensory systems. (B599; emphasis added)

Each type of nucleotide in DNA has its *component parts* joined together in much the same way as the others. (B208; emphasis added)

10. *range words:* words and phrases that indicate a range of quantity; e.g., *varies from, ranges between, varies in size.* Notice the sample sentences:

Every two to seven years, the warm reservoir and the associated heavy rainfall move eastward. (B871; emphasis added)

The patch [of desert] may have ocotillo, which can drop leaves *more than once a year,* then grow new ones *within a week.* (B854; emphasis added)

Annual rainfall can *exceed 200 centimeters* and is *never less than 130 centimeters.* (B858; emphasis added)

11. *metaphors.* Though metaphors are rhetorically rather than semantically based, our corpus contains an interesting, if minor, use of metaphors to express quantity; in this case, distance and speed:

Now, through implementation of DNA technology, that *long road* of basic research is forking almost daily in new directions. (B251; emphasis added)

[re: bottom-dwelling fish] Their . . . bodies are easy to conceal, but the shape tells us that these fishes have to be sluggish, not *the Corvettes of the deep.* (B449; emphasis added)

Inclusive Subsets

Inclusive subsets include those into which all nonnumerical quantifiers can be divided. In the manner of Chinese boxes, we can immediately list (1) partials and universals, (2) scalars and nonscalars, and (3) numericals and nonnumericals (i.e., general and specific). Another traditional category (4) is that of *ascenders, descenders,* and what we might call (5) neutrals: words that indicate an increasing, decreasing, or medial but indeterminate quantity:

> The *increased* [↑] acidity switches on an enzyme that can digest the chicken protein. (B30; emphasis added)

> As we move out from the tropical rain forests, we enter regions where temperatures remain mild but rainfall *dwindles* [↓] during part of the year. (B858; emphasis added)

> *Some* [↔] substances release one or more protons. (B30; emphasis added).

To these we might add the following:

6. *assignables* and *nonassignables.* Assignables are nonnumerical quantifiers that can be assigned a reasonably specific numerical value; for example probability words (*very unlikely* is about a 5% chance). Also universals, which by definition, are 100%, plus several others we will discuss below (vanishing point, itemizers, some range words).

7. *inherents* (and by default, noninherents) are words whose meanings denote more than one (*assemble, combined, partner, mosaic).* Notice the following sentences:

> Other enzymes *assemble* a new DNA strand on the exposed regions of the parent strand. (B211; emphasis added)

> The number of species [of bony fish] possibly exceeds the number of all species of land vertebrates *combined.* (B450; emphasis added)

> The platypus is a *mosaic* of reptilian, avian, and mammalian traits. (B442; emphasis added)

8. *implicits:* words whose secondary connotation is quantitative (*severe, book, battery,* as in a battery of tests). We will discuss inherents and implicits at length in the section "Context and Precision."

9. and finally *contextual* and *noncontextual* words. Noncontextuals are those words whose quantitativeness exists independent of context. Inherent quantifiers are noncontextual. So are words like *group* and *collection, amount* and *variety, differentiate* and *multiply.*

Contextuals, on the other hand, are words whose quantitativeness is derived from their context. Contextuality is a major theme in our study and will be discussed at greater length in the next section.

Here we return to our original question: "Why the great variety of quantifiers?" There are probably hundreds of them, all used to cover a limited field of information. True, we can subdivide them into categories such as degree, frequency, and probability, as we have seen. Yet their huge number remains. This is all the more curious, considering that many scholars—linguists and others—tend to feel there are no true synonyms in a language. Why, then, do we find such clustering among quantifiers? Our suggestion is that the need is more rhetorical than semantic. Bolinger also notes the need for novelty in degree words and emphasizers in general, areas where terms "quickly grow stale and need to be replaced" (1972, 18). Since quantification plays such an important role in scientific discourse—and comparable measurements occur with such frequency—it is necessary to have a variety of words for expressing those measures.

Still, a wide variety is also found in speech. In one experiment, for example, subjects were asked to describe drawings that contained different proportions of male and female pin figures, so that a person listening to the description could select the correct one from a set. From a total of 825 descriptions, people produced 182 different expressions. Presumably these expressions did not correspond to 182 different numerical values, but to many identical numbers or a similar range of proportions (Moxey and Sanford 1993, 4).

Context and Precision

Two of the forces influencing the creation and behavior of quantifiers are *context* and *precision*.

Context

Many words acquire a quantitative meaning solely because of the context they appear in. We thus speak of *contextual* and *context-free* quantifiers. Notice the following examples of contextual quantifiers:

> Blood pressure *plummets* and can lead to circulatory collapse. (B693; emphasis added)

> The pharynx . . . has a *good* supply of blood. (B445; emphasis added)

> The boy *remained* free of infection. (B680; emphasis added)

> The *breathtaking* simplicity of the structure [DNA] enabled them [Watson and Crick] to solve a long-standing riddle about life. (B204; emphasis added)

Out of context, to plummet means to fall, *good* is normally associated with the paradigm *good, better, best*. And the verb *remain* normally has a more locative than temporal meaning. In the above sentences, *plummeting* means a sharp decrease in temperature, *good* becomes a large or considerable supply, and *remain* refers to the fact that a boy inoculated by Jenner with the diphtheria vaccine remained free of infection for the duration of his life.

In like manner, many words assume a quantitative meaning by virtue of their *collocations*. Consider these sentences:

> The x-ray diffraction images provided *convincing* evidence that DNA had the following features . . . (B209; emphasis added)

> Plasmid genes are transmitted through *successive* generations of bacterial cells. (B246; emphasis added)

> Individuals with *severely* compromised immune systems have *drastically* reduced numbers of these infection-fighting cells. (B245; emphasis added)

Out of context, the terms *convincing* and *successive* have no inherent quantitative meaning. That meaning is acquired by their reasonably common collocation with the following terms *(convincing evidence, successive generations)*; similarly, in the last sentence with the words *severely* and *drastically*. Their primary adjective forms *(severe, drastic)* have a slightly quantitative feel to them, which is strengthened by their conversion to adverbials with the addition of the -ly suffix.

Indeed, we may ask the questions: How many words (1) have quantification as a secondary connotation or (2) acquire a quantifying meaning solely by collocation? This leads us to two concepts that we might call inherent and implicit quantifiers. An *inherent quantifier,* as we have seen, is a word that contains the meaning of more than one item, apart from its context. An *implicit quantifier* is a word with a secondary connotation of quantity (admittedly, this may be an overly fine distinction). These sample words from our corpus are inherent quantifiers: *divide, generation, collection, colony, partner.* Here are some sentences with inherent quantifiers:

> Hundred of *generations* of bacteria descended from the transformed cells. (B206; emphasis added)

> With that track record, who are we to chuckle at the curious *collection* of platypus traits? (B443; emphasis added)

> Each parent strand is twisted into a double helix with a *partner* strand. (B210; emphasis added)

> All of the cells may *reproduce* to form *large colonies.* (B250; emphasis added)

IMPLICIT QUANTIFIERS. Implicit quantifiers include words like *book, battery, generation,* and *library,* as in the following sentences:

> The [DNA] molecule . . . serves as a *book* of genetic information in every living cell. (B204; emphasis added)

It takes a *battery* of enzymes . . . to unwind the [DNA] molecule. (B211; emphasis added)

We now have a DNA *library*—a collection of DNA fragments. (B248; emphasis added)

Syntactically, we may also regard *generalizations* as containing quantifiers. Compare the following sentences:

People need water.

People love Italians.

Even though both sentences lack explicit quantifiers, their quantities differ. The first implies that *all* people need water. The second implies that *some* people love *some* Italians. In our corpus, we find a few rare cases in which a specific figure follows the generalized quantifier:

In each round, the DNA first is denatured by exposure to *near-boiling temperatures* (about 94°C). (B249; emphasis added)

Where regular, heavy rainfall coincides *with high humidity* (80 percent or more) . . . , you will find highly productive tropical rain forests. (B858; emphasis added)

Precision

Clearly, the thing that differentiates numerical from nonnumerical quantifiers is the matter of *precision,* or *specificity.* The matter therefore deserves a few comments.

Studies suggest that people have little common agreement on numerical values in a nonnumerical scale such as the following:

0%   very small   small   medium   large   very large   100%

In one study, subjects were asked to give an arbitrary value for the word *some;* say, 50. They were then asked to assign numerical values for forty-three other expressions, in relation to the value of *some.* The study revealed a large overlap among the other expressions. Even with a scale of only nine expressions, there was an overlap of 20% between adjacent words (Moxey and Sanford 1993, 20).

One way of dealing with this is the well-known use of *approximators:* words like *about, just, almost,* and *much,* as in the following sentences:

Each type of nucleotide in DNA has its component parts joined together in *much* the same way as the others. (B206; emphasis added)

Adult amphibians eat *just about* any animal they can catch. (B454; emphasis added)

As a subset of approximators, we might include *diminishers,* words that reduce the amount of a quantity:

> With their *potentially limitless* combination of amino acid subunits, proteins *almost certainly* could function as the sentences [genes] in each cell's book of inheritance. (B204; emphasis added)

In a sense, all nonnumericals are approximators (apart from words indicating 0 and 100%). Our corpus reveals that even numerical quantifiers often contain an element of approximation. An analysis of one chapter (Chapter 47), for example, shows the existence of twenty-seven numerical quantifiers (compared to several hundred nonnumericals). Of these, only three contained exact figures *(three general types, at 4 °C, six distinct realms).* Among the others, fourteen contained range words (words that include a range of measurement). Nine included approximators *(about 80 percent);* and one, an approximator plus a range word *(about 40 to 100 centimeters).*

TOLERANCE. Even in (numerical) measurements, *tolerances* are allowed that do not compromise the results of the work. These tolerances are normally specified, such as "one part per thousand," or "plus or minus 10," although they may be stated or unstated. Thus, tests of scientific statements are generally reported within a range of precision. The degree of precision needed relates to the task at hand.

Fine-tuning

In addition to approximators, there are many more ways in which quantifiers are used to achieve greater precision, or *fine-tuning.* Indeed, fine-tuning seems to be the main reason for the existence of numerous classes, and an important reason for others. Among these classes are: vanishing point, degree words, frequency words, probability words, multiple quantifiers, and intensifiers. Let's examine a few of these classes and the fine-tuning function that they serve.

Just as some quantifiers reach 100% and beyond (the infinites), others aim in the opposite direction. They approach zero (a universal), but hold out the smallest amount possible. We might call them quantifiers of the *vanishing point:*

> Air descends to the polar regions, where low temperatures and *almost* nonexistent precipitation create cold, dry, polar deserts. (B848; emphasis added)

> *All but about 5 percent* of the carbon in the Arctic is locked up in peat. (B861; emphasis added)

> The amount of DNA in a library is *almost vanishingly small.* (B248; emphasis added)

MULTIPLE QUANTIFIERS. Notice how the use of multiple quantifiers in the following sentences—three in the first two and four in the third—helps fine-tune the information:

> *All* of the *36 or so* species live in moderately deep water. (B450; emphasis added)

> Existing species are *generally quite small.* (B459; emphasis added)

> *Nearly all* of the *150 or so* species live in humid forests. (B455; emphasis added)

INTENSIFIERS (EMPHASIZERS). Intensifiers may serve a chiefly rhetorical or semantic function, depending on their sentence context. Rhetorically, they add no new information in modifying these numerical statements:

> This may have no effect *whatsoever* on survival and reproduction. (B277; emphasis added)

> Each B cell . . . makes many copies of *just* one kind of antibody. (B686; emphasis added)

> Protein-degrading enzymes had no effect *at all* on the transforming activity. (B207; emphasis added)

Semantically, they do serve a fine-tuning function in the following:

> And so peat became *even* more compact, with a higher percentage of carbon. (B34; emphasis added)

> As the specimen shown in Figure 26 *so* adequately suggests . . . (B454; emphasis added)

The phrase *so adequately* seems almost overly fine-tuned and presses against the next higher level (e.g., It *strongly* suggests).

HEDGES. At the same time, many quantifiers may be viewed as *hedges:* words that provide a greater degree of tentativeness, or margin of error, to a statement. Looking back at some of our recent examples, we can say that *much the same way* is *less* precise than *the same way. Just about any animal* is *less* precise than *any animal.* And *almost nonexistent precipitation* is *less* precise than *nonexistent precipitation.* But while these statements may be less precise, they are also presumably *more accurate.*

Scales, Scalars, and Scalarity

To the extent that there is a common thread among quantifiers, that common thread is *scalarity.* As we saw early on, a great number of classes are based on relative positions in a set. For this reason, we might explore this concept a bit further. As one study so well puts it: "How many is many, how many is few . . . how often is seldom, how probable is likely?" (Moxey and Sanford 1993, ix). More specifically, we might also ask: What correspondences can we find between different subsets of scalars? How do scales divide up; that is, are the points or ranges on a scale evenly divided, or do they tend to cluster? What about overlap? Do certain sets have greater accuracy than others? Can we discern any underlying patterns or relationships within the order of scalarity?

Our list from early on includes the following sets (a total of twelve): default words, degree words, descriptors, frequency words, infinites, normatives, quantity-count words, quantity-mass words, probability words, size words, sufficiency words, and universals. To make comparing easier, I have arranged them in a table (Table 9.1). A capital *Y* (for yes) means that the item is used for a particular quantity; e.g., degree words are used for items from 0 to 100%. An *X* means that it is not; e.g., normatives are not used to describe very small (VS) quantities. A *Y* in parentheses *(Y)* means that the item *can* occur but is not very likely.

What can we learn from the table? Working our way down, we find that only six of the twelve classes have full sets, apart from 100%+, which is unique to infinites. Of these, only three (frequency, quantity-mass, and quantity-count) share several of the quintessential quantity words: *a few, some(times), much, many,* and *all.* Accordingly, they may have a closer correspondence in people's minds in general. In addition, they may well represent more clearly delineated quantities than some of the sets that use highly contextual words.

Default words, in our corpus *(the rest, the remainder, the remaining),* cluster around the small value *(S);* a default would not be zero or 100%. *Descriptors* also cluster, specifically around the value of large *(L).* Things tend to be oversized, long-legged, or simply large (B682, B462, B256). We can also say that *normatives,* judging from their use in our corpus *(tend to, normally, usually, generally),* cluster around large–very large–100% *(L, VL, 100%).* That which is typical or prevailing is, in all likelihood, more than 50%.

As for *sufficiency words (not enough, not quite enough, enough, excess, too much),* zero sufficiency does not occur. One could have not enough to survive, but that would still be a very small amount *(VS).* A problem arises with the phrase *too much.* How much is too much? My sense is that, in general, a medium or large amount is still not too much. For something to be too much, it would have to be very large or 100%. And as for *universals,* we can regard them as *polar* rather than scalar since they exist only at the two ends of the scale.

SET	0	VS	S	M	L	VL	100%	100%+
Default	X	Y	Y	(Y)	Y	Y	X	
Degree	Y	Y	Y	Y	Y	Y	Y	
Descriptors	X	(Y)	Y	(Y)	Y	Y	X	
Frequency	Y	Y	Y	Y	Y	Y	Y	
Infinites	X	X	X	X	X	X	X	Ⓨ
Normatives	X	X	X	X	←Y	Y	Y→	
Qnty/Mass	Y	Y	Y	Y	Y	Y	Y	
Qnty/Count	Y	Y	Y	Y	Y	Y	Y	
Probability	Y	Y	Y	Y	Y	Y	Y	
Size	Y	Y	Y	Y	Y	Y	Y	
Sufficiency	X	Y	Y	Y	(Y)	←too Y	much→ Y	
Universal	Ⓨ	X	X	X	X	X	Ⓨ	

Table 9.1. Table of Quantities

RHETORICAL EFFECTS. A rhetorical effect that appears in the very large *(VL)* column—and that cuts across several sets of quantifiers—is the occurrence of dramatic, or "emotional," terms, words like *severe* (B858), *immense* (B850), *frighteningly* (B851), *alarmingly* (B854), *massively* (B871). We also find a strong rhetorical flavor in the very large and 100% cells of *degree words;* for example, phrases such as *profound effort* (B6), *total darkness* (B13), *severely injured* (B2).

Two Sample Passages

As I noted at the beginning of the chapter, quantifiers are an integral part of the language, especially the language of science. To illustrate their subtlety and pervasiveness, I have reproduced two sample passages for analysis. The first, admittedly, is chosen for its variety and abundance of quantifiers. I have labeled each quantifier with an abbreviation of the set that it belongs to (NORM = normative, e.g.):

Sample 1

Within *each* [UNIV] biogeographic realm are *major* [NORM] ecosystems in which *certain* [QNTY/COUNT] plants and other organisms *predominate* [NORM]. *Each* [UNIV] *major* [NORM] type of ecosystem is a biome. Biomes *dominated* [NORM] by *short plant species* [DESCRIPTOR] *tend to*

[NORM] *prevail* [NORM] in *dry* [QNTY/COUNT] regions, at *high altitude* [QNTY/COUNT] and at *high elevations* [QNTY/COUNT]. Those *dominated* [NORM] by *tall* [QNTY/COUNT], leafy plant species *prevail* [NORM] at *tropical* [QNTY/COUNT] and *temperate* [QNTY/COUNT] latitudes and *low elevations* [QNTY/COUNT] where *warm temperatures* [QNTY/ COUNT] combine with *high rainfall* [QNTY/COUNT]. Such plants are *typical* [NORM] of *tropical* [QNTY/COUNT] rain forests, which show the *highest* [QNTY/MASS] *annual* [FREQ] *primary* [SEQ] *productivity*. (B851; emphasis added)

Sample 2

[A passage describing grasslands and savannas] The land is *usually* [FREQ/ NORM] flat or rolling. *Warm temperatures* [QNTY/COUNT] *prevail* [NORM] during summer in the *temperate zones* [QNTY/COUNT] and throughout the *year* [FREQ] in *the tropics*. The *25 to 100 centimeters* [RANGE] of *annual rainfall* [FREQ] is *enough* [SUFFIC] to keep the regions from turning into deserts but *not enough* [SUFFIC] to support forests. Grazing and burrowing species are the *dominant* [NORM] forms of animal life. Grazing activities and *periodic* [FREQ] fires stop the encroachment of the forests. . . . Where winds are *strong* [DEGREE], rainfall *light* [DEGREE/ COUNT?] and *infrequent* [FREQ], and evaporation *rapid* [MASS/TEMPORAL?], we find *shortgrass prairie* [DESCRIPTOR]. Plant roots above the *permanently dry subsoil* [FREQ] soak up the *brief* [FREQ], *seasonal* [FREQ] rainfall. *Much of* [QNTY/MASS] the shortgrass prairie of the American Great Plains was *overgrazed* [SUFFIC] and plowed under for wheat, which requires *more* [QNTY/MASS] moisture than the region provides. (B856; emphasis added)

Sample 1 contains five sentences and 25 quantifiers, an average of 5 quantifiers per sentence. Sample 2 contains eight sentences and 22 quantifiers, an average of 2.75 quantifiers per sentence. How typical is this? Another section of our corpus (B386)—with six paragraphs and twenty-five sentences—reveals 31 quantifiers. This yields an average of 1.24 quantifiers per sentence, which is probably more typical. In addition, the first forty-two definitions in the glossary contain 28 quantifiers, an average of 0.6 quantifiers per definition. These figures further indicate how integral the process of quantifying is to our thinking.

I have marked the phrase *primary productivity* in Sample 1 as SEQ, short for sequence. *Sequence words*, or *itemizers*, may be considered quantifiers. They imply additional items in a series (secondary, tertiary; first, second, third; the following . . .). Ultimately—psychologically—it depends on whether an item has "a quantifying feel" for the reader. Consider the following sentences:

In short, the inflammatory response involves *these events:* . . . (B683; emphasis added)

the images . . . provided convincing evidence that DNA had the *following features* . . . First . . . Second . . . Third . . . (B209; emphasis added)

A *first-time* encounter with an antigen elicits a *primary immune response.* (B686; emphasis added)

Does a first-time encounter suggest a second-time encounter? Does a primary immune response suggest a secondary immune response? If we accept our original definition of quantifying as making "assertions about the number of things being talked about," then itemizers need to be accepted as quantifiers.

A problem arises with the word *rapid,* meaning quickly, in a short period or amount of time. In this sense, we might place it in the set that quantifies mass nouns. But this doesn't "feel" quite right. An alternative is to include it in a class that we might call *temporals,* or time words of a scalar nature (the job takes no time/very little time/not much time/a bit of time/a lot of time/a great deal of time/forever).

A further area of interest involves the use of *high* and *low* in discussions of rainfall and altitudes, elevations and productivity. We can define high rainfall as a large amount of rainfall (MASS); high altitude as anything above, say, 8,000 feet (COUNT); low elevation as anything below, say, 1,000 feet (COUNT); and high productivity as a MASS measurement. Ultimately, however, our earlier question returns: Does the word give the reader a quantifying feel in these contexts?

Let me offer a final comment, on the words *tropical* and *temperate,* in the context of zones, latitudes, and rain forests. Things tropical are characterized by having consistently high temperatures and high humidity; things temperate, by having mild temperatures. To the extent that these quantifying elements are activated in the mind of the reader, the terms may be considered quantifiers.

Conclusion

We have examined the language of quantifying in a science text. In all likelihood, the occurrence of quantifiers is lower in nonscience texts and much lower in nonscience writing. Yet it stands as a major mode of perception and thinking in general.

We have explored some of the myriad semantic sets that quantifiers belong to and some of their special properties and behaviors. We have observed that quantifying statements are overwhelmingly nonnumerical and nonspecific; that nonnumerical quantifiers use a variety of ways to fine-tune their claims; and that even numerical statements of quantity often use verbal quantifiers in their statements.

We have also seen how context plays a primary role in the formation of quantifiers and how it invests nonquantifying words with a quantifying meaning.

My thesis has been that the seemingly endless proliferation of quantifiers is due more to rhetorical than semantic reasons: the need for variety, novelty, even accuracy, in making quantitative statements.

I hope this chapter has not quantified you to death. Those who believe in devils see devils everywhere. Those who believe in angels see angels everywhere. I hope I have not been guilty of this. Still, the significance of our study—if there is one—is to realize how important and subtle a role quantifying plays in our thinking. As we have seen, it is not a matter of numbers, but of a general quantifying sense. As such, it is an element of language—and of thought—that deserves more careful attention than most of us have given it.

A List of Quantifiers

As a handy reference, I have appended a list of quantifiers that were discussed or mentioned in the chapter:

approximators

ascenders and descenders

context-free (noncontextual) quantifiers

contextual quantifiers

default quantifiers

degree words

descriptors

false quantifiers

frequency words

implicit quantifiers

infinites

itemizers/sequence words

multiple quantifiers

numerical quantifiers

partial quantifiers

partition words

probability words

range words

sufficiency words

temporals

universal quantifiers

Chapter 10

The Language of Comparison

No two snowflakes are the same. How so should two of any other
things in the universe?

S. DARIAN

❋

To understand lions and tigers and bears, you first need to know the
basic chemistry that makes them tick, for they are chemical machines,
as you are.

Every carbon atom in your body was created in a star.

RAVEN AND JOHNSON,

Biology, 1989

❋

Sound familiar? Yes. Well, primal analogies die hard. And not just among
the ancients. Our corpus for this chapter was a biology text published in
1989. Yet even here we find our primal analogies: Man the Machine and
Man the Microcosm. Though we can assume our authors are using these
images in a more figurative sense, they still seem to cast their spell, in however attenuated a form.

Originally, I had not intended to write a chapter on comparison. But the
topic interposed itself further and further . . . until I had no choice.

The Comparative Sense

The Structure of Comparison

Comparison is one of the most loosely structured of our thought modes. It
has four elements, two of which are sometimes omitted. In what we might
call its canonical—or full—form, a comparison contains:

- two or more items being compared *(X and Y);*
- the basis—or bases—of comparison. Let's call them *criteria;*
- a word or phrase indicating a comparison. Let's call it a *comparitor.*

THE ITEMS BEING COMPARED. The two or more items being compared need not be two separate items but can be the same item, compared

to itself at different times, as in this example from our biology text (Raven and Johnson 1989):

> The book [Darwin's *Origin of Species*] created a sensation when it was published *in 1859,* and the ideas expressed in it have played a central role in human thought *ever since.* (B7; emphasis added)

Or in the case of superlatives, we are comparing an item (X) to all the items in its class (Y). That Y may be *stated* ("One of the greatest advances in physics in this century [SD: compared to other great advances] was the discovery that electrons orbit a nucleus only at certain distances" [B24]) or *implied* ("He's the greatest").

CRITERIA. A comparison may contain one or more criteria for comparing the items. We'll examine specific criteria further on, at the semantic level. The criterion can be (A) stated or (B) implied:

> [A] The earliest vertebrates had far *more complex* brains than their ancestors. (B903; emphasis added)

> [B] The oaks, beeches, and chestnuts are grouped, along with other genera, in the beech family Fagaceae, because of the *many similar features* they have in common. (B555; emphasis added)

COMPARITORS. Comparitors—terms like *compared to, in contrast, differ, like, unlike, related to*—occur in a great variety of forms, which we'll examine in our section "Lexical Items." Like criteria, the comparitor is sometimes absent.

In analyzing our quote above—on Darwin—we could say that:

- *X* = the first time period (1859)
- *Y* = the second time period: up to the present *(ever since)*
- the criterion is the effect of Darwin's ideas
- there is no comparitor

Categories of Comparison

We can classify comparisons in several ways. Linguist Michael Halliday divides them into two groups: General and Particular. Under *General Comparisons,* he includes items of likeness and unlikeness that have no specified property, or in our terms, no criteria:

> The brains of all vertebrates are organized along similar lines. (B900)

> Plants, animals, amoebas—individuals that belong to distinct major groups of organisms—differ so greatly from one another that it is difficult at first to identify the features they have in common. (B429)

The X and Y, as we have seen, may refer to the same thing ("It's the same bird we saw yesterday") or to two different things (Halliday and Hasan 1976, 80). *Particular Comparisons,* on the other hand, include a specific quality or quantity; in other words, one or more criteria.

Professor Lee Kok Cheong groups them somewhat differently, suggesting comparisons of: (1) *equality,* (2) *inequality,* (3) *similarities and differences,* and what he calls (4) relationships of *opposition* (Cheong 1978, 137–160). His uses of equality ("X is as successful as classical physics") and inequality ("X is more efficient than Y") both include criteria (successfulness and efficiency). His meaning of similarities and differences includes examples with and without criteria, which thus differ somewhat from the items in Halliday's general class. As for category #4—opposition— Cheong includes words of contrast, such as *however, yet, still, in spite of, on the other hand,* words that relate items in a negative or surprising way. Take this example:

> *Although* the two hemispheres of the brain contain *all of the cortexes,* the two hemispheres are responsible for different *associative functions.* (B909; emphasis added)

In comparing the two hemispheres of the brain (our X and Y), our textbook notes that they are alike in one way and different in another. Accordingly, the sentence contains two criteria: *all of the cortexes* and *associative functions.*

Here's a rough comparison of Cheong's and Halliday's concepts:

	Halliday	Cheong
General:	Like	Similar
	Unlike	Different
Particular:	Smaller than	Inequality
	Bigger than	Inequality
	As big as	Equality
	————	Opposition

In the three *traditional* categories of comparison (positive, comparative, and superlative), the positive form may or may not compare things. There is an implied comparison in the sentence "It's heavy" (compared to other similar items). Or a stated comparison in "CO_2 is 30 times as soluble as oxygen" (B992). Interestingly, this has the same meaning as its comparative form: "CO_2 is 30 times more soluble than oxygen." The comparative form compares two items against a lesser-or-greater criterion of some sort. And the superlative compares three or more items, against some absolute standard.

The Movement of Thought

At the start of the book, we looked at the direction of thought—the linear, recursive, reciprocal turns taken by various thought patterns. We observed specific examples of this in our chapter on cause and effect. Comparison as well shows distinct movement in its referents and relationships. As we will see, one of the major functions of comparisons is as a cohesive device, tying together different segments of discourse: between sentences, between paragraphs, and between subsections of a chapter.

Here are the three basic movements in the language of comparison, with an example of each:

ANAPHORIC (←——). An item in a sentence refers back to a preceding clause or sentences:

> The apple in your hand is said to possess energy . . . because of its position— if you were to release it, the apple would fall. ←—— *Similarly,* electrons have energy of position. (B23; emphasis added)

> On the primitive earth . . . [certain] molecules were bound to one another in strongly linked crystalline arrays . . . which combined and formed rocks. ←—— *In contrast to the others,* the molecules of one compound . . . did not form crystals: water. (B31; emphasis added)

The words *similarly* and *others* derive their meaning from reference to previous statements.

CATAPHORIC (——→). The meaning, or referent, of an item depends on information further on in the sentence, or in a later sentence. Both Cheong and Halliday found cataphoric use of comparatives not very common (Cheong 1978, 145; Halliday and Hasan 1976, 78). My findings were similar in our biology text. Some examples:

> The heart of a vertebrate faces *the same problem* ——→ as a closed garden hose: it must push a pulse of fluid through a closed system of vessels that meets a resistance at one end—a network of small capillaries. (B1010; emphasis added)

> The brains of fishes continue growing throughout their lives. This is in marked *contrast to* ——→ the brains of the more advanced classes of vertebrates, which complete their development by infancy. (B905; emphasis added)

> The cerebrum [X], which is at the very front of the human brain, is so large *relative to* ——→ the rest of the brain [Y] that it appears to envelop it. (B907; emphasis added)

In both cases, the reader must read on to determine what that *same problem* is and also how the fish's development compares to that of other vertebrates.

RECIPROCAL (←——→). A balanced comparison of items within a sentence:

> Species on oceanic islands show ←—— *strong affinities* to ——→ those on the nearest mainland. Thus the finches on the Galapagos Islands ←—— *closely resemble* ——→ a finch seen on the western coast of South America. The Galapagos finches ←—— *do not resemble* ——→ the birds of the Cape Verde islands in the Atlantic Ocean off Africa ←—— that are *very similar* to ——→ the Galapagos. (B9; emphasis added)

The paragraph contains a surprisingly high incidence of reciprocal comparisons: a total of four. All the cases are simple statements of similarity or difference, analogous to Halliday's general categories of like and unlike.

Haptics

As I suggested earlier—in our chapter on classifying—language was probably *perceptual* before it was *conceptual:* We had words for kangaroos and koalas before we had the word *mammal* (Linnaeus's term). Another level of language is its substratum of feeling, movement, balance, direction, what scholars in the performing arts call the *haptic* sense. Above all, comparison is a *relationship*—something palpable. It is a relationship—or set of relationships—that we can *feel* and, often, visualize. The four basic types of comparisons might be depicted as they are in Figure 10.1.

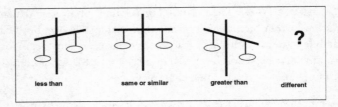

Figure 10.1. Kinds of Comparisons

Is there any significance to the fact that the last item—*difference*—does not fit into our visual paradigm? But we won't explore that here.

Comparison in Other Thought Patterns

Back in Chapter 1, we touched on the historical role of comparison in other thought patterns. Classifying and several figures of speech *are* comparisons. As we saw in Chapter 2, several elements of definitions also include comparison; for example, the limiting features.

This section will illustrate the role of comparison in several thought patterns from our text. Unless otherwise indicated, I have added the emphasizers (italics and boldface).

Definition

Consider the following examples:

> A classification based on many correlated features is said to be a **natural classification,** *whereas* one based on one or a few stated features is said to be an *artificial classification.* (B557)

Here, the authors are defining two terms by comparing them with each other. The criteria are the number and types of features. The comparitor is *whereas.*

> **Arterioles** *differ* from **arteries** simply in that they are smaller in diameter. (B1011)

The sentence provides a partial definition by comparison.

> A circulatory system may be either open or closed. In a **closed system** the fluid in the circulatory system is enclosed within the blood vessels and so is separated from the rest of the body's fluids and does not mix freely with them. . . .
> In an **open system,** *by contrast,* there is no distinction between circulating fluid and body fluid in general. (B1007)

As we will see below, in the section "Discourse-Level Features," this is a frequent pattern, in which the definition by contrast is reinforced (1) with a pair of boldfaced terms (boldfaced in the text) and (2) with the explicit comparitor *by contrast.* The use of these additional markers ties the paragraph together nicely.

Figurative Language

Our text makes considerable use of figurative language, especially simile, metaphor, analogy, and what we might call "simple comparison," that is, a statement that something resembles something else that is quite different but functions in a very similar way.

The quotes at the start of the chapter reflect the two dominant analogies of science: those of Man the Machine and Man the Microcosm. Recall, as well, from our chapter on figurative language, the analogy of the classical physician Galen, who compares the veins of the portal system, which carries the chyle to the liver, with the streets of a city, which carry food to the city's shops and bakeries. We find surprising echoes of this in our modern text:

> The vertebrate body is a complete colony of many cells. *Like a city,* it contains many individuals that carry out specialized functions. It has its own *police* (macrophages), its own *construction workers* (fibroblasts), and its own *telephone company* (the nervous system). The many individual cells of the vertebrate body, like the people in a city, need to be fed with *food that is trucked in from elsewhere.* (B968)

> If the circulatory system is thought of as the "highway" of the vertebrate body, the blood contains the "traffic" passing on that highway. (B1015)

We also find this extended metaphor comparing the liver to a savings bank:

> The liver, the body's "metabolic reservoir," thus acts much like a bank, making deposits and withdrawals in the "*currency*" of glucose molecules. . . . Also like a bank, the liver *exchanges currencies, converting* other molecules, such as amino acids and fats, to glucose for storage. . . . The first step in this conversion is the removal of the amino acid group (NH^+_4) from the amino acid. (B980)

Quantifying

Quantity and comparison are closely related. Cheong even suggests that "for every comparative sentence, there is an implied measurement sentence." And that these implications of measurement and quantity play a major part "in distinguishing logico-deductive texts from purely descriptive ones" (Cheong 1978, 241, 222).

Notice the following paragraph, in which each sentence contains a comparison. In fact, every sentence in the passage is a comparison of quantity. While not a typical proportion (30% of Cheong's sample contained comparative sentences), it illustrates the reciprocity between the two thought patterns:

> [1] *Since the time of Linnaeus,* about 1.4 million species have been named. [2] This is a far *greater* number of organisms *than* Linnaeus suspected to exist when he was developing his system of classification in the 18th century. [3] The actual number of species in the world . . . is undoubtedly much *greater,* judging from the very large numbers that are still being discovered. [4] Basing their estimates on numbers of species found in *different* parts of the world and the *proportions* of unknown species obtained in samples of *different* kinds, taxonomists have concluded that at least 5 million species of organisms exist on earth. [5] *At least* ⅔ *of these*—more than 3 million species—occur in the tropics. [6] Considering that only about 500,000 tropical species have been named so far, we may conclude that at least ⅚ of them are still unknown. (B555)

Here's an analysis of the passage, in table form:

entence #	X	Y	Criterion	Comparitor
	the time of Linnaeus	Y = now (implied)	number of species (1.4m)	————
	18th century	now	number of species (1.4m)	-er . . . than
	actual no. of species	1.4m	greater number	-er
	5 million	1.4m	actual number of species	proportion
	tropics	nontropical regions	number of species	(⅔) of these
	numbers already named	total number in tropics	unknown no. of tropical species	————

Another comparative feature of quantity is found in "allness" words: those that compare a particular item to all of the potential items in a set (100%). This would include words like: *each, all, every,* and the percent sign (%). We can consider the percent sign a comparative marker:

> *Over 90%* of *all* ulcers are duodenal. (B975)

> *Of all* its many functions [referring to the liver], *one of the most important* is its regulation of the blood's metabolic levels. (B979)

Here, *all* functions as an intensifier, emphasizing the great number and variety of functions. We could delete it and still have the same basic meaning. *Of* has the equivalency of *compared to,* and thus serves as a comparitor. A final item (and you could probably do a paper on the comparative elements of quantifiers) is the use of the word *times* (in the multiplication sense), which functions in the following sentence as a comparitor:

> In humans, the total surface area devoted to diffusion can be as much as 80 square meters; an area about **42 times** the surface of the body (B997). [SD: that is, compared to the remaining surface area of the body]

Visuals

In Chapter 8 we discussed the role of visuals in comparing. About 40% of the visuals in our biology text—pictures, drawings, charts, and graphs— are for the purpose of comparison. *All* of the tables are. In a table listing

Darwin's evidence in support of evolution, for example, all six of the items mentioned involve comparison (B9). We can also say that the chief function of charts and graphs is to allow for comparison: changes in quantities between periods of time.

Experiments

In his *Syntax of Scientific English,* Cheong emphasizes that "the ability to understand the relationship of comparison (with its implied contrast) is most significant in reading descriptive scientific texts where experiments are explained and discussed" (Cheong 1978, 241). This is also the case in our biology text. So the authors of the text explain how the Greek Eratosthenes, in the second century B.C., determined the circumference of the earth, by comparison:

> On the day when sunlight shone directly down into a deep well at Syene, near the present location of the Aswan Dam in Egypt, he measured the length of the shadow cast by a tall obelisk in the city of Alexandria. (B3)

By using several principles from the newly developed Euclidean geometry and an estimate of the distance between the two locations, he was able to determine the angle of the shadow cast by the obelisk. His estimate of the earth's circumference (correcting for the distance between the two locations) was 40,000 kilometers. The actual distance is 40,075.

In explaining the energy relationship between electrons and a nucleus, our text compares the relationship to a bowling ball, released from the top of a building, that "impacts with greater force than one dropped from a distance of a meter" (B24) (shades of Galileo).

Classifying

As we saw back in Chapter 1 and again in Chapter 3, classifications are based on comparisons: comparing various objects with different degrees of similarity and arranging them into hierarchical relationships. Notice this excerpt on classifying and the comparative elements that it contains:

> As an example of the way in which systems of classification are constructed according to evolutionary principles, consider the [accompanying] essay on the *relationships* of the giant panda and the red panda, as interpreted in light of modern evidence. Using morphological evidence alone, scientists were not sure about the *relationship between* these two unique mammals *to one another* and *to other groups;* with the addition of evidence derived from detailed *comparison* of some of their proteins and segments of nucleic acid, however, these *relationships* have become clear. (B557)

Levels of Analysis

Comparative elements exist at every level of the text. In exploring our topic, we will find discourse and syntactic, lexical and semantic considerations. But while these levels overlap, I would like to approach them as somewhat discrete topics.

The Discourse Level

As I noted earlier, a considerable number of comparative statements are unmarked—they have no comparitor or other type of marker to indicate the nature of the relationship. On the other hand, there are a diverse number of comparison markers that we will examine a little further on, apart from the obvious comparatives, superlatives, and other comparitors. Let's look at some of these diverse markers, as they operate at the discourse level.

Boldface and Parallel Structures

While these two elements are quite distinct, I've listed them under the same heading since they often occur together. Parallel structures in our text often indicate a comparison. Notice the following examples:

> The human stomach has a volume of about 50ml *when empty; when full* it may have a volume 50 times larger, from 2 to 4 liters. (B976)

Here we have a simple statement, whose comparative nature is implied by the pair of phrases (italics mine). The next sample uses boldface as a comparison device, in this case, reinforced by comparitors *(one kind of, a different kind)* (my italics):

> An **ionic bond** is *one kind of* chemical bond by which atoms are held together in molecules. A *different kind* of chemical bond results when two atoms share one or more electron pairs, an attraction called a **covalent bond**. (B26)

Notice the number of devices in the next sample that signal a comparison. The passage discusses the influence of Malthus's *Essay on Population* on Darwin's thinking:

> [1] In his book, Malthus pointed out that populations of plants and animals (including human beings) tend to increase *geometrically, whereas* in the case of people, our ability to increase our food supply increases only *arithmetically.* [2] A **geometric** progression *is one in which* the elements progress in a constant factor, as 2, 6, 18, 54, *and so forth . . .* [3] An **arithmetic** progression, *in contrast, is one in which* elements increase by a constant difference, as 2, 6, 10, 14, *and so forth.* (B10)

The first sentence sets up a parallelism between the two major terms of the passage by presenting them both in adverbial form *(geometrically* and *arithmetically)*. Sentences #2 and #3 contrast them again, this time by using boldface for both. They also enforce the comparison with a series of parallel phrases: *is one in which,* a series of numbers, followed by *and so forth.* The comparative nature of the passage is further emphasized by the two comparitors *whereas* and *in contrast.*

Numbers

Numbers are sometimes used to set up or indicate a comparison. In this way, they may serve as a type of forecasting statement. Notice, in the following two examples, the use of the word *different,* which has a comparative flavor to it. However, we could delete the word in both cases without affecting the comparison, since the comparison depends on what follows, that is, whether or not the actual comparisons are made. In both cases they *are,* and at great length:

> Blood plasma is a complex solution of **three** very *different* components dissolved in water: . . . (1) . . . (2) . . . (3) . . . (B1015; emphasis added)

> There are **five** *different* classes of heavy [antibody] chains: IgM, IgG, IgA, IgD and IgF . . . M chains are . . . G chains are . . . E chains . . . (B1045; emphasis added)

The next example combines three different indicators of comparison: (1) the number three, (2) the comparitor *differ,* and (3) parallelism, in this case, repetition of the word *possess:*

> The **three** principal kinds of white blood cells *differ* in the particular cell surface proteins they possess: . . . (1) B cells *possess* . . . (2) T cells *possess* . . . (3) Macrophages do not *possess* . . . (B1037; emphasis added)

Examine the following passage. See how the "potential" comparitors in the first two sentences—*different, three,* and *all of which*—focus the reader more and more on the upcoming comparison. Yet it is still possible not to *make* that comparison. The upcoming comparison is only established by the phrase the *most common* and "confirmed" by the sequencing words *remaining* and *third*—the latter carrying the comparison across the paragraph boundary:

> [1] Most elements in nature exist as a mixture of *different* isotopes. [2] There are, for example, **three** isotopes of the element carbon, *all of which* possess six protons (Figure 2-3). [3] The *most common* isotope of carbon has six neu-

trons. [4] Because its total mass is 12 . . . , it is referred to as carbon-12. . . . [5] Over 99% of the carbon in nature is like this. [6] The *remaining* carbon is almost all carbon-13. . . .

[7] The *third* isotope of carbon is carbon-14, with 8 neutrons. . . . [8] Unlike the other *two* isotopes of carbon, carbon-14 is unstable. (B22; emphasis added)

Series Words

This leads directly to our next comparison marker: series words. The numbers in our example above indicate a series of items, as do the phrases *the most common, the remaining,* and *the third.* This use of series to indicate a comparison is very common in our text. Notice this additional example:

An injury to *one* speech center produces halting but correct speech; injury to *another* speech center produces fluent, grammatical, but meaningless speech; injury to *a third* center abolishes speech altogether. Injuries to *other* sites on the surface of the brain's left hemisphere result in impairment of the ability to read, write, or do arithmetic. (B909)

Comparison in the Structure of the Paragraph

We've seen—in several cases above—where all the sentences in a paragraph contain a comparison (e.g., the influence of Malthus's *Essay on Population*). We have also seen where a comparison provides a cohesive structure *across* paragraph boundaries (the passage on kinds of isotopes, B22). In addition, comparison may provide a single unifying structure of a paragraph. We saw this in the passage on injuries to various speech centers, above, and we see it in the following example:

[Describing the major sections in the first half of the book] *At the molecular, subcellular, and cellular levels of organization,* you will be introduced to the principles of **cell biology,** and learn how cells are constructed and how they grow, divide, and communicate. *At the organismal level,* you will learn the principles of **genetics,** which deals with the way that individual traits are transmitted from one generation to the next. *At the population level* you will examine **evolution,** a field that is concerned with the nature of population changes from one generation to the next. . . . Finally, *at the community and global level,* you will study **ecology,** which deals with how organisms interact with their environments and with one another. (B18; emphasis added)

The sentences in the paragraph are perfectly parallel. Each of them describes a different level of topic and contains the following structure: *At the X level, you will* . . . **boldface.**

In this final example, we can observe a pattern of *generalization* and *detail,* in which the paragraph opens with a generalization (a noun plural without an article) and is developed by two examples as comparisons:

> *Organisms* live or die on the basis of their ability to capture . . . water and incorporate it into their bodies. *Plants* take up water from the earth in a continuous stream. . . . *Animals* obtain water directly from the plants or other animals they eat. (B484; emphasis added)

The Syntactic Level

Patterns of comparison also operate at the syntactic level, including: relative and subordinate clauses, what I call inclusives (comparison to 100% of an item), and the level of prosody. Let's examine some of these patterns. The majority of comparisons in our text involve two items. At this point, it is worth distinguishing between the two, which we can designate as *topic,* the focus of the discussion, and *referent,* the item you are comparing it to (Cheong's topic and target).

Prosody: Stress

To the extent that we subvocalize—pronouncing in our heads part of what we read—certain words tend to be stressed. Comparison lends itself naturally to such patterns, which usually occur at the syntactic level. Take the following sentence:

> It is one thing to observe the resúlts of evolution, but quite another to understand how it háppens. (B10; emphasis added)

The two items being compared both receive primary stress; we could arguably place the second primary stress instead over *how*. Here's another example, along with the logical places for primary stress:

> Although bacterial digestion within the gut plays a relatively small role in húman metabolism, it is an essential element in the metabolism of many óther vertebrates (B981; emphasis added)

We might say the first primary stress in a pair is cataphoric, since it does not arise until the reader reaches the second word in the pair; unless, of course, the reader is scanning the entire sentence at one time. Here's another excerpt. It contrasts Jenner and Pasteur, two of the founders of immunology. Where would *you* locate the primary stresses?

> A long time passed before people learned how one microbe can confer resistance to another. A key step was taken more than half a century later after Jen-

ner, when the famous French scientist Louis Pasteur showed that immunity was not created by the injected material, but rather invoked by it. (B1032)

We have here two sets of primary stress for comparison: óne microbe . . . anóther. A second set would be in the words creáted and invóked.

Relative Clause Patterns

Restrictive relative clauses ("The man that you spoke to . . .") tend to carry with them an implied comparison. "The man that you spoke to" implies that there were one or more other men present that you *didn't* speak to. Here are some examples from our text:

> Bacteria **that** live within the digestive tract of cows and other ruminants play a key role in the ability of those mammals to digest cellulose. (B976; emphasis added)

The implication: Bacteria in the tracts of other animals (nonruminants) do not do this.

> Carnivores **that** engage in sporadic gouging as an important survival strategy [SD: compared to those that don't] possess stomachs that are able to destroy much more than our stomachs can. (B976; emphasis added)

> Vertebrates lack the enzymes **that** are necessary to digest some kinds of potentially useful foodstuffs. (B981; emphasis added) [Implication: Compared to the other kinds of enzymes that they *do* have.]

As a subset, we also find sentences starting with *Those people who . . .* or *Those individuals that . . .*

> Those individuals **that** possess superior physical, behavioral, or other attributes are *more likely* to survive than those **that** are not so well endowed. (B11; emphasis added)

In this case, the comparison is specified.

Subordinate Clauses and Detached Phrases

Comparisons often occur in subordinate clauses and detached phrases (those separated from the main clause by a comma). I've examined several of these in the hope of finding distribution patterns of our various elements: the locations of X, Y, comparitors, and criteria. There do not seem to be many regularities. Here are four sample sentences, followed by a brief analysis:

Even though capillaries collectively have **the same** flow rate **as** arteries, the velocity of flow of individual capillaries is much less than in an artery, [because there are so many capillaries that the total cross-sectional area is far greater than in the arteries]. (B1011; emphasis added)

Arterioles differ from arteries simply in that they are **smaller** in diameter. (B1011; emphasis added)

The walls of the veins, although **similar** in structure to arteries, have much thinner layers of muscle and elastic fiber. (B1013; emphasis added)

Unlike arterial blood, the blood in the veins is far from the heart and does not get pushed hard when the heart beats. (B1013; emphasis added)

Analysis. The topic appears in the independent clause, which sometimes contains the referent in addition. The free phrases and subordinate clauses all contain a comparitor.

Inclusives

I have used the term *inclusives* for patterns that indicate some proportion or percentage of the whole. We examined the concept earlier in our discussion of quantifying. Inclusives come in various forms. Superlatives, for example, are inclusives, since they compare an individual to all the others in its class. We can also think of *part-whole* relationships as inclusives:

There are at least 5 million different kinds of organisms living on earth, of which about 1.4 million have been catalogued. (B553)

Percentages are inclusives, as in this double comparison:

In a mouse . . . 95% of the surface of the cerebral cortex is occupied by motor and sensory areas; in humans, only 5% of the surface is devoted to motor and sensory functions; the remainder is associative cortex. (B909)

The great number of inclusive words can be divided into two groups: those that apply to the entire set (all, each, every, none), and those that apply to a portion of it (a few, most, one of, some). We also find a few interesting patterns, including:

Of (all) the X, only the Y

Of the approximately 6m length of the human small intestine, only the duodenal region (the first 25cm) is actively involved in digestion. (B978) [Analysis: Compared to 100%, only about 5% is . . .]

Of the 92 elements that formed the crust of the cooling earth, only 11 are common in living organisms. (B29)

Of all its [the liver's] many functions, one of the most important is its regulation of the blood's metabolic level. (B979)

Plural Noun *without an Article*

Take a sentence like "Men talk of such things," with its implication that it is something *all* men do. While the following excerpts do contain comparitors *(differ, simplest)*, we can consider them inclusive comparisons as well:

Species *differ* from one another in at least one characteristic and generally do not interbreed freely with one another where their ranges overlap in nature. (B555; emphasis added)

Capillaries have the *simplest* structure of any element in the cardiovascular system. (B1011; emphasis added)

Semantic-Level Criteria

As might be expected, we find a near-endless variety of criteria that are used for comparisons, criteria that may be stated or unstated. They include— as a bare sampling—such elements as: time and duration, processes and properties, complexity, efficiency, size, and location.

Unstated Criteria

This category would include those items in Halliday's General Comparison, which we mentioned earlier. They are statements that the items are similar or different, but no criteria are offered for the comparison. Such forms are not very common in our text:

The oaks, beeches, and chestnuts are grouped, along with other genera, into the beech family Fagaceae, because of the many similar features they have in common. (B555)

Darwin was the first to present evidence that the animals and plants living on oceanic islands resemble most closely the forms of the nearest continent. (B395)

The chapter does not discuss in what ways Darwin's two groups differ. The book, however, does analyze some of these differences earlier on—in Chapters 1 and 21. In the following excerpt, the type of similarity is not stated. But a specific criterion (their lack of charge) is added in the second coordinate clause:

Neutrons are similar to protons, but as their name implies, they have no charge. (B21)

Stated Criteria

Statements with stated criteria are by far the more common of the two:

> The proportion of brain mass to body mass is much greater in birds than in reptiles, and even greater in mammals. (B907)

> Electrons have very little mass (only $\frac{1}{1840}$ the mass of a proton). (B22)

The criterion for a comparison may be found within a sentence, in an adjoining sentence, or in one later on. In the following example, the reader needs to leave the text and examine the photographs in order to discover the exact points of comparison. In fact, it is necessary to read the photo's caption text, which describes the differences in more meaningful detail.

> On the Galapagos Islands, off the coast of Ecuador, Darwin encountered giant land tortoises. Surprisingly, these tortoises **were not all identical.** Indeed, local residents and the sailors who captured the tortoises for food could tell which island a particular animal had come from just **by looking at its shell** (Figure 1-7). (B9)

Lexical and Morphological Level

Morphological Elements

Several morphological elements bear on the topic of comparison. The most obvious, of course, is the comparative form of adverbs and adjectives, which contains the comparitor *and* criterion. For example, in the sentence "John is taller than Bill," the suffix -er plus **than** = comparitor, and **tall** = criterion. Similarly with the form: **more** *(interesting)* **than.**

Superlatives as well indicate comparison, since superlative statements compare the item in question to *all* other items in its set:

> The associative cortex represents a *far greater* portion of the total cortex in primates *than* it does in many other mammals and reaches its *greatest* extent in human beings. (B909; emphasis added)

We also observed in the section on syntax that the plural marker, in nouns without articles, often implies a comparison.

Lexical Elements

Lexically, comparitors come in all sizes and shapes—phrases, single words—and in all parts of speech. We can divide them up in a host of ways: stated or implied. Or, recalling Halliday's and Cheong's categories, we can view them as symmetrical and asymmetrical, overt and covert. We can also think of them as:

- Contrast Words, or Differentiators: *compared to, contrast, differ, differ(ly), distinction, as opposed to, on the other hand, unlike.*
- Like-, Comparison Words, Like, or Resemblers: *affinity, both, just as, in like manner, likewise, related, similar(ly), in the same way.* Also time words, such as *now* and *ever since.*

We also find in our corpus several *exemplars:* words that appear in various forms (e.g., noun, adverb, and adjective). These include:

- *comparable, compare, comparison*
- *contrast* (verb), *contrast* (noun), *in contrast, contrasting*
- *different, differ, difference, differently*
- *distinct, distinguished, distinction*
- *like, likewise, unlike, -like* (e.g., a gemlike brightness)
- *related, relationship, relative to*
- *similar, similarly*

There already exist several excellent analyses of individual words and word groups (Cheong, Huddleston, and Bolinger).

Teaching the Language of Comparison

After all is said and done, the language of comparison remains—on the one hand—subtle and elusive, and on the other, apparent and obvious. In teaching the language of comparison, several considerations arise, especially if you are dealing with non-native speakers.

THE DIRECTION OF THOUGHT. One consideration is the direction of thought. As we have seen, comparisons tend to be anaphoric: the meaning of the referent derives from the topic, which appears earlier in the sentence or in a previous sentence:

> *Mammals* and birds maintain a constant body temperature by expending metabolic energy. They differ ⟵ in this respect from *most other organisms.* (B1008; emphasis added)

Since this is contrary to the normal movement of the eye (⟶), students need practice in recall, or backward, referential skills, as Cheong calls them. For cataphoric sentences, they need work in anticipatory skills. One way to do this is simply provide a list of comparative sentences (from the science text being used) and have students decide which element is topic and which is referent.

OTHER PROBLEMS. In addition to the direction of thought, other problems arise in processing sentences of comparison. As we have seen, the criterion may be unstated. Sometimes the referent is omitted. Sentences often appear without comparitors. All of these may cause difficulties in understanding, and accordingly, deserve a bit of attention.

REFERENT OMITTED. Again, working from a list or directly from the textbook, ask students what the Y may be (in some cases, the answer will be found in an accompanying visual).

> One of the obstacles that blocked the acceptance of any theory of evolution was the incorrect notion, still widely believed at that time, that the earth was only a few thousand years old. (B8; emphasis added)

Question: "Can you think of any **other** obstacles to such a theory?"

> The **molecule** that is most important to the evolution of life is water. (B20; emphasis added)

Question: "What are some **other** molecules that are important to the evolution of life?"

COMPARITOR UNSTATED. In this case, have students paraphrase the information and add a comparitor:

> Smallpox was a common and deadly disease in those days, and only those who had previously had the disease and survived it were immune from the infection—except, Jenner observed, milkmaids. (B1032)

Paraphrase: "**Like** those who had previously had the disease and survived, the only people who developed immunity from smallpox were milkmaids."

> Allergy shots work best for pollen allergies and for allergy to the venom of bee and wasp stings; they are not effective against food or drug allergies. (B1049)

Paraphrase: "**In contrast to** shots against pollen allergies and allergy to bee venom and wasp stings, allergy shots do not work against food or drug allergies."

CRITERION UNSTATED. Where possible, have students find the criterion, which may be elsewhere in the section (or chapter) and add it to the comparison:

> The brains of primitive chordates [vertebrates] are little more than swellings at the end of the nerve cord. In the ancestors of the vertebrates, such primitive

brains served primarily as sensory centers, receiving messages from eyes and other sensory receptors. (B903)

The passage contains no criterion for comparing primitive chordates and their ancestors. That criterion does appear, however, six lines later, in another subsection:

The earliest vertebrates had far more **complex** brains than their ancestors. (B903)

In this and other ways, it is important to teach comparison in a larger (discourse) context rather than in isolated sentences.

PROSODY: STRESS. As we have seen, both items in a comparison tend to take a primary stress. Students can be made aware of this if provided with a few oral examples, then a list of comparison sentences from a text so they can add the pairs of primary stress. How many sets of primary stress occur in this passage? Where would you place them?

In many simple animals digestion is intracellular; in vertebrates it is extracellular. (B967)

CHANGING THE GENRE. Another very useful technique is having students change the genre from text to visual, specifically from text to table. Such an activity is good for both testing and developing comprehension. Notice the following information from the text, and the table derived from it (Table 10.1). The topic is a comparison between groundwater and surface water:

Much less obvious than the surface waters, which we see in streams, lakes, and ponds, is the groundwater, which occurs in aquifers—permeable, saturated, underground layers of rock, sand, and gravel. In many areas, ground-

Surface Water	Groundwater
Found in streams, lakes, & ponds	In aquifers
4% of freshwater	96% of freshwater
Flows faster	Flows slower
75% of all water use	25% of all water use
50% of drinking water	50% of drinking water
Negligible	Provides almost 100% of water for rural areas

Table 10.1. Ground and Surface Water

water is the most important reservoir for water; for example, it amounts to more than 96% of all fresh water in the United States. . . .

Groundwater flows much more slowly than surface water. . . . In the Unites States, groundwater provides about 25% of the water used for all purposes and provides about 50% of the population with drinking water. Rural areas depend on groundwater almost exclusively, and its use is growing at about twice the rate of surface water. (B484)

LEXICAL CONSIDERATIONS. Especially with non-native students, it is advisable to include a few of the most common comparitors from each category of relationships: *same, different, more than,* and *less than.* It is also worth including the most "productive" words: those that appear in several forms. As we saw earlier, these would include: *compare, different, like,* and *related.*

Bibliography

Abelson, R. 1967. "Definitions." In *Encyclopedia of Philosophy*, 1:323–325. New York: Macmillan.

Abramov, P. 1976. *An Experimental Approach to Biology*. San Francisco: Freeman.

Achinstein, P. 1983. *The Concept of Evidence*. New York: Oxford University Press.

Achinstein, P., and O. Hannaway, eds. 1985. *Observation, Experiment, and Hypotheses in Modern Physical Science*. Cambridge, Mass.: MIT.

Ackoff, R. 1961. *Scientific Method*. New York: Wiley.

Adler, M. 1929. *Dialectic*. New York: Harcourt Brace.

Altham, J. 1971. *The Logic of Plurality*. London: Methuen.

American Heart Association. n.d. *Controlling Your Risk Factors for Heart Attack*. N.p.: n.p.

Arber, A. 1947. "Analogy in the History of Science." In *Studies and Essays in the History and Science of Learning Offered in Homage to George Sarton*, ed. M. F. Ashley-Montague, pp. 219–233. New York: Shuman.

———. 1964. *The Mind and the Eye*. London and Cambridge: Cambridge University Press.

Antilla, R. 1977. *Analogy*. The Hague: Mouton.

Aristotle. 1984. *Complete Works*. Ed. J. Barnes. 2 vols. Princeton, N.J.: Princeton University Press.

Arnheim, R. 1969. *Visual Thinking*. Berkeley: University of California Press.

Audesirk, G., and T. Audesirk. 1993. *Biology: Life on Earth*. New York: Macmillan.

Bacon, F. 1937 [1627]. *Essays, Advancement of Learning, New Atlantis, and Other Pieces*. Ed. Richard Foster Jones. New York: Odyssey.

———. 1960. *The New Organon and Related Writings*. Ed. Fulton Anderson. New York: Liberal Arts Press.

———. 1962. *The Advancement of Learning*. Ed. G. W. Kitchin. London: Dent.

Baker, J., and G. Allen. 1968. *Hypothesis, Prediction, and Implication in Biology*. Reading, Mass.: Addison-Wesley.

Baker, S., and L. Talley. 1972. "The Relationship of Visualization Skills to Achievement in Freshman Chemistry." *Journal of Chemical Education* 49 (11): 775–777.

Barker, S. F. 1957. *Induction and Hypothesis*. Ithaca, N.Y.: Cornell University Press.

Barwise, J., and R. Cooper. 1981. "Generalized Quantifiers and Natural Language." *Language and Philosophy* 4: 159–219.

Bauerle, C., et al., eds. 1983. *Meaning, Use and Interpretation in Language*. Berlin: W. de Gruyter.

Bazerman, C. 1989. *Shaping of Written Knowledge*. Madison: University of Wisconsin Press.

Beament, J. W. L., ed. 1960. *Models and Analogies in Biology*. Symposium of the Society for Experimental Biology No. 14. Cambridge: Cambridge University Press.

Bean, T. W., et al. 1990. "Learning Concepts from Biology Texts through Pictorial Analogies." *Journal of Educational Research* 83: 233–237.

Bergenholtz, H., and S. Tarp. 1995. *Manual of Specialized Lexicography.* Amsterdam and Philadelphia: John Benjamins.

Bernard, C. 1961. *An Introduction to the Study of Experimental Medicine.* Trans. H. C. Greene. New York: Collier.

Bernard, C., and C. D. Epp. 1987. *Laboratory Experiments in College Physics.* New York: Wiley.

Beveridge, W. I. 1957. *The Art of Scientific Investigation.* New York: Vintage.

Black, M. 1961. *Models and Metaphors.* Ithaca, N.Y.: Cornell University Press.

Blake, R. M., et al., eds. 1960. *Theories of Scientific Method: The Renaissance through the 19th Century.* New York: Gordon & Breach.

Boas, M. 1962. *The Scientific Renaissance 1450–1630.* New York: Harper & Row.

Bobrow, D., and A. Collins, eds. 1975. *Representation and Understanding.* New York: Academic Press.

Bolinger, D. 1972. *Degree Words.* The Hague: Mouton.

Bradford, A., and D. Bradford. 1983. "Practical and Empirical Knowledge of Photo Illustration." *Journal of Technical Writing and Communication* 13 (3): 259–268.

Bragg, G. 1974. *Principles of Experimentation.* Englewood Cliffs, N.J.: Prentice-Hall.

Bridgman, P. 1961 [1927]. *The Logic of Modern Physics.* New York: Macmillan.

Bruner, J., et al. 1956. *A Study of Thinking.* New York: Wiley.

Buchanan, S. 1962 [1929]. *Poetry and Mathematics.* Philadelphia: Lippincott.

Bunge, M. 1968. "Analogy in Quantum Theory, from Insight to Nonsense." *British Journal for the Philosophy of Science* 18 (February): 265–286.

———. 1979. *Causality and Modern Science.* New York: Dover.

Burtt, E. A. 1925. *The Metaphysical Foundations of Modern Science.* Atlantic Highlands, N.J.: Humanities Press.

Butterfield, H. 1985. *Origins of Modern Science 1300–1800.* New York: Random House.

Butts, R. E., and J. W. Davis, eds. 1970. *The Methodological Heritage of Newton.* Toronto: University of Toronto Press.

Cajori, F. 1928. *A History of Mathematical Notations.* LaSalle, Ill.: Open Court.

Campbell, N. R. 1957. *The Foundations of Science: The Philosophy of Theory and Experiment.* New York: Dover.

Canguilhelm, G. 1963. "The Role of Analogies and Models in Biological Discoveries." In *Scientific Change,* ed. A. C. Crombie, pp. 507–520. New York: Basic Books.

Carden, G. 1976. *English Quantifiers.* New York: Academic Press.

Chamberlin, T. 1981. "On Multiple Hypotheses." In *On Scientific Thinking,* ed. W. Tweney et al., pp. 100–104. New York: Columbia University Press.

Chauvet, J., et al. 1996. *Dawn of Art: The Chauvet Cave.* New York: Abrams.

Cheong, L. K. 1978. *Syntax of Scientific English.* Singapore: University of Singapore Press.

Churchman, C. W. 1948. *Theory of Experimental Inference*. New York: Macmillan.

Cippola, C. 1981. *Fighting Plague in the 17th Century*. Madison: University of Wisconsin Press.

Cohen, M. 1931. *Reason and Nature*. New York: Harcourt Brace.

———. 1965. *A Preface to Logic*. Cleveland: World.

Cohen, M., and E. Nagel. 1934. *An Introduction to Logic and Scientific Method*. New York: Harcourt Brace.

Conant, J. B., ed. 1950–1954. *Harvard Case Studies in Experimental Science*. 2 vols. Cambridge, Mass.: Harvard University Press.

Crombie, A. C. 1952. *Augustine to Galileo: The History of Science*. London: Falcon.

Crosland, M. P. 1962. *Historical Studies in the Language of Chemistry*. Cambridge, Mass.: Harvard University Press.

Crowson, R. 1970. *Classification and Biology*. New York: Atherton Press.

Cruse, D. A. 1986. *Lexical Semantics*. Cambridge: Cambridge University Press.

Cushings, S. 1976. "The Formal Semantics of Quantifiers." PhD. diss., University of California at Los Angeles.

Dampier, W. 1936. *A History of Science*. Cambridge: Cambridge University Press.

Dantzig, T. 1939. *Number: The Language of Science*. New York: Macmillan.

Darian, S. 1973. "Similes and the Creative Process." *Language and Style* 6 (1): 48–57.

———. 1982. "The Role of Definitions in Scientific and Technical Writing." In *Pragmatics and LSP*, ed. J. Hoedt et al., pp. 27–49. Copenhagen: Copenhagen School of Economics/UNESCO.

———. 1991. "More than Meets the Eye: The Role of Visuals in Science Textbooks." *LSP & Professional Communication* 1 (1): 10–37.

———. 1995. "Hypotheses in Introductory Science Texts." *IRAL* 33 (2): 84–108.

———. 1996. "Cause and Effect in Science Textbooks." *ESP Malaysia* 4: 65–83.

———. 1997a. "The Language of Classifying in Introductory Science Texts." *Journal of Pragmatics* 27: 815–839.

———. 1997b. "The Language of Experiments in Introductory Science Texts." *Fachsprache* 19 (1–2): 28–42.

———. 2000a. "The Language of Comparison in an Introductory Science Textbook." *ESP Malaysia* 6: 29–50.

———. 2000b. "The Language of Quantifying in Introductory Science Texts." *Fachsprache* 22 (1–2): 59–72.

———. 2000c. "The Role of Figurative Language in Science Texts." *International Journal of Applied Linguistics* 10 (2): 3–26.

———. 2001. *Skills Workshop: Reading in the Content Areas*. Austin: Holt Rinehart.

Darwin, C. 1859. *The Origin of Species and the Descent of Man*. New York: Random House.

Darwin, F., ed. 1958 [1892]. *The Autobiography of Charles Darwin and Selected Letters*. New York: Dover.

Davies, J. T. 1965. *The Scientific Approach*. New York: Academic Press.

da Vinci, L. 1939. *The Notebooks of Leonardo da Vinci*. Ed. and trans. J. Richter. 2 vols. New York: Dover.

de Santillana, G. 1970. *The Origins of Scientific Thought*. Chicago: University of Chicago Press.

Descartes, R. 1956. *Discourse on Method*. Trans. L. Lafleur. Indianapolis: Bobbs-Merrill.

Deutsch, M. 1959. "Evidence and Inference in Nuclear Research." In *Evidence and Inference*, ed. D. Lerner, pp. 96–106. Glencoe, Ill.: Free Press.

Doblin, J. 1980. "A Structure for Nontextual Communications." In *Processing of Visible Language*, ed. P. A. Kolers et al., pp. 2:89–111. New York: Plenum.

Dondis, D. A. 1973. *A Primer of Visual Literacy*. Cambridge, Mass.: MIT.

Dreyer, E. L. E. 1953. *A History of Astronomy from Thales to Kepler*. New York: Dover.

Dubos, R. 1960. *Pasteur and Modern Science*. New York: Anchor Books.

Duhem, P. 1954. *Aim and Structure of Physical Theory*. Princeton, N.J.: Princeton University Press.

Dwyer, F. M. 1972. *A Guide for Improving Visual Instruction*. State College, Pa.: State College Learning Services.

Ebbing, D., and M. Wrighton. 1990. *General Chemistry*. Boston: Houghton Mifflin.

Ehrenberg, A. 1977. "Rudiments of Numeracy." *Journal of the Royal Statistical Society* 140: 277–297.

Ellen, R. F. 1979. *Classifications in Their Social Context*. New York: Academic Press.

Ellis, B. 1966. *Basic Concepts of Measurement*. Cambridge: Cambridge University Press.

Elstein, A., et al. 1978. *Medical Problem Solving: An Analysis of Clinical Reasoning*. Cambridge, Mass.: Harvard University Press.

Empson, W. 1951. *The Structure of Complex Words*. New York: New Directions.

Estes, W. 1994. *Classification and Cognition*. New York: Oxford University Press.

Evans, G. E. 1988. "Metaphors as Learning Aids in University Lectures." *Journal of Experimental Education* 56: 91–99.

Ewing, A. C. 1951. *The Fundamental Questions of Philosophy*. London: Routledge.

Farber, E. 1956 [1950]. "Chemical Discoveries by Means of Analogies." *Isis* 41: 20–26.

Farrington, B. 1936. *Science in Antiquity*. London: Oxford University Press.

Fiumara, G. C. 1995. *The Metaphoric Process: Connections between Language and Life*. London: Routledge.

Fleming, M. 1970. *Perceptual Principles for the Design of Instructional Material*. Bloomington: Indiana University AV Center.

Fleming, M. L. 1977. "The Picture in Your Mind." *AV Communication Review* 25: 43–62.

Fogelin, R. J. 1988. *Figuratively Speaking*. New Haven, Conn.: Yale University Press.

Franklin, A. 1986. *The Neglect of Experiment*. Cambridge: Cambridge University Press.

Frege, G. 1950. *The Foundations of Arithmetic.* Oxford: Blackwell.

French, J. 1965. "The Relationship of Problem Solving to Factor Composition of Tests." *Educational and Psychological Measurement* 25: 9–28.

French, R. 1994. *Ancient Natural History.* London: Longman.

Funkhauser, H. G. 1937. "Historical Development of the Graphical Representation of Statistical Data." *Osiris* 3: 269–404.

Gabbay, D., and F. Guenthnerm, eds. 1989. *Handbook of Philosophical Logic,* Vol. 4. Dordrecht, Holland: Reidel.

Gabriel, M. J., and S. Fogel, eds. *Great Experiments in Biology.* Englewood Cliffs, N.J.: Prentice-Hall.

Galilei, G. 1957. *Discoveries and Opinions.* Trans. S. Drake. Garden City, N.Y.: Doubleday.

———. 1967. *Dialogue Concerning the Two World Systems.* Trans. S. Drake. Berkeley and Los Angeles: University of California Press.

———. 1974 [1638]. *Dialogues Concerning Two New Sciences.* Trans. S. Drake. Madison: University of Wisconsin Press.

Gardenfors, P., ed. *Generalized Quantifiers.* Dordrecht, Holland: Reidel.

Garrett, A. B., ed. 1963. *The Flash of Genius.* Princeton, N.J.: Van Nostrand.

Gattegno, C. 1969. *Towards a Visual Culture.* New York: Outerbridge and Dienstfrey.

Geach, P. 1962. *Reference and Generality.* Ithaca, N.Y.: Cornell University Press.

Gega, P. 1994. *Science in Elementary Education.* New York: Macmillan.

Gelb, I. J. 1963. *A Study of Writing.* Chicago: University of Chicago Press.

———. 1980. "Principles of Writing Systems within a Frame of Visual Communication." In *Processing of Visible Language,* ed. P. A. Kolers et al., pp. 2:7–24. New York: Plenum.

Gelman, R., and E. Speike. 1981. *The Development of Thoughts about Animate and Inanimate Objects.* Cambridge: Cambridge University Press.

Gentner, D., et al. 1997. "Analogy and Creativity in the Works of Johannes Kepler." In *Creative Thought,* ed. T. Ward et al., pp. 403–461. Washington, D.C.: American Psychological Association.

Gentner, D., and M. Jeziorski. 1993. "The Shift from Metaphor to Analogy in Western Science." In *Metaphor and Thought,* ed. A. Ortony, pp. 447–480. Cambridge: Cambridge University Press.

Gentner, D., and A. Stevens, eds. 1983. *Mental Models.* Hillsdale, N.J.: Erlbaum.

Ghiselin, M. 1984. *The Triumph of the Darwinian Method.* Chicago: University of Chicago Press.

Gholsen, B., et al., eds. 1989. *The Psychology of Science and Metascience.* Cambridge: Cambridge University Press.

Giere, R. 1979. *Understanding Scientific Reasoning.* New York: Holt Rinehart.

Giere, R., and R. Westfall, eds. 1973. *Foundations of Scientific Method: The Nineteenth Century.* Bloomington: Indiana University Press.

Gilbert, S. W. 1989. "An Evaluation of the Use of Analogy, Simile and Metaphor in Science Texts." *Journal of Research in Science Teaching* 26: 315–327.

Godolphin, F., ed. 1942. *The Greek Historians.* 2 vols. New York: Random House.

Goldsmith, E. 1984. *Research into Illustration.* Cambridge: Cambridge University Press.

Goldstein, M., and I. Goldstein. 1984. *The Experience of Science.* New York: Plenum.

Goldstein, P. 1957. *How to Do an Experiment.* New York: Harcourt Brace.

Gombrich, E. H. 1972. "The Visual Image." *Scientific American* 227: 82–96.

Goodman, S., and D. Graddol. 1997. *Redesigning English.* New York: Routledge.

Gordon, D. 1978. *Therapeutic Metaphors.* Cupertino, Calif.: Meta Publications.

Gordon, W. J. J. 1973. *The Metaphoric Way of Knowing.* Cambridge, Mass.: Porpoise Books.

Gross, A. G. 1990. *The Rhetoric of Science.* Cambridge, Mass.: Harvard University Press.

Hacking, I. 1983. *Representing and Intervening.* Cambridge: Cambridge University Press.

Hall, A. R. 1954. *The Scientific Revolution 1500–1800.* New York: Longman.

Halliday, M. A. K., and R. Hasan. 1976. *Cohesion in English.* London: Longman.

Halliday, M. A. K., and J. R. Martin. 1993. *Writing Science.* Pittsburgh: University of Pittsburgh Press.

Hamilton, E., and H. Cairns, eds. 1971. *The Collected Dialogues of Plato.* Princeton, N.J.: Bollingen.

Harré, R. 1969. *Scientific Thought 1900–1960.* Oxford: Oxford University Press.

———. 1976. *Philosophies of Science.* London: Longman.

———. 1981. *Great Scientific Experiments.* Oxford: Phaidon.

Harris, E. E. 1970. *Hypothesis and Perception: The Roots of Scientific Method.* New York: Humanities Press.

Harvey, D. 1969. *Explanation in Geography.* New York: St. Martins.

Haskins, C. H. 1927. *Studies in the History of Medieval Science.* Cambridge, Mass.: Harvard University Press.

Hein, M. 1992. *Laboratory Manual for College Chemistry.* Pacific Grove, Calif.: Brooks/Cole.

Hein, M., et al. 1993. *College Chemistry.* Pacific Grove, Calif.: Brooks/Cole.

Helman, D., ed. 1988. *Analogical Reasoning.* Dordrecht, Holland: Kluwer.

Hempel, C. G. 1965. *Aspects of Scientific Explanation and Other Essays in the Philosophy of Science.* New York: Free Press.

Herschell, J. 1842. *Discourse on the Study of Natural Philosophy.* London: Longman.

Hesse, M. 1966. *Models and Analogies in Science.* Notre Dame, Ind.: Notre Dame University Press.

Higgonbotham, J., and R. May. 1981. "Questions, Quantifiers, and Crossings." *Linguistics Review* 1: 41–79.

Hoenigswald, H., and L. Wiener, eds. 1987 *Biological Metaphor and Cladistic Classification.* Philadelphia: University of Pennsylvania Press.

Hogben, L. T. 1949. *From Cave Painting to Comic Strip: A Kaleidoscope of Human Communication.* London: Parrish.

———. 1960. *Mathematics in the Making.* London: Macdonald.

Hogg, R. 1977. *English Quantification System.* New York: North-Holland.

Holmes, J. 1988. "Doubt and Uncertainty in ESL Textbooks." *Applied Linguistics* 9 (1): 21–44.

Honeck, R. P., and R. R. Hoffman, eds. 1980. *Cognition and Figurative Language.* Hillsdale, N.J.: Erlbaum.

Hübler, A. 1983. *Understatements and Hedges in English.* Amsterdam: John Benjamins.

Huddleston, R. D. 1967. "More on English Comparative Construction." *Journal of Linguistics* 3: 91–102.

———. 1971. *The Sentence in Written English.* London: Cambridge University Press.

Hume, D. 1955 [1748]. *An Inquiry Concerning Human Understanding.* Indianapolis: Bobbs-Merrill.

Hutchins, Edward. 1983. "Understanding Micronesian Navigation." In *Mental Models,* ed. D. Gentner and A. Stevens, pp. 191–227. Hillsdale, N.J.: Erlbaum.

Hutton, E. 1953. "The Role of Models in Physics." *British Journal for the Philosophy of Science* 4: 284–301.

Johnson, M. 1987. *The Body in the Mind: The Bodily Basis of Meaning, Imagination, and Reasoning.* Chicago: University of Chicago Press.

———. 1988. "Embodied Analogical Understanding." In *Analogical Reasoning,* ed. D. Helman, pp. 25–40. Dordrecht, Holland: Kluwer.

Kanazawa, M., and C. Piñón, eds. 1994. *Dynamics, Polarity, and Quantification.* Stanford, Calif.: CSLI Publications.

Kearney, H. 1971. *Science and Change.* New York: McGraw-Hill.

Kedar-Cabelli, S. 1988. "Analogy—from a Unified Perspective." In *Analogical Reasoning,* ed. D. Helman, pp. 65–105. Dordrecht, Holland: Kluwer.

Kleinmutz, B., ed. 1966. *Problem Solving.* New York: Wiley.

Klima, E. S. 1964. "Negation in English." In *The Structure of Language,* ed. J. Fodor and J. Katz. Englewood Cliffs, N.J.: Prentice-Hall.

Knorr-Cetina, K. D. 1981. *The Manufacture of Knowledge.* Oxford: Pergamon.

Kockelmans, J., ed. 1968. *Philosophy of Science: The Historical Background.* New York: Free Press.

Koestler, A. 1949. *Insight and Outlook.* London: Macmillan.

———. 1960. *The Watershed.* Garden City, N.Y.: Doubleday.

———. 1964a. *The Act of Creation.* New York: Macmillan.

———. 1964b. *The Sleepwalkers: A History of Man's Changing Vision of the Universe.* London: Penguin.

Kolers, P. A., et al., eds. 1979. *Processing of Visible Language,* Vol. 1. New York: Plenum.

———. 1980. *Processing of Visible Language,* Vol. 2. New York: Plenum.

Kourilová, M. 1993. "Epistemic Modality in Written Scientific Discourse." *UNESCO ALSED-LSP Newsletter* 15 (2): 4–18.

Koyrè, A. 1964. "The Exact Sciences." In *The Beginnings of Modern Science,* ed. R. Taton, pp. 2:11–105. New York: Basic Books.

Krynicki, M., and M. Mostowski, eds. 1992. *Quantifiers.* Dordrecht, Holland: Kluwer.

Kuhn, T. 1962. *The Structure of Scientific Revolutions.* Chicago: University of Chicago Press.

Lakoff, G. 1987. *Women, Fire, and Dangerous Things: What Categories Reveal about the Mind.* Chicago: University of Chicago Press.

Lakoff, G., and M. Johnson. 1980. *Metaphors We Live By.* Chicago: University of Chicago Press.

Langer, S. 1948. *Philosophy in a New Key.* New York: Mentor.

Larrabee, Harold. 1945. *Reliable Knowledge.* Boston: Houghton Mifflin.

Latour, B., and S. Woolgar. 1986. *Laboratory Life.* Princeton, N.J.: Princeton University Press.

Leatherdale, P. 1974. *The Role of Analogy, Model and Metaphor in Science.* New York: Elsevier.

Lees, R. B. 1961. "Grammatical Analysis of the English Comparative Constructions." *Word* 17: 171–185.

Lemke, J. 1990. *Talking Science: Language, Learning, and Values.* Norwood, N.J.: ABLEX.

———. 1995. *Textual Politics.* London: Taylor & Francis.

———. 1988. "Multiplying Meaning: Visual and Verbal Semiotics in Scientific Texts." In *Reading Science,* ed. J. R. Martin and R. Veel, pp. 87–114. New York: Routledge.

Lerner, D., ed. 1959. *Evidence and Inference.* Glencoe, Ill.: Free Press.

———. 1985. *Cause and Effect.* Glencoe, Ill.: Free Press.

Levie, W. 1987. "Research on Pictures." In *The Psychology of Illustration,* ed. D. M. Willows and H. A. Houghton, 1:1–51. New York: Springer-Verlag.

Levin, J., et al. 1987. "On Empirically Validating Functions of Pictures in Prose." In *The Psychology of Illustration,* ed. D. M. Willows and H. A. Houghton, 1:51–86. New York: Springer-Verlag.

Lloyd, G. E. R. 1987. *The Revolutions of Wisdom.* Berkeley and Los Angeles: University of California Press.

Loftus, G., and S. Bell. 1975. "Two Types of Information in Picture Memory." *Journal of Experimental Psychology: Human Learning and Memory* 104: 103–113.

Longwell, C., et al. 1969. *Physical Geology.* New York: Wiley.

Lord, T. 1983. "The Effects of Visual-Spatial Aptitude on the Study of College Biology." Ed.D. diss., Rutgers University, New Brunswick, New Jersey.

———. 1985. "Enhancing the Visuo-Spatial Aptitude of Students." *Journal of Research in Science Teaching* 22 (5): 395–405.

Lynch, M. 1985. *Art and Artifact in Laboratory Science: A Study of Shop Work and Shop Talk in a Research Laboratory.* London: Routledge.

Lynch, M., and L. Woolgar. 1990. *Representation in Scientific Practice.* Cambridge, Mass.: MIT.

McCarthy, M. 1990. *Vocabulary*. London: Oxford University Press.

MacCormack, E. 1979. *Metaphor and Myth in Science and Religion*. Durham, N.C.: Duke University Press.

———. 1985. *A Cognitive Theory of Metaphor*. Cambridge, Mass.: MIT.

———. 1986. *Myths of Science and Technology*. Madras, India: Madras University.

Macdonald-Ross, M. 1977. *Research in Graphic Communication*. Milton Keynes, UK: Institute of Educational Technology.

———. 1981. *Language in Text: Bibliography*. Milton Keynes, UK: Open University.

McKim, R. 1980. *Thinking Visually*. Belmont, Calif.: Lifetime Learning.

Madden, E. 1960. *The Structure of Scientific Thought*. Boston: Houghton Mifflin.

Mandel, S. 1970. *Writing for Science and Technology*. New York: Dell.

Mandl, H., and J. Levin, eds. 1989. *Knowledge Acquisition through Text and Pictures*. Amsterdam: Elsevier.

Martin, J. R., and R. Veel. 1988. *Reading Science*. New York: Routledge.

Mason, S. F. 1953. *Main Currents in Scientific Thought*. New York: Schuman.

May, R. 1990. *The Grammar of Quantification*. New York: Garland.

Mayer, R. 1993. "The Instructive Metaphor: Metaphoric Aids to Students' Understanding of Science." In *Metaphor and Thought*, ed. A. Ortony, pp. 561–578. Cambridge: Cambridge University Press.

Mayer, R., et al. 1995. "A Generative Theory of Textbook Design: Using Annotated Illustrations to Foster Meaningful Learning of Science Text." *Educational Technology Research and Development* 43 (1): 31–43.

Mayr, E. 1985. "Cause and Effect in Biology." In *Cause and Effect*, ed. D. Lerner, pp. 33–51. Glencoe, Ill.: Free Press.

Medawar, P. 1969a. *The Art of the Soluble*. Harmondsworth, England: Penguin.

———. 1969b. *Induction, Intuition, and Scientific Thought*. Philadelphia: American Philosophical Society.

Meltzer, E. 1980. "Remarks on Ancient Egyptian Writing." In *Processing of Visible Language*, ed. P. A. Kolers et al., pp. 2:43–66. New York: Plenum.

Mill, J. S. 1950. *John Stuart Mill's Philosophy of Scientific Method*. Abridged and ed. by E. Nagel. New York: Hafner.

Miller, A. 1981. "Visualizability as a Criterion for Scientific Acceptability." In *On Scientific Thinking*, ed. W. Tweney et al., pp. 383–395. New York: Columbia University Press.

Miller, A. J. 1984. *Imagery in Scientific Thought: Creating 20th Century Physics*. Boston, Basle, and Stuttgart: Birkhauser.

Miller, G. A. 1978. "Semantic Relations among Words." In *Linguistic Theory and Psychological Reality*, ed. M. Halle et al. Cambridge, Mass.: MIT.

Miller, T. 1998. "Visual Persuasion: A Comparison of Visuals in Academic Texts and the Popular Press." *English for Specific Purposes* 17 (1): 29–47.

Moxey, L., and A. Sanford. 1993. *Communicating Quantities*. Hillsdale, N.J.: Erlbaum.

Myers, G. 1989. "The Pragmatics of Politeness in Scientific Articles." *Applied Linguistics* 10 (1): 3–35.

————. 1990. *Writing Biology: Texts in the Social Construction of Knowledge.* Madison: University of Wisconsin Press.

————. 1992. "Textbooks and the Sociology of Scientific Knowledge." *English for Specific Purposes* 11 (1): 3–17.

Nagel, E. 1961. *The Structure of Science.* New York: Harcourt, Brace, & World.

————. 1985. "Types of Causal Explanations in Science." In *Cause and Effect,* ed. D. Lerner. Glencoe, Ill.: Free Press.

Newell, A., and H. Simon. 1972. *Human Problem Solving.* Englewood Cliffs, N.J.: Prentice-Hall.

Newton, I. 1952 [1730]. *Opticks . . . ,* 4th ed. Reprint. New York: Dover.

————. 1959–1977. *The Correspondence.* Ed. H. W. Turnbull et al., 7 vols. Cambridge: Cambridge University Press.

————. 1978. *Isaac Newton's Papers and Letters on Natural Philosophy.* Ed. I. Bernard Cohen and R. Schofield. Cambridge, Mass.: Harvard University Press.

Nishigauchi, T. 1990. *Quantifiers in the Theory of Grammar.* Dordrecht, Holland: Kluwer.

Ogden, C. K., and I. A. Richards. 1946. *The Meaning of Meaning.* New York: Harcourt Brace.

Ohanian, H. C. 1989. *Physics,* 2d ed. New York: Norton.

Olsen, R. 1990. *Science Deified and Science Defied.* Berkeley: University of California Press.

Oppenheimer, J. R. 1956. "Analogy in Science." *American Psychologist* 11 (March): 127–135.

Ortony, A., ed. 1993. *Metaphor and Thought.* Cambridge: Cambridge University Press.

Paine, H. 1980. "Some Problems of Illustration." In *Processing of Visible Language,* ed. P. A. Kolers et al., pp. 2:143–156. New York: Plenum.

Paivio, A. 1986. *Mental Representations: A Dual Coding Approach.* Oxford: Oxford University Press.

Palmer, F. 1978. *Grammar.* Harmondsworth, England: Penguin.

Palmer, F. R. 1979. *Modality and the English Modals.* London: Longman.

Panchen, A. 1992. *Classification, Evolution, and the Nature of Biology.* Cambridge: Cambridge University Press.

Pelletier, F. 1979. *Mass Terms.* Dordrecht, Holland: Reidel.

Pepper, S. 1942. *World Hypotheses.* Berkeley: University of California Press.

Perkins, D. 1980. "Pictures and the Real Thing." In *Processing of Visible Language,* ed. P. A. Kolers et al., pp. 2:259–278. New York: Plenum.

Perkins, M. 1983. *Modal Expressions in English.* Norwood, N.J.: ABLEX.

Peters, F. E. 1970. *The Harvest of Hellenism.* New York: Barnes & Noble.

Pierce, C. S. 1957. *Philosophical Writings of Pierce.* Ed. J. Buchler. New York: Dover.

Plato. 1971. *Collected Dialogues.* Ed. Edith Hamilton and Huntington Cairns. Princeton, N.J.: Princeton University Press.

Poincaré, H. 1952. *Science and Hypothesis.* New York: Dover.

————. 1958. *The Value of Science*. New York: Dover.

Polya, G. 1954. *How to Solve It*. Garden City, N.Y.: Doubleday.

Popper, K. 1959. *The Logic of Scientific Discovery*. New York: Basic Books.

Pressley, G. M. 1976. "Mental Imagery Help Eight-Year-Olds Remember What They Read." *Journal of Educational Psychology* 658 (3): 355–359.

Prigogine, I., and I. Stengers. 1984. *Order out of Chaos*. New York: Praeger.

Quirk, R., et al. 1976. *A Grammar of Contemporary English*. London: Longman.

Rapaport, A. 1953. *Operational Philosophy*. San Francisco: International Society for General Semantics.

Raven, P., and G. P. Johnson. 1989. *Biology*. St. Louis: Times Mirror/Mosby.

Ray, W. 1960. *An Introduction to Experimental Design*. New York: Macmillan.

Régent, O. 1985. "A Comparative Approach to the Learning of Specialized Written Discourse." In *Discourse and Learning*, ed. Philip Riley, pp. 105–121. London: Longman.

Reid, W. 1991. *Verb and Noun Number in English*. London: Longman.

Rescher, N. 1970. *Scientific Explanation*. New York: Free Press.

Richards, I. A. 1965. *Philosophy of Rhetoric*. New York: Oxford University Press.

————. 1973. *On Interpretation in Teaching*. New York: Humanities Press.

Ridgman, W. J. 1975. *Experimentation in Biology*. New York: Wiley.

Riley, P., ed. 1985. *Discourse and Learning*. London: Longman.

Ritchie, A. 1958. *Studies in the History and Methods of the Sciences*. Edinburgh: Edinburgh University Press.

Robinson, R. 1954. *Definition*. London: Oxford University Press.

Roe, S. 1952. "A Psychologist Examines 64 Eminent Scientists." *Scientific American* 187: 21–22.

Roller, B. 1980. "Graph Reading Abilities of Thirteen-Year-Olds." In *Processing of Visible Language*, ed. P. A. Kolers et al., pp. 2:305–314. New York: Plenum.

Rosch, E., and B. Lloyd, eds. 1978. *Cognition and Categorization*. Hillsdale, N.J.: Erlbaum.

Rubens, P. 1986. "A Reader's View of Text and Graphics." *Journal of Technical Writing and Communication* 16 (1–2): 73–86.

Sacks, S., ed. 1979. *On Metaphor*. Chicago: University of Chicago Press.

Sadock, J. 1993. "Figurative Speech and Linguistics." In *Metaphor and Thought*, ed. A. Ortony, pp. 42–57. Cambridge: Cambridge University Press.

Saha, P. K. 1988. "Metaphoric Style as Message." In *Analogical Reasoning*, ed. D. Helman, pp. 41–65. Dordrecht, Holland: Kluwer.

Salager-Meyer, F. 1994. "Hedges and Textual Communicative Function in Medical English Writing." *English for Specific Purposes* 13 (2): 149–170.

Samuels, M., and N. Samuels. 1975. *Seeing with the Mind's Eye: The History, Techniques, and Use of Visualization*. New York: Random House.

Sarton, G. 1927–1947. *Introduction to the History of Science*. 3 vols. Baltimore: Carnegie Institution.

————. 1957. *Six Wings: Men of Science in the Renaissance*. Bloomington: Indiana University Press.

————. 1959. *A History of Science.* 2 vols. Cambridge, Mass.: Harvard University Press.

Schiller, J. 1973. "The Genesis and Structure of Claude Bernard's Experimental Method." In *Foundations of Scientific Method: The Nineteenth Century,* ed. R. Giere and R. Westfall, pp. 133–161. Bloomington: Indiana University Press.

Schlesinger, G. 1991. *The Sweep of Probability.* Notre Dame, Ind.: Notre Dame University Press.

Schon, D. A. 1967. *Invention and the Evolution of Ideas.* London: Tavistock.

Schwartz, S., and T. Griffin. 1986. *Medical Thinking: The Psychology of Medical Judgment and Decision Making.* New York: Springer-Verlag.

Seese, W., and W. Daube. 1988. *Basic Chemistry.* Englewood Cliffs, N.J.: Prentice-Hall.

Shapin, S. 1984. "Pump and Circumstance: Robert Boyle's Literary Technology." *Social Studies of Science* 14: 481–520.

————. 1993. *The Scientific Revolution.* Chicago: University of Chicago Press.

Sharlin, H. 1966. *The Convergent Century: The Unification of Science in the 19th Century.* New York: Abelard-Schuman.

Shepherd, R. 1966. "Learning and Recall as Organization and Search." *Journal of Verbal Learning and Verbal Behavior* 5: 201–204.

Shepherd, R., and J. Chipman. 1970. "Second Order Isomorphism of Representations." *Cognitive Psychology* 1: 1–17.

Shibles, W. 1971. *An Analysis of Metaphor.* The Hague: Mouton.

Silberner, J. 1986. "Metaphor in Immunology." *Science News* 130 (October 18: 254.

Simon, H. 1969. *The Science of the Artificial.* Cambridge, Mass.: MIT.

————. 1977. *Models of Discovery.* Dordrecht, Holland: Reidel.

Singer, C. 1922. *Greek Biology and Medicine.* Oxford: Oxford University Press.

————. 1925. *The Evolution of Anatomy.* Oxford: Oxford University Press.

————. 1928. *A Short History of Medicine.* Oxford: Oxford University Press.

————. 1931. *A Short History of Biology.* New York: Abelard-Schuman.

————. 1959. *A History of Scientific Ideas.* New York: Barnes & Noble.

Singer, C., ed. 1956. *History of Technology,* Vol. 2. Oxford: Oxford University Press.

Smith, D. E. 1958. *History of Mathematics.* 2 vols. New York: Dover.

Smith, R. 1973. *Materials of Construction.* New York: McGraw-Hill.

Solomon, J. 1986. "Children's Explanations." *Oxford Review of Education* 12 (1): 41–50.

Spiro, R., et al. 1989. "Multiple Analogies for Complex Concepts." In *Similarity and Analogical Reasoning,* ed. S. Vosniadou and A. Ortony, pp. 499–532. Cambridge: Cambridge University Press.

Stanford, W. B. 1972. *Greek Metaphor.* Oxford: Blackwell.

Starr, C. 1984. *Biology: Concepts and Applications.* Belmont, Calif.: Wadsworth.

Starr, C., and R. Taggart. 1990. *Biology.* Belmont, Calif.: Wadsworth.

Stebbings, L. S. 1933. *Modern Introduction to Logic*. London: Methuen. New York: Humanities Press.

Stillman, J. M. 1960. *The Story of Alchemy and Early Chemistry*. New York: Dover.

Stimson, D., ed. 1962. *Sarton on the History of Science*. Cambridge, Mass.: Harvard University Press.

Suppe, F., ed. 1977. *The Structure of Scientific Theories*. Urbana: University of Illinois Press.

Swales, J. 1971. *Writing Scientific English*. London: Nelson.

———. 1990. *Genre Analysis*. Cambridge: Cambridge University Press.

Szlichcinski, K. P. 1979. "Diagrams and Illustrations as Aids to Problem-Solving." *Instructional Science* 8 (3): 253–274.

Taton, R., ed. 1964. *The Beginnings of Modern Science*. New York: Basic Books.

Temkin, O. 1949. "Metaphors of Human Biology." In *Science and Civilization*, ed. R. C. Stauffer, pp. 169–194. Madison: University of Wisconsin Press.

Thayer, H. S., ed. 1953. *Newton's Philosophy of Nature*. New York: Hafner.

Thomas, O. 1969. *Metaphor*. New York: Random House.

Thorndike, L. 1923–1958. *A History of Magic and Experimental Science*. 8 vols. New York: Columbia University Press.

Toulmin, S. 1953. *Philosophy of Science*. New York: Harper & Row.

Trigg, G. L. 1975. *Landmark Experiments in 20th Century Physics*. London: Edward Arnold.

Trimble, L. 1985. *English for Science and Technology: A Discourse Approach*. Cambridge: Cambridge University Press.

Tuersky, B. 1969. "Pictorial and Verbal Encoding in a Short-Term Memory Task." *Perception and Psychophysics* 6: 225–233.

Tufte, E. 1983. *The Visual Display of Quantitative Information*. Cheshire, Conn.: Graphics Press.

———. 1990. *Envisioning Information*. Cheshire, Conn.: Graphics Press.

———. 1997. *Visual Explanations*. Cheshire, Conn.: Graphics Press.

Turbayne, C. M. 1962. *The Myth of Metaphor*. New Haven, Conn.: Yale University Press.

Tweney, W., et al., eds. 1981. *On Scientific Thinking*. New York: Columbia University Press.

Upton, A. 1961. *Design for Thinking*. Palo Alto, Calif.: Pacific Books.

Urban, W. 1961. *Language and Reality*. New York: Macmillan.

Van Naappen, J. P. 1990. *Metaphor II: A Classified Bibliography*. Philadelphia: John Benjamins.

Vernon, M. D. 1951. "Learning and Understanding." *Quarterly Journal of Experimental Psychology* 3: 19–23.

Vosniadou, S., and A. Ortony, eds. 1989. *Similarity and Analogical Reasoning*. Cambridge: Cambridge University Press.

Wallace, W. 1972. *Causality and Scientific Explanation*. Volume I: *Medieval and Early Modern Science*. Ann Arbor: University of Michigan Press.

Ward, T., et al., eds. 1997. *Creative Thought*. Washington, D.C.: American Psychological Association.

Wartofsky, M. 1968. *Conceptual Foundations of Scientific Thought*. London: Macmillan.

Watson, J. 1968. *The Double Helix*. New York: Atheneum.

Webber, P. 1996. "Metaphor in Medical English Abstracts." *UNESCO ALSED-LSP Newsletter* 19: 35–52.

Westaway, F. 1937. *Scientific Method*. New York: Hillman-Curl.

Wheelwright, P. 1962. *Metaphor and Reality*. Bloomington: University of Indiana Press.

Whewell, W. 1858. *History of Scientific Ideas*. 2 vols. London: Cass.

Willows, D. M., and H. A. Houghton, eds. 1987. *The Psychology of Illustration*. 2 vols. New York: Springer-Verlag.

Wilson, J. 1981. *Physics Laboratory Experiments*. Lexington, Mass.: Heath.

Winn, B. 1987. "Charts, Graphs, and Diagrams in Educational Material." In *The Psychology of Illustration*, ed. D. M. Willows and H. A. Houghton, pp. 1: 152–190. New York: Springer-Verlag.

Yates, F. 1966. *The Art of Memory*. Chicago: University of Chicago Press.

Ziman, J. 1984. *An Introduction to Science Studies*. Cambridge: Cambridge University Press.

Index